Shopping for local products in the Mutrah Souk of Muscat, Oman

The opulent Emirates Palace Hotel in Abu Dhabi, UAE

Modern and traditional skyline of Abu Dhabi, UAE

The many pleasures of the United Arab Emirates

Marine Towers at night in Dubai

Gold market in Deira, Old Dubai

Outdoor camel art in Abu Dhabi

Waterfront in Deira, Old Dubai

Mall life for locals in Abu Dhabi

Spice Market in Deira, Old Dubai

Waterfront in Muscat, Oman

Shopping treasures in Oman

Buying silver in the Nizwa Souk

More shopping treasures in Oman

Minaret in Nizam, Oman

Resort Life in Muscat, Oman

Fort in Oman

Skyline of Sana'a, Yemen

Architecture of Sana'a

Merchants of Sana'a

Shopping treasures of Yemen

Shopping in Yemen

The many faces of Yemen

Praise for The Impact Guides

The World's Only Travel-Shopping Series

What Travel Critics and Professionals Say

"YOU LEARN MORE ABOUT A PLACE you are visiting when Impact is pointing the way." – **The Washington Post**

"THE DEFINITIVE GUIDE to shopping in Asia." – **Arthur Frommer**, The Arthur Frommer Almanac of Travel

"THE BEST travel book I've ever read." – Kathy Osiro, **TravelAge West**

"AN EXCELLENT, EXHAUSTIVE, AND FASCINATING look at shopping in the East . . . it's difficult to imagine a shopping tour without this pocket-size book in hand." – **Travel & Leisure**

"BOOKS IN THE SERIES help travelers recognize quality and gain insight to local customs." – **Travel-Holiday**

"THE BEST GUIDE I've seen on shopping in Asia. If you enjoy the sport, you'll find it hard to put down . . . They tell you not only the where and what of shopping but the important how, and all in enormous but easy-to-read detail." – **Seattle Post-Intelligencer**

"ONE OF THE BEST GUIDEBOOKS of the season – not just shopping strategies, but a Baedeker to getting around . . . definitely a quality work. Highly recommended." – **Arkansas Democrat**

"WILL WANT TO LOOK INTO . . . has shopping strategies and travel tips about making the most of a visit to those areas. The book covers Asia's shopping centers, department stores, emporiums, factory outlets, markets and hotel shopping arcades where visitors can find jewelry, leather goods, woodcarvings, textiles, antiques, cameras, and primitive artifacts." – **Chicago Tribune**

"FULL OF SUGGESTIONS. The art of bartering, including everyday shopping basics are clearly defined, along with places to hang your hat or lift a fork." – **The Washington Post**

"A WONDERFUL GUIDE . . . filled with essential tips as well as a lot of background information . . . a welcome addition on your trip." – **Travel Book Tips**

"WELL ORGANIZED AND COMPREHENSIVE BOOK. A useful companion for anyone planning a shopping spree in Asia." – **International Living**

"OFFERS SOME EXTREMELY VALUABLE INFORMATION and advice about what is all too often a spur-of-the-moment aspect of your overseas travel." –**Trip & Tour**

"A MORE UNUSUAL, PRACTICAL GUIDE than most and is no mere listing of convenience stores abroad . . . contains unusual tips on bargaining in Asia . . . country-specific tips are some of the most valuable chapters of the guidebook, setting it apart from others which may generalize upon Asia as a whole, or focus upon the well-known Hong Kong shopping pleasures." – **The Midwest Book Review**

"I LOVED THE BOOK! Why didn't I have this book two months ago! . . . a valuable guide . . . very helpful for the first time traveler in Asia . . . worth packing in the suitcase for a return visit." – Editor, **Unique & Exotic Travel Reporter**

"VERY USEFUL, PERFECTLY ORGANIZED. Finally a guide that combines Asian shopping opportunities with the tips and know-how to really get the best buys." – **National Motorist**

"INFORMATION-PACKED PAGES point out where the best shops are located, how to save time when shopping, and where and when to deal . . . You'll be a smarter travel shopper if you follow the advice of this new book." – **AAA World**

"AN ABSOLUTE 'MUST HAVE' for international travelers." – Midwest Library Review

"DETAILED, AND RELEVANT, EVEN ABSORBING in places . . . The authors know their subject thoroughly, and the reader can benefit greatly from their advice and tips. They go a long way to removing any mystery or uneasiness about shopping in Asia by the neophyte." – **The Small Press Book Review**

What Seasoned Travelers Say, Including Stories That Changed Lives

"IMMENSELY USEFUL . . . thanks for sharing the fruits of your incredibly thorough research. You saved me hours of time and put me in touch with the best." – **C.N.**, DeKalb, Illinois

"FABULOUS! I've just returned from my third shopping trip to Southeast Asia in three years. This book, which is now wrinkled, torn, and looking much abused, has been my bible for the past three years. All your suggestions (pre-trip) and information was so great. When I get ready to go again, my 'ebible,' even though tattered and torn, will accompany me again! Thanks again for all your wonderful knowledge, and for sharing it!" – **D.P.**, Havertown, Pennsylvania

"I LOVE IT. I've read a lot of travel books, and of all the books of this nature, this is the best I've ever read. Especially for first timers, the how-to information is invaluable." – **A.K.**, Portland, Oregon

"THE BEST TRAVEL BOOK I'VE EVER READ. Believe me, I know my travel books!" – **S.T.**, Washington, DC

"MANY MANY THANKS for your wonderful, useful travel guide! You have done a tremendous job. It is so complete and precise and full of neat info." – **K.H.**, Seattle, Washington

"FABULOUS BOOK! I just came back from Hong Kong, Thailand, and Singapore and found your book invaluable. Every place you recommended I found wonderful quality shopping. Send me another copy for my friend in Singapore who was fascinated with it." – **M.G.**, Escondido, California

"THIS IS MY FIRST FAN LETTER TO A BOOK . . . you made our trip to Indonesia more special than I can ever say. I not only carried it in my backpack everyday, I shared it with everyone I met, including a friend in Hong Kong, who liked it so much he kept it and I had to go out and buy another copy for myself when I got back stateside. The book taught us the customs, and through your teachings on how to bargain, I would even draw crowds to watch the Westerner bargain, and some wonderful chats afterwards, always starting off with 'ëYou good bargainer. Where you from?' It was a wonderful trip and we credit your book for making it so. Thank you from my husband and myself, and everyone else we shared your book with." – **N.H.**, New York, New York

"YOU SAVED ME . . . hurry up with the next book so I can find out what I did wrong in Burma!" – **N.H.**, Chiang Mai, Thailand

"I FURNISHED MY HOME IN FLORIDA using your wonderful books. What countries are you doing next?" – **A.A.**, New York City

"I WANT YOU TO KNOW HOW MUCH I ENJOYED YOUR BOOK. Like many people, I picked up a ton of guide books to China before we took off on our trip in May. However, yours was totally unique, and it was not until we had finished our trip that I fully appreciated everything you covered. It was also the only guidebook I took with us. Your book was the only one that mentioned the Painter's Village in Chongqing. When we arrived in Chongqing early in the morning, our guide told me the village was included in the tour, but several people wanted to skip it and go to the zoo. Fortunately, I was able to lobby the many art lovers on the tour by showing them what you had to say about the village and we did end up visiting it. It was a lovely day and the flowers were in bloom in the gardens surrounding the village. We were greeted warmly and enjoyed visiting some of the artists. I purchased two numbered prints and, although I did not meet the artist, I did get his business card. Once home, the prints were framed and I took a picture of them and wrote to the artist to see what he could tell me about them. Imagine my surprise when several weeks later I received an e-mail from him. His mother and father, both famous artists, lived in the village and his mother had forwarded my letter to their son who now lives in Tokyo. He is a well known illustrator . . . We have been corresponding by e-mail for nearly a year and I have been helping him with his English and in doing his website in English . . . We are looking forward to the day when we can have him visit us in California. Thank you for leading us to one of the highlights of Chongqing for without that experience we would not have found a new and valued friend who has taught us much about China and life under Mao." – **C.S.**, California

"I'VE USED YOUR BOOKS FOR YEARS – earlier, the book on shopping in Thailand was wonderful and more recently your best of India has been very useful." – **S.M.**, Prince George, British Columbia, Canada

"I WOULD JUST LIKE TO SAY HOW MUCH I ENJOY YOUR SERIES. I have been an avid shopper and traveler for many years and it has often been difficult finding even a decent chapter on shopping, let alone an entire book. Your guides are a wonderful contribution to the industry." – **H.P.**, Honolulu, Hawaii

"GREAT! I followed your advice in Bangkok and Hong Kong and it was great. Thanks again." – **B.G.**, Los Angeles, California

"WE ADORE ASIA! We like it better than any other part of the world . . . We have copies of your earlier editions and they are our "Asian Bibles." We also want to compliment you on doing such a masterful research job, especially on what to buy and where. Thanks to you we have some beautiful and treasured pieces from Asia. We could not have done it without your books." – **L.C.**, Palm Beach, Florida

"WE TOOK YOUR BOOK (to China) and had to concur with everything you said. We could hardly believe that 80-90% discounts were in order, but we soon found out that they were!! The Friendship Stores were everything you described. Many thanks for the book, it certainly was a help." – **L.G.**, Adelaide, Australia

"AFTER REVIEWING MANY TRAVEL GUIDES, I chose this book (China) to buy because it gave me not only insight to the same cities I am about to tour, but the how to's as well. With limited time in each city, I can go directly to the "best of the best" in accommodations, restaurants, sightseeing, entertaining, and shopping. It has also supplied me with advice on how to bargain!" – an Amazon.com buyer

"WE LOVED THE GUIDE. It's wonderful (Rio and São Paulo). We don't have anything like this in São Paulo." – **M.M.**, São Paulo, Brazil

"LOVE YOUR GUIDE to India. Thanks so much." – **B.P.**, Minneapolis, Minnesota

"THANK YOU so much for the wonderful shopping recommendations on Johannesburg and Namibia. I did want to let you know how grateful we were to have your recommendations with us." – **M.S.**, Los Angeles

"I JUST WANTED TO THANK YOU for your shopping guide to Vietnam and Cambodia. We just spent our month-long honeymoon in Vietnam and it was very helpful to have read your book and to use it as a reference as we went along." – **H.F.**, San Francisco

"A MUST HAVE read for our travel group to Vietnam." – **S.B.**, Maryland

The Treasures and Pleasures
of Dubai, Abu Dhabi,
Oman, and Yemen

By Ron and Caryl Krannich

TRAVEL AND INTERNATIONAL BOOKS

Best Resumes and CVs for International Jobs
The Directory of Websites for International Jobs
Jobs for Travel Lovers
Shopping in Exotic Places
Travel Planning On the Internet
Treasures and Pleasures of Australia
Treasures and Pleasures of Bermuda
Treasures and Pleasures of China
Treasures and Pleasures of Egypt
Treasures and Pleasures of Ethiopia
Treasures and Pleasures of Hong Kong
Treasures and Pleasures of India
Treasures and Pleasures of Jordan
Treasures and Pleasures of Kenya and Tanzania
Treasures and Pleasures of Mexico
Treasures and Pleasures of Paris
Treasures and Pleasures of Rio and São Paulo
Treasures and Pleasures of Singapore
Treasures and Pleasures of South America
Treasures and Pleasures of Southern Africa
Treasures and Pleasures of Syria
Treasures and Pleasures of Thailand and Myanmar
Treasures and Pleasures of Turkey
Treasures and Pleasures of the Dubai, Abu Dhabi, Oman, and Yemen

CAREER AND BUSINESS BOOKS

101 Secrets of Highly Effective Speakers
201 Dynamite Job Search Letters
America's Top 100 Jobs for People Without a Four-Year Degree
America's Top Jobs for People Re-Entering the Workforce
America's Top Internet Job Sites
Best Resumes and Letters for Ex-Offenders
Blue Collar Resume and Job Hunting Guide
Change Your Job, Change Your Life
The Complete Guide to Public Employment
Discover the Best Jobs for You!
The Ex-Offender's Job Hunting Guide
Get a Raise in 7 Days
Give Me More Money!
High Impact Resumes and Letters
I Can't Believe They Asked Me That!
I Want to Do Something Else, But I'm Not Sure What It Is
The Job Hunting Guide: Transitioning From College to Career
Job Hunting Tips for People With Hot and Not-So-Hot Backgrounds
Job Interview Tips for People With Not-So-Hot Backgrounds
Jobs and Careers With Nonprofit Organizations
Military-to-Civilian Resumes and Letters
Military Transition to Civilian Success
Nail the Cover Letter!
Nail the Job Interview!
Nail the Resume!
No One Will Hire Me!
Overcoming Barriers to Employment
Savvy Interviewing
The Savvy Networker
The Savvy Resume Writer
Win the Interview, Win the Job

THE IMPACT GUIDES

THE TREASURES AND PLEASURES OF

Dubai, Abu Dhabi, Oman, and Yemen

BEST OF THE BEST IN TRAVEL
AND SHOPPING

RON AND CARYL KRANNICH, PH.DS

IMPACT PUBLICATIONS
MANASSAS PARK, VA

The Treasures and Pleasures of Dubai, Abu Dhabi, Oman, and Yemen

Photos: Cover and text photos by Ron and Caryl Krannich.

Warning/Liability/Warranty: The authors and publisher have made every attempt to provide the reader with accurate, timely, and useful information. However, some information will inevitably change. The information presented here is for reference purposes only. The authors and publisher make no claims that using this information will guarantee the reader a trouble-free trip. The authors and publisher shall not be liable for any losses or damages incurred in the process of following the advice in this book.

ISBNs: 1-57023-274-1 (10-digit); 978-1-57023-274-9 (13-digit)

Library of Congress: 2007943864

Publisher: For information on Impact Publications, including current and forthcoming publications, authors, press kits, online bookstore, and submission requirements, visit the left navigation bar on the front page of www.impactpublications.com.

Publicity/Rights: For information on publicity, author interviews, and subsidiary rights, contact the Media Relations Department: Tel. 703-361-7300, Fax 703-335-9486, or email: query@impactpublications.com.

Sales/Distribution: All bookstore sales are handled through Impact's trade distributor: National Book Network, 15200 NBN Way, Blue Ridge Summit, PA 17214, Tel. 1-800-462-6420. All special sales and distribution inquiries should be directed to the publisher: Sales Department, IMPACT PUBLICATIONS, 9104 Manassas Drive, Suite N, Manassas Park, VA 20111-5211, Tel. 703-361-7300, Fax 703-335-9486, or email: query@impactpublications.com.

Contents

PART III
Yemen

Preface

WELCOME TO THE TREASURES and pleasures of the Arabia Peninsula. Join us as we explore the many appealing markets, shops, restaurants, hotels, sites, and entertainment venues of the United Arab Emirates (UAE), Oman, and Yemen. We'll put you in touch with the best of the best they have to offer visitors. We'll take you to popular tourist sites, but we won't linger long since combining great shopping with terrific dining, sightseeing, and activities is our passion. If you follow us to the end, you'll discover there is a lot more to the Arabian Peninsula, and travel in general, than taking tours, visiting popular sites, and acquiring an unwelcome weight gain attendant with new on-the-road dining habits.

The United Arab Emirates, Oman, and Yemen offer wonderful travel-shopping experiences for those who know what to look for and where to go. While they are especially popular for outdoor sports activities and adventure travel, for us they are also important shopping destination offering many attractive imported goods and local products as well as excellent restaurants and resort hotels. Their people, products, sights, and activities may truly enrich your life.

If you are familiar with our other Impact Guides, you know this will not be another standard travel guide to history, culture, and sightseeing in the UAE, Oman, and Yemen. Our approach to travel is very different. We operate from a particular perspective, and we frequently show our attitude rather than just present you with the sterile "travel facts." While we seek good travel value and offer tips on cutting travel costs), we're not budget travelers in search of cheap travel experiences.

❑ Our approach to travel is very different from most guidebooks – we offer a very different travel perspective and we frequently show our attitude.

❑ We're not obsessed with local history, culture, and sightseeing. We get just enough history and sightseeing to make our travels interesting rather than obsessive.

❑ Through shopping, we meet many interesting and talented people and learn a great deal about their country.

❑ We're street people who love "the chase" and the serendipity that comes with our style of travel.

At the same time, we're not obsessed with local history, culture, and sightseeing. We get just enough of this to make our travels interesting rather than obsessive. When we discuss history, culture, and sightseeing, we do so in abbreviated form, highlighting what we consider to be the essentials. We also assume interested travelers will have that information covered from other resources.

As you'll quickly discover, we're very focused—we're in search of quality shopping and travel. Rather than spend eight hours a day sightseeing, we may only devote two hours to sightseeing and another six hours learning about the local shopping scene. As such, we're very people- and product-oriented when we travel. Through shopping, we meet many interesting and talented people and learn a great deal about their country.

What we really enjoy doing, and think we do it well, is shop. For us, shopping makes for great travel adventure and contributes to local development. Indeed, we're street people who love "the chase" and the serendipity that comes with our style of travel. We especially enjoy discovering quality products, meeting local artists and crafts people, getting good deals, unraveling new travel and shopping rules, forming friendships with local business people, staying in special places, and dining in great restaurants where we often meet the talented chefs and visit their fascinating kitchens. Like Winston Churchill and many other travelers, our travel philosophy is very simple and focused: *"My needs are very simple—I simply want the best of everything."* When we travel, we seek out the best of the best—just like we often do back home.

The chapters that follow represent a particular travel perspective. We purposefully decided to write more than just another travel guide with a few pages on shopping. While some travel guides include a brief and usually dated section on the "whats" and "wheres" of shopping, we saw a need to also explain the "how-tos" of shopping in this part of the Arab world. Such a book would both educate and guide you through our Arabian shopping mazes as well as put you in contact with the best of the best in restaurants, accommodations, sightseeing, and other activities. It would be a combination travel-shopping guide designed for people in search of quality travel experiences.

The perspective we develop throughout this book is based on our belief that traveling should be more than just another adventure in eating, sleeping, sightseeing, and taking pictures of unfamiliar places. Whenever possible, we attempt to bring to life the fact that the UAE, Oman, and Yemen have real people and interesting products that you, the visitor, will find exciting. They have many talented artists, craftspeople, and entrepreneurs. When you leave the Arabian Peninsula, you will take with you not only some unique experiences and memories but also quality products that you will certainly appreciate for years to come.

We have not hesitated to make qualitative judgments about the best of the best in the UAE, Oman, and Yemen. If we just presented you with travel and shopping information, we would do you a disservice by not sharing our discoveries, both good and bad. While we know that our judgments may not be valid for everyone, we offer them as reference points from which you can make your own decisions. Our major emphasis is on quality shopping, accommodations, dining, sightseeing, outdoor activities, entertainment, and in that order. We look for shops which offer excellent quality and styles. If you share our concern for quality shopping, as well as fine restaurants, hotels, and resorts, you will find many of our recommendations useful in planning and implementing your own Arabian adventure. Best of all, you'll engage in what has become a favorite pastime for many of today's discerning travelers—lifestyle shopping!

Throughout this book we have included "tried and tested" shopping information. We make judgments based upon our experience—not on judgments or sales pitches from others. Our research method was quite simple: we did a great deal of shopping and we looked for quality products. We acquired some choice items, and gained valuable knowledge in the process. However, we could not make purchases in every shop, nor do we have any guarantee that your experiences will be the same as ours. Shops close, ownership or management changes, and the shop you visit may not be the same as the one we shopped. So use this information as a starting point, but ask questions and make your own judgments before you buy. For related information on our featured countries, including many of our recommended shops, please visit our two companion websites: www.i shoparoundtheworld.com and www.middleeasttravellover.com.

Whatever you do, enjoy the Arabian Peninsula. While you need not *"shop 'til you drop,"* at least shop these places well and with the confidence that you are getting good quality and value. Don't just limit yourself to small items that will fit into your suitcase or pass up something you love because of shipping concerns. Consider acquiring larger items that can be safely and conveniently shipped back home. Indeed, shipping is something that needs to be *arranged* rather than lamented or avoided.

We wish to thank the many people who contributed to this book. They include many shop owners and personnel who took time to educate us on their products and the local shopping, dining, and travel scenes.

We wish you well as you prepare for a unique travel-shopping adventure. The book is designed to be used in the streets, roads, markets, and shopping malls of the UAE, Oman, and Yemen. If you plan your journey according to the following chapters, you should have an absolutely marvelous time. You'll discover some exciting places, acquire some choice items, and return home with many fond memories of a terrific adventure. If you put this book to use, it will indeed become your best friend—and passport—to the many unique treasures and pleasures of Dubai, Abu Dhabi, Oman, and Yemen. Enjoy!

Ron and Caryl Krannich
krannich@impactpublications.com

Liabilities and Warranties

WHILE WE HAVE attempted to provide accurate information, please keep in mind that names, addresses, phone and fax numbers, e-mails, and website URLs do change, and shops, restaurants, and hotels do move, go out of business, or change ownership and management. Many new shops, shopping venues, hotels, resorts, restaurants, and entertainment complexes are continually opening in fast-changing Dubai and Abu Dhabi. We regret any inconvenience such changes may cause to your travel and shopping plans.

Inclusion of shops, restaurants, hotels, and other hospitality providers in this book in no way implies guarantees nor endorsements by either the authors or publisher. Recommendations are provided solely for your reference. The honesty and reliability of shops can best be ensured by **you**. It's okay to be a little paranoid when travel-shopping. Indeed, always ask the right questions, request proper receipts and documents, use credit cards, take photos, and observe our shopping tips as well as tips given on our companion websites: www.ishoparoundtheworld.com and www.middleeasttravellover.com.

The Treasures and Pleasures of Dubai, Abu Dhabi, Oman, and Yemen provides numerous tips on how you can best experience a trouble-free adventure. As in any unfamiliar place or situation, and regardless of how trustworthy strangers may appear, the watchwords are always the same—*"watch your wallet!"* If it seems too good to be true, it probably is. Any *"unbelievable deals"* should be treated as such.

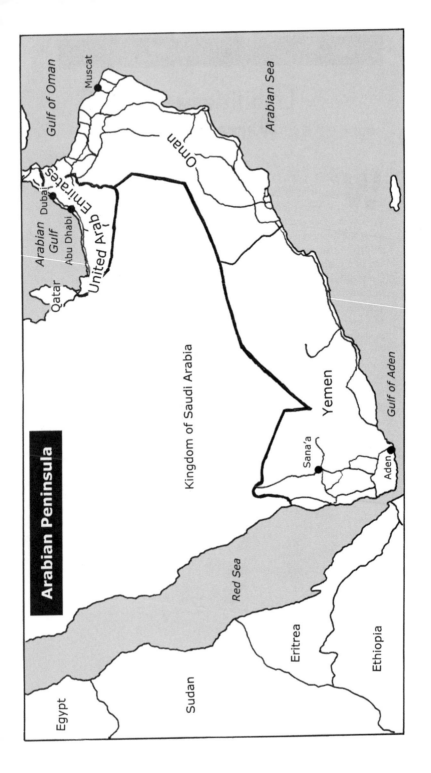

Arabian Peninsula

Welcome to
Fascinating Arabia

WELCOME TO THREE FABULOUS and intriguing destinations on the eastern and southern sections of fabled Arabia
(the Arabian Peninsula)—the United Arab Emirates (UAE),
Oman, and Yemen. Relatively small in size, they have, nonetheless, a
powerful presence in international politics, finance, and trade. They
are "must see" travel and shopping destinations that may forever enrich
your understanding of the Arab world as well as enhance your collection of earthly possessions. A two- to four-week visit here may well
change your travel-shopping life!

Safe Havens for Sorry Travelers

Let's address the safety issue up front since it's an important one for
many travelers who would love to visit this part of the world but are
afraid something terrible, such as being kidnapped, could happen to
them. They just can't bring themselves to cross a self-imposed safety
chasm that has little basis in reality.

Not surprisingly, most people living outside this region, and
especially Americans, have little understanding of Arabia, the Gulf

States, and the Middle East beyond what is portrayed in the popular media. For many, all Arabs and Muslims seem the same. Therefore, in the perception of many people, our recommended destinations most likely occupy forbidden travel territory that should be avoided.

Arab countries in the Middle East are frequently lumped together and marginalized as problematic. They occupy a stereotyped world of deserts, camels, oil, mysterious veiled women, radical Islam, terrorism, kidnappings, war, and tribalism that is often perpetuated in the news media and promoted by parochial governments preoccupied with national security issues. And shopping . . . well, that's another matter altogether, as you'll see throughout this book.

If, for example, you announce your intentions to visit the UAE, Oman, and Yemen, friends may think you're crazy to venture into what they believe is an unsafe area for anyone to travel to these days. They will wish you well and say goodbye with these cautious yet ostensibly encouraging words: "*Be very careful! Don't worry about bringing me something—just take good care of yourself!*" However, nothing could be further from the truth. And how sad so many people know so little about this part of the world.

❑ Arab countries are frequently lumped together and marginalized as problematic.

❑ These tend to be safe destinations, perhaps more so than your country of origin.

❑ Major safety issues are traffic accidents and drinking tap water.

❑ Don't avoid these places simply because of perceived safety and security issues.

These tend to be safe destinations, perhaps more so than your country of origin. Crime and violence rarely occur and seldom affect tourists in these extremely civil and hospitable countries. Just make sure you don't commit a crime and thus come into contact with the seemingly exotic criminal justice systems, which include a combination of civil and Islamic Shariah courts. Local justice is often swift and jails unpalatable to foreigners who violate local laws, especially those relating to drugs and anti-Islamic behavior.

Major safety issues relate to traffic accidents and the local drinking water—the same as in other countries you've probably visited. The proof is on the ground and regularly reported by enthusiastic visitors who discover new realities that are at major odds with their preconceived notions of safety. In fact, those who were initially reluctant to visit this part of the Middle East, and thus planned a short trip because of perceived safety issues, often leave saying, "*What a wonderful trip. Sorry I didn't plan to stay longer. I'll be back soon!*"

Don't avoid these places or shorten your trip simply because of perceived safety issues and lack of accurate information on these generally safe and hospitable places. We address safety and security issues in the separate country chapters. For example, safety issues in the UAE and Oman are similar yet different from those in Yemen, a country that has one of the world's highest per capita ownership of guns—nearly the same as the U.S. and Finland.

Sizing Up the Area

Covering an area of 823,310 square kilometers (317,881 square miles), together these three countries are approximately the same size as Pakistan, Namibia, or the U.S. states of Texas and Louisiana combined, or one-half the size of neighboring Saudi Arabia. Their combined population is nearly 27 million (4 million in the UAE, 3 million in Oman, and 19 million in Yemen), which makes them approximately the same size as Saudi Arabia, Iraq, Nepal, Uganda, or Peru, but smaller than the U.S. state of California (34 million).

❑ The combined population of the UAE, Oman, and Yemen is 27 million —about the same as Saudi Arabia but less than California.

❑ The geographic area of 823,310 square kilometers is about the same as Pakistan or the U.S. states of Texas and Louisiana combined.

Packed into this area are some amazing treasures and pleasures. From the towering buildings, glittering shopping malls, fast-paced traffic, and noisy 24/7 construction sites of the UAE's ultra-modern cities of Dubai and Abu Dhabi to the traditional Arab markets (souks), friendly peoples, and striking architecture of Oman and Yemen, these neighboring countries are among the world's most fascinating and contrasting places that will forever change your view of this region. Depending on where you shop and what you buy, you may even reinterpret the joys of shopping abroad!

Go Quickly and Then Come Back

Visit these three countries now before too many others get there first. And then return in three years to witness what a remarkable transformation took place in the intervening 36 months as more and more oil-based wealth spreads from north to south throughout the Arabian Peninsula, from the Arabian (Persian) Gulf and Arabian Sea to the Gulf of Aden and the Red Sea.

A great deal of local wealth acquired by powerful sheikhs and their families, along with other international financiers from countries within the region, currently flows into the construction of new hotels, restaurants, commercial buildings, residential complexes, and shopping malls. Stereotypical images of underdevelopment, violence, deserts, camels, and poor and uneducated Bedouins are quickly giving way to the realities of ultra-modern cities, legendary Arab hospitality, well-lighted multi-lane expressways, four-wheel drive vehicles, pick-up trucks transporting compliant and seemingly contented camels, and ubiquitous cell phones and satellite dishes that continue to revolutionize communication from the boardroom to the Bedouin tent.

Contrasting Shopping Adventures

Best of all for travel-shoppers, the UAE, Oman, and Yemen offer many unique shopping experiences for an interesting array of locally produced and imported goods. If you're a high-flying lifestyle traveler who enjoys shopping in the air-conditioned comfort of the world's largest shopping malls overflowing with imported duty-free goods—as well as seeks five-star comfort associated with great hotels and their accompanying luxurious spas, fine restaurants, and lively entertainment and sports venues—then you'll have a great time exploring the many familiar, and often decadent, treasures and pleasures of Dubai in the United Arab Emirates.

❑ The UAE is a new creation financed by oil money and other interesting sources of international wealth.

❑ Oman and Yemen represent authentic Arab adventures, complete with history, culture, and traditional markets.

❑ Yemen is a very special place—unlike any you will encounter elsewhere in the world.

Especially in the UAE's three major urban areas—**Dubai**, **Abu Dhabi**, and **Sharjah**—you'll encounter over-the-top destinations where traffic, construction, hotels, high-rise commercial buildings, shopping malls, condos, theme parks, entertainment centers, and a large expatriate presence tend to be the predominant sights and sounds. Except for mosques and a few markets and desert oases, not much here fits the stereotypical perception. For most visitors, it's all so familiar, just like back home, but to an extreme not seen elsewhere in the world. The UAE is basically a new creation financed by a seemingly unlimited amount of local oil money and other interesting sources of international wealth in search of a safe and tax-free haven. A real field of dreams, much of the UAE is a make-believe world with all the creature comforts and pleasures, including indoor snow skiing and an underwater hotel, for avoiding the harshness of a forbidding desert environment. Make no mistake, this is one of the new wonders of the world!

On the other hand, if you want to combine unique history, culture, sightseeing, and eco-adventures with shopping in traditional Arab markets, then you'll have a wonderful time exploring the engaging cities, towns, villages, roads, and waters of **Oman** and **Yemen**. Indeed, if you're looking for authentic Arab adventures—complete with traditional markets jam-packed with locally produced arts, crafts, clothes, spices, and jewelry—be sure to set your sights on laid-back Oman and ancient Yemen.

If fascinating architecture and people are two of your travel passions, be sure to spend some extra time in one of the world's most underrated and neglected destinations—relatively tourist-free **Yemen**. You'll be glad you did. Especially in the beautiful capital city of Sana'a, with its distinctive gingerbread/icing-cake architecture and extensive, colorful, and crowded market complexes overflowing with tempting locally produced arts, crafts, jewelry, and spices, this World Heritage site will enthrall you with its many exotic sights, sounds, and shopping treasures.

In fact, both Oman and Yemen may well become the highlights of your travels to the Gulf States and the Arabian Peninsula. They are a breath of fresh air after indulging in the often congested worlds of highly urbanized, sanitized, and increasingly narcissistic United Arab Emirates.

So pack your bags for what may well become one of the greatest travel-shopping adventures. In the following pages we'll prepare you for three very different shopping cultures. Join us as we put a **shopping face** on three of the Arab world's most interesting and welcoming places for visitors.

United Arab Emirates

You've probably heard a great deal about this special place that continues to attract investors, entertain journalists, and fascinate even the most jaded travelers—a real-life build-it-and-they-will-come phenomenon. Little of what you hear about the UAE relates to its history or culture. Much of the buzz has to do with today's financial complex, property development schemes, and a huge and increasingly restless expatriate labor force involved in creating new urban wonders of the world.

Rising like a phoenix from an ostensibly inhospitable desert floor, the UAE, and especially the booming city of Dubai, has become an international symbol of savvy business, instant wealth, and sometimes tasteless excess—a sort of post-Singapore along the Gulf. Positioning itself as a major financial, transportation, and communication hub, as well as a world-class tourism and recreation center, the UAE has to be seen to be believed. Reinventing itself every six months with new high-rise commercial buildings, five-star hotels, and mega shopping centers, the UAE is well on its way to creating two of the world's most impressive and competitive cities—Dubai and Abu Dhabi. It's a financial powerhouse challenging the roles of many other major cities around the world.

An expensive destination primarily catering to upscale travelers, business people, and investors, the UAE is all about wealthy investors making their dreams come true by spending billions of dollars on ambitious commercial and residential projects. Indeed, the UAE testifies to the fact that the toys of the very wealthy are bigger but not necessarily better. This is the ultimate "Wow!" destination for people impressed with new construction and seemingly unlimited wealth in action. In many respects, the UAE is one huge financial center and construction site busily trying to become the Middle East's number one destination. Flush with oil revenue, real estate schemes, and questionable sources of wealth, the UAE includes many of the world's biggest buildings, shopping malls, man-made islands, and property developments. Above all, this is a shopper's paradise for all types of imported goods and property, with special emphasis on duty-free designer goods and condos. The UAE is the ultimate place for what we call **desert retailing**!

Oman

Neighboring Oman is much more laid back and authentic than the UAE. In fact, relatively closed and isolated Oman has been open to tourists for fewer than 25 years. In many respects, Oman deliberately stands in sharp contrast to the commercial excesses lining the shores of the UAE. Visitors to Oman have an opportunity to tour a very scenic country noted for its rugged mountains, gravel and sand deserts, empty interior, beautiful beaches, and charming forts, villages, towns, and cities. This is a sparsely populated and conservative land of sultans, tribes, friendly people, mosques, frankincense, oil, sardines, camels, four-wheel drive vehicles, and a slowly emerging tourist industry centered in and around the rapidly developing capital city of Muscat.

❑ The UAE represents savvy business, instant wealth, and sometimes tasteless excess.

❑ Dubai is one huge financial center and construction site busily trying to become the Middle East's number one destination.

The good news is that Oman is a relatively easy two-hour drive along excellent paved roads from the UAE's major cities. If you enjoy renting a car and exploring a country on your own, you'll have a wonderful time discovering Oman behind the wheel. The bad news is that many visitors to the Arabian Peninsula overlook or spend too little time in this charming country, which is so near but at times seems so far from the fancy hotels, restaurants, shopping malls, and huge expatriate crowds of neighboring Dubai. Allow yourself at least five days to sample Oman's many treasures and pleasures. You won't be disappointed.

> ❏ Relatively closed and isolated, Oman has been open to tourists for fewer than 25 years.
>
> ❏ Yemen is an extremely beautiful, diverse, and fun country—an ancient, authentic, and legendary land with very accessible and friendly people.

Sprawling low-rise Muscat is the major center for shopping and other tourist activities. Eschewing the runaway commercial development of high-rise Dubai and Abu Dhabi, Muscat boasts several new five-star hotels and resort complexes, a new expatriate residential and tourism complex (The Wave), and a few excellent

restaurants for expatriates and tourists. Muscat and the town of Nizwa are Oman's major centers for acquiring Omani, Yemeni, and South Asian arts, crafts, antiques, and jewelry. Here you'll encounter traditional souks offering a wide range of attractive products (handicrafts, clothes, spices, jewelry) as well as a few art and antique galleries primarily catering to expatriates and tourists. If you're looking for original Omani products, you'll have to do lots of sleuthing. Much of what you find in Oman's markets is produced elsewhere—primarily imported from India, Pakistan, Iran, China, and Yemen. Nonetheless, you can find unique products in Oman, especially arts, antiques, and jewelry.

Yemen

Ancient, **authentic**, and **legendary** are perhaps the best words to characterize this storied land called Yemen. This place shows a lot of age, spirit, and greenery, especially if you've traveled north to nearby Oman and the UAE, which lack a strong sense of history, culture, and geographic diversity. Unfortunately, much of the greenery is devoted to growing the water-thirsty tree (*Catha edulis*) that produces the infamous *qat* leaves that most Yemeni men are addicted to chewing daily to get a mild narcotic high.

Compared to the UAE and Oman, the Yemeni people are more

accessible and social. They spend a great deal of time outdoors in the company of friends and family. The daily male *qat*-chewing ritual tends to drive much of this outdoor activity, from buying fresh *qat* leaves in the markets to sitting around with friends in the afternoon chewing and chatting their way to another daily buzz. In fact, you'll see many more people on the streets and roads in Yemen that you will in the UAE and Oman. Accordingly, you'll probably come into greater contact with the locals in Yemen than you will with locals elsewhere in Arabia.

Rugged, raw, unspoiled, and unique, Yemen is an extremely beautiful, diverse, and fun country. It's the real thing—real people, real sounds, real sights, real culture, real history, real climate, and real cities, towns, and villages. Except for a few five-star hotels, there's nothing artificial about this place, since developers have yet to have a significant impact on this country noted for its unique tower architecture, fairytale houses, mud and brick construction, mountain villages perched over awesome valleys and canyons, breathtaking scenery, excellent food, pristine islands and white beaches, mosques and minarets, frankincense and myrrh, Queen of Sheba, Noah, Arabian horses, amazing diving and trekking, and fiercely independent tribal society.

But it's the distinctive looking and joyful people that stand out as really special: *qat*-chewing men wearing mustaches, head dresses, dark sports coats, white shirts, and the legendary *jambiya* (curved dagger); mysterious black-veiled women; and friendly, noisy, and exuberant children.

While the roads may be rough and dusty, the ancient mud and brick buildings may crumble from the lack of regular maintenance, the aging vehicles may look a bit worn and battle-scarred, and the men may look fierce wearing their traditional daggers, nonetheless, this is one of the friendliest and most enticing places you may ever visit. Indeed, especially noted for its very proud, honest, and hospitable people, Yemen is a very special place that will forever fascinate and charm you.

Rugged, romantic, but still reeling from bad press attendant with some unfortunate terrorist activities in recent years, Yemen is a unique experience. There's nothing like it in the Arab world for travel-shoppers who love exploring traditional markets, meeting friendly and engaging people, taking incredible photos, and exploring the rich history, culture, and architecture of a truly special place. Primarily centered in and around the capital city of Sana'a, Yemen is a shopper's paradise for traditional arts, crafts, antiques, jewelry, textiles, and spices. It's also a photographer's paradise with storybook scenes and where everyone, except women, seems to welcome being photographed! Best of all, you'll have a great time wandering Sana'a's labyrinth of streets and shopping its traditional crowded and noisy markets where you'll also experience daily life in Yemen, from shopping for household goods to acquiring the addictive *qat* leaves, which men chew with puffy cheeks and near abandonment each afternoon.

Whatever you do, and despite some fearful travel warnings to the contrary, don't overlook Yemen. It may well change your travel life!

Primary Focus on Treasures

The Treasures and Pleasures of Dubai, Abu Dhabi, Oman, and Yemen is a different kind of travel book for a very special type of traveler— lifestyle travel-shoppers. It doesn't present the typical smorgasbord of history, culture, popular sites, and sightseeing tours, nor does it promote cheap travel or the latest travel fads.

While we love understanding the history and culture of unfamiliar places, we're not preoccupied with trying to see the past without first understanding the present, especially the people, their products, and other joys of travel. You'll find several other travel guides (see the order form at the end of this book) that primarily cover history and culture along with cheap eats and sleeps. We, on the other hand, primarily focus on quality shopping (treasures) as well as include useful tips on dining, accommodations, sightseeing, and entertainment (pleasures) appropriate for discriminating travel-shoppers.

We want you to experience the best of the best the UAE, Oman, and Yemen have to offer discriminating travelers. Accordingly, we uncover a different slice of travel reality—shopping for local treasures and experiencing the best in local pleasures. When, for example, most tourists spend four hours sightseeing, including climbing over piles of rocks, we may spend only one hour sightseeing and three hours sleuthing through quality shops, shopping malls, and markets. We leave with lots of photos of both the sights and vendors, a few choice purchases, and a wider range of experiences than the other sightseers.

We mine destinations for *both* treasures and pleasures.

The book is designed to provide you with the necessary knowledge and skills to enjoy the UAE's, Oman's, and Yemen's many wonderful treasures and pleasures. Going beyond the typical tourist attractions, we focus on how you can acquire treasures by becoming a savvy shopper. We especially designed the book with three major considerations in mind:

- Learn a great deal about the society and culture of these three countries by meeting their many talented artists, craftspeople, and shopkeepers and exploring major shops and shopping centers.

- Do quality shopping for items having good value.

- Discover unique items that can be integrated into your home and/or wardrobe.

As you will quickly discover, this is not a book on how to find great bargains in the UAE, Oman, and Yemen, although we do show you how to find good deals. Nor are we preoccupied with shopping for expensive brand-name luxury goods—primarily imported from the Europe and North America—which appear in the many shopping malls and airports of Dubai and Abu Dhabi. These items reflect an "imported" shopping culture and are frequently overpriced despite duty-free claims to the contrary.

While you will find some bargains in these countries, this book focuses on quality shopping for unique items. As such, we are less concerned with shopping to save money and to get great bargains than with shopping for local and unique products that can be taken home, integrated into one's wardrobe and home decor, and appreciated for years to come. Rather than purchase an inexpensive piece of jewelry or art, we prefer finding the best of what there is available and selectively choosing those items we both enjoy and can afford. If, for example, you buy a single piece of exquisite jewelry or a special work of art that fits nicely into your wardrobe or home, chances are these purchases will last much longer and you will appreciate them for many more years to come than if you purchased several cheap pieces of jewelry or tourist kitsch that quickly lose their value and your interest.

Our general shopping rule is this: *A "good buy" is one that results in acquiring something that has good value; when in doubt, go for quality because quality items will hold their value and you will enjoy them much more in the long run.*

Indeed, some of our most prized possessions from our shopping sojourns around the world are those we felt we could not afford at the time, but we purchased them nonetheless because we knew they represented excellent quality and thus we would continue to value them. In retrospect our decision to buy quality items was a wise one because we still love these items today.

Our general rule for doing comparative shopping in places with many other foreign shoppers is this: *If you see something you love, buy it now; if you wait to find it elsewhere, chances are you won't find a comparable item, and the one you left behind may be gone when you return!* Indeed, too much comparative shopping can lead to disappointments.

We have learned one other important lesson from shopping abroad: *good craftsmanship everywhere in the world is declining* due to the increased labor costs, lack of interest among young people in pursuing traditional craft skills, and erosion of traditional cultures. Therefore, any items requiring extensive hand labor and traditional craft skills—such as Omani chests and doors, brass pots, textiles, silver and bronze work, ceramics, furniture, basketry, and handcrafted jewelry—are outstanding values today, because many of these items are disappearing as fewer craftspeople are trained in producing quality products.

❑ Focus on quality shopping for unique items that will retain their value.

❑ When in doubt, go for quality products—you will enjoy them much more in the long run.

❑ Good craftsmanship everywhere in the world is declining. Any items requiring extensive hand labor and traditional craft skills are outstanding values today.

Throughout this book we attempt to identify the best quality shopping in the UAE, Oman, and Yemen. This does not mean we have discovered the cheapest shopping nor the best bargains. Our search for unique shopping and quality items that retain their value in the long run means many of our recommended shops may initially appear expensive. But they offer top value or unique items that you may not find in other shops.

Organize for Arabia

The chapters that follow primarily take you into the best shops, hotels, restaurants, and attractions of the UAE, Oman, and Yemen. In so doing, we've attempted to construct a completely user-friendly book that first focuses on the shopping process but also includes the best of many other treasures and pleasures in these places.

The chapters are organized as one would organize and implement a travel and shopping adventure. Each chapter incorporates basic details, including names and addresses, to get your adventure started.

Indexes and a table of contents are especially important to us and others who believe a travel book is first and foremost a guide to unfamiliar places. Therefore, our index includes both subjects and shops. The shops are printed in bold for ease of reference; the table of contents is elaborated in detail so it, too, can be used as another handy reference index for subjects and products. By using the table of contents and index together, you can access most any information from this book.

The remainder of this book is divided into three parts and seven additional chapters. The five chapters in Part I, *"The United Arab Emirates,"* focus on the treasures and pleasures of the UAE's major destinations—Dubai, Abu Dhabi, and Sharjah.

Part II examines the treasures and pleasures of Oman with special emphasis on Muscat and Nizwa.

Part III takes you into Yemen where we primarily focus on the treasures and pleasures of the capital city, Sana'a, and a few nearby villages and towns.

Beware of Recommended Shops

Throughout this book we concentrate on providing you with the necessary **knowledge and skills** to become an effective shopper. We would prefer not recommending and listing specific shops and services—even though we have our own favorite shops. We know the pitfalls of doing so. Shops that offered excellent products and service during one of our visits, for example, may change ownership, personnel, and policies from one year to another, and some popular products may disappear altogether due to high demand but discontinued production or supply. In addition, our shopping preferences may not be the same as yours.

We believe it is much more important for you to **know how to shop** than to be told where to shop. This knowledge especially comes in handy when shopping in traditional markets where names, addresses, and other locational markers of specific shops are largely nonexistent. There, you'll largely be on your own navigating through crowds to make your own shopping discoveries.

This type of "discovery shopping" is especially prevalent in the meandering souks, streets, and lanes of Oman and Yemen and to a lesser extent in the markets of the UAE's Old Dubai. While we try our best to give you preferred names and addresses in these places, you also need to venture on your own with an eye for quality and the ability to effectively bargain for good deals. In the process, you may get lost for a few minutes, but you'll have a wonderful time experiencing some very special shopping cultures as you find your way out of a charming labyrinth of streets, alleys, shops, and stalls with a few treasures in hand!

Our major concern is to outline your shopping options, show you where to locate the best shopping areas, and share some useful shopping strategies and tips that you can use anywhere, regardless of particular shops we or others may suggest. Armed with this knowledge and some basic shopping skills, you will be better prepared to locate your own shops and determine which ones offer the best products and service in relation to your own shopping needs and travel goals.

However, we also recognize the "need to know" when shopping on limited time in the UAE, Oman, and Yemen. We believe you should benefit from reliable advice on the what, where, and how of quickly shopping in these places. Indeed, we hope to save you time and money by cutting through the shopping mazes and focusing on the really good shops and buys. Therefore, throughout this book, we list the names and locations of various shops we have

found to offer good quality products. In some cases we have purchased items in these shops and can also recommend them for service and reliability. But in most cases we surveyed shops to determine the type and quality of products offered without making purchases. To buy in every shop would be beyond our budget, as well as our home storage capabilities! When we do list specific shops, we do so only as reference points from which to start your shopping.

We do not guarantee the quality of products or service. In many cases our recommended shops offer exceptional quality, honesty, and service. While we believe you should have the advantage of this information, we also caution you to again evaluate the business by asking the necessary questions. Like any hotel or restaurant, quality, service, value, and personnel do change from time to time. You need to read the signs and make your own decisions accordingly. Most shopping problems our readers encounter are usually outlined as cautionary rules in this book. Failure to read and adhere to these rules—from buying jewelry and shipping your treasures home—can result in some unpleasant "*I told you so!*" shopping and travel experiences.

If you rely solely on our listings, you will miss out on one of the great adventures of shopping in the UAE, Oman, and Yemen—discovering your own special shops that offer unique items, exceptional value, and excellent service.

Should you encounter any problem with our recommended shops, we would appreciate hearing about your experience. We also welcome readers' recommendations and success stories! We can be contacted through the publisher:

Ron and Caryl Krannich
IMPACT PUBLICATIONS
9104 Manassas Drive, Suite N
Manassas Park, VA 20111-5211
Fax 703-335-9486
E-mail: krannich@impactpublications.com

While we cannot solve your problems, future editions of this book will
reflect the experiences of our readers.

You also may want to stay in contact with our two travel websites:

www.ishoparoundtheworld.com
www.middleeasttravellover.com

These websites are designed to complement the *Impact Guides* with
numerous additional resources and advice, including video clips and
photo galleries. The sites provide travel and shopping tips, updates,
profiles of shops, recommended resources, and an online travel
bookstore. They also include some of the world's best deals on hotels,
car rentals, cruises, airlines, and travel packages around the world.

Expect a Rewarding Adventure

Whatever you do, enjoy your travel-shopping adventure to the UAE,
Oman, and Yemen. These are very special places that offer many
unique items for discerning travel-shoppers.

So arrange your flights and accommodations, pack your credit cards,
ATM card, and traveler's checks, take your sense of humor, wear a smile,
and head for three of the world's delightful travel and shopping destinations. You should return home with much more than a set of photos and
travel brochures and a weight gain attendant with new eating habits. You
will acquire some wonderful products and accumulate many interesting
travel tales that can be enjoyed and relived for a lifetime.

Experiencing the treasures and pleasures of the UAE, Oman, and
Yemen only takes time, money, a sense of adventure, and many key
references found in this book as well as on our travel websites. Take the
time, be willing to part with some of your money, and open yourself to
a whole new travel-shopping world. If you are like us, you will
encounter an exciting new travel world of quality products, friendly
people, and interesting places that you might have otherwise missed had
you passed through these countries as a typical tourist or traveler who
came here to only eat, sleep, see sights, be entertained, and take
pictures. When you travel and shop in the UAE, Oman, and Yemen,
you learn about wonderful places by way of the people, products, sights,
and activities that define their many treasures and pleasures. Enjoy!

PART I

The United Arab Emirates

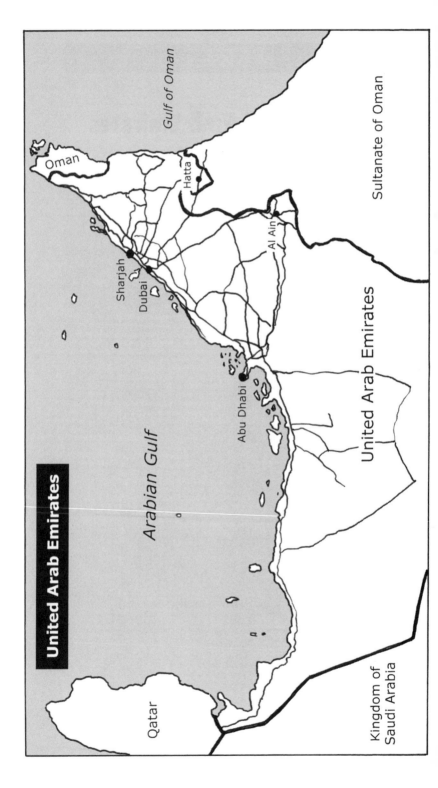

2

UAE Basics

THERE'S NOTHING LIKE a little background information and a few good statistics and visuals to give one a sense of place. The UAE is very different from most countries you have ever encountered. For some interesting introductions to the UAE, be sure to check out the many text links, video clips, and photo galleries included in the UAE section of our website: www.ishoparoundthe world.com.

Getting There

Visas and Entry

Most visitors do not need to get a visa in advance, pay visa fees, or carry photos for a visa. In fact, they don't even have to complete paperwork upon arrival—just present a valid passport!

Visitors from the following countries automatically receive a free 60-day tourist visa stamped into their passport by immigration officials upon arrival in the UAE by air, sea, or land: all Arab Gulf Cooperation Countries (GCC), Andorra, Australia, Austria, Belgium, Brunei, Canada, Denmark, Finland, France, Germany, Greece, Hong Kong, Iceland, Ireland, Italy, Japan, Lichtenstein, Luxembourg, Malaysia, Monaco, New Zealand, Norway, Portugal, San Marino, Singapore, South Korea, Spain, Sweden, Switzerland, The Netherlands, UK, USA, and Vatican City. Make sure your passport is valid for at least six months from the date of your arrival.

Avoid any paper associated with Israel since Israeli passport holders, or anyone found with an Israeli visa stamped in their passport, will be denied entry into the UAE. In the name of Arab unity, Israel and their passport friends don't exist, nor are they encouraged to come to this part of the world. If you ever visit Israel, ask the immigration officials to give you a separate visa paper rather than a passport stamp, which they routinely do for visitors who plan to go on to nearby Arab countries that are officially anti-Israel.

If you have a question about visa requirements, including visa extensions, check this website:

http://guide.theemiratesnetwork.com/living/visa.php

Airlines and Airports

The UAE is a major hub for international airlines serving Asia, Europe, Africa, and the Middle East. By air, Dubai is seven hours from London, six hours from Frankfurt, three hours from Mumbai, four hours from Hong Kong, four hours from Nairobi, and 14 hours from New York City.

The UAE operates three airlines—Emirates, Etihad Airways, and Air Arabia. The oldest (since 1985) national carrier is **Emirates** (www.emirates.com), which is based in Dubai and has a reputation for being one of the world's finest airlines with its excellent safety and service records. It flies to 93 cities in 59 countries in the Middle East, Europe, Asia, the South Pacific, Africa, and the Americas. It now offers direct flights (11,023 kilometers in 14 hours) from New York City to Dubai.

The newest national carrier (since 2003) is **Etihad Airways** (www.etihadairways.com), which is based in Abu Dhabi. It, too, flies to numerous destinations in the Middle East, Europe, Asia, the South Pacific, Africa, and the Americas. Within North America, it offers direct flights from New York City and Toronto to Abu Dhabi.

Air Arabia (www.airarabia.com), which is based in Sharjah, is a relatively new (since 2003) no-frills budget airline. It services 35 cities in the Middle East and Asia.

Including the three UAE companies, over 90 airlines fly into the UAE. Numerous flights come from Pakistan and India, the home countries for millions of expatriate workers in the Middle East. Major airlines regularly servicing the **Dubai International Airport** (www.dubaiairport.com), which processes over 32 million visitors a year, include:

- Aer Lingus
- Aeroflot
- Air France
- Air India

- Alitalia
- British Airways
- Cathay Pacific Airways
- China Airlines
- China Southern Airlines
- Delta Airlines
- EgyptAir
- Ethiopian Airlines
- Gulf Air
- Kenya Airways
- KLM

- Korean Air
- Lufthansa Airlines
- Malaysia Airlines
- Pakistan International Airlines
- Qatar Airways
- Royal Brunei Airlines
- Royal Jordanian Airlines
- Saudi Arabian Airlines
- Singapore Airlines
- SriLankan Airlines
- Swissair
- Thai Airways International
- Turkish Airlines
- United Airlines
- Virgin Atlantic

International airlines servicing the **Abu Dhabi International Airport** (www.abudhabiairport.ae), which processes over 5 million passengers a year, include:

- Air India
- British Airways
- China Airlines

- EgyptAir
- Ethiopian Airlines
- Etihad Airways
- Garuda Indonesia
- Gulf Air
- KLM

- Kuwait Airway
- Lufthansa
- Pakistan International Airlines
- Qatar Airways
- Royal Jordanian
- Saudi Arabian Airlines
- Singapore Airlines
- SriLankan Airlines
- Turkish Airlines

Both the Dubai and Abu Dhabi international airports, with a combined passenger load quickly approaching 40 million a year, continue to grow at phenomenal rates. Expect both airports to be undergoing expansion and renovation as they try to cope with 15-percent annual growth rates in passenger arrivals as well as a continuing boom in duty-free shopping operations.

Both airports also have extensive **duty-free shopping** operations, both upon arrival and departure. Indeed, the Dubai International Airport alone takes in over US$800 million a year (2007), making it the world's third largest duty-free airport operation—after London's Heathrow and Seoul, Korea. Experiencing annual growth rates of 15 to 20 percent, this airport may soon become the world's number one duty-free airport.

Selecting Airports

While international airlines service both Dubai and Abu Dhabi, you are well advised to fly into the much larger **Dubai International Airport**, unless you are planning to spend most of your time in Abu Dhabi. With the construction of a huge new terminal, Dubai International Airport is currently expanding its capacity to handle an additional 46 million passengers a year—up from 24 million in 2007 to a projected 70 million in 2010—an anticipation of annually attracting 9 million more tourists (from 6 to 15 million) by 2010.

While the cities of Dubai and Abu Dhabi are connected by an excellent expressway, they are nearly 200 kilometers from each other, or a 1 1/2—to 2-hour drive. Since you'll find much more to see and do in Dubai than in Abu Dhabi, make Dubai your base for both entering and exiting the country. From there you can easily rent a car to visit other parts of the UAE via its excellent four—to eight-lane road system.

Airport to City (Dubai)

Chances are you will initially arrive in the UAE through the Dubai International Airport. This large facility is located adjacent to the city, immediately to the east of the Deira area. Arrival is extremely efficient. The time between getting off your plane and finally getting into a taxi may take as little as 30 minutes. You can even speed up the process by following this little-known tip: Once you deplane, take the elevators from the arrival gate to the immigration floor rather than follow the crowds which ride three different escalators to the immigration area.

As you exit the airport on the lower level, you'll find several car rental agencies, money changers, and hotel representatives manning small booths near the exit. If you haven't arranged for a car, you may want to check with these rental agencies. We decided on Dollar since they allowed us to take a car into Oman at the best rates. Exchange some money here since you'll need it if you're taking a taxi to your hotel or apartment.

Taxis are located just outside this arrival area and to your left. Get into the taxi queue and wait your turn. You'll shortly be in a taxi and off to your destination. Taxis are metered. Airport taxis drop their flag at Dhs.20 or US$5.45. City taxis drop the flag at Dhs.3 (US$.80). Depending on your destination, your taxi ride could cost from Dhs.30

to Dhs.80 (US$8.20 to US$21.80). Depending on traffic, which at times can be horrendous, you should arrive at your destination within 30 minutes, if not sooner.

Since many taxi drivers are very friendly and talkative, you may want to strike up a conversation about Dubai . . . and hear about his country of origin and his complaints about the traffic and high cost of living. Welcome to the UAE!

Background Information

For quick overviews of the history of the UAE, visit these three useful websites:

- www.arab.de/arabinfo/uaehis.htm
- http://wikitravel.org/en/United_Arab_Emirates
- www.uaeinteract.com/travel

For background information on the UAE, including history, economics, government, population, language, religion, and transportation, we recommend the following websites:

- UAE   http://en.wikipedia.org/wiki/United_Arab_Emirates
               www.cia.gov/cia/publications/factbook
- Dubai   http://en.wikipedia.org/wiki/Dubai
- Abu Dhabi   http://en.wikipedia.org/wiki/Abu_Dhabi
- Sharjah   http://en.wikipedia.org/wiki/Sharjah

The following travel websites also provide useful information on the UAE:

Dubai

- www.timeoutdubai.com
- www.lonelyplanet.com
- http://dubaitourism.co.ae
- www.dubailife.com
- www.dubaicityguide.com/main/index.asp?ref=vis
- www.wordtravels.com/Cities/United+Arab+Emirates/Dubai
- www.world66.com/asia/middleeast/unitedarabemirates/dubai

Abu Dhabi

- www.timeoutabudhabi.com
- www.abudhabitourism.ae/Corp/en/default.aspx
- www.wordtravels.com/Cities/United+Arab+Emirates/Abu+Dhabi
- www.executivetravelmagazine.com/page/Abu+Dhabi
- www.miceonline.net/abudhabi/introConvention.htm

Sharjah

- www.sharjah-welcome.com
- www.dubaicityguide.com/sharjah/index.asp
- www.expo-centre.co.ae/about/Sharjah.html

Areas, Borders, and Coastline

Located directly across the Arabian (Persian) Gulf from Iran and occupying the southeastern tip of the Arabian Peninsula, the United Arab Emirates is an oil-rich federation of seven sovereign emirates headed by families of self-appointed sheikhs: Abu Dhabi, Dubai, Sharjah, Ras Al Khaimah, Fujairah, Umm Al Quiwain, and Ajman. This federation of sheikdoms was formed in 1971 after the withdrawal of the British from the region. Abu Dhabi, which occupies 87 percent of the country's landmass, is the largest emirate in terms of area. Dubai is the country's largest and most diverse city in terms of population and economic activity. In fact, about one-third of the country's population resides in Dubai.

Today the UAE occupies an area of 83,600 square kilometers (32,278 square miles), which makes it about the size of the U.S. states of South Carolina, Maine, or Indiana, or the countries of Austria or Azerbaijan. It's bordered by Qatar (northwest), Saudi Arabia (west, south, and southeast), and Oman (southeast and northeast).

The UAE also has 1,318 kilometers of coastline, which primarily run along the Arabian (Persian) Gulf, although it has a small section of coastline along the Gulf of Oman in the east. This coastline is constantly expanding as both Dubai and Abu Dhabi continue to reclaim land for ambitious oceanfront real estate projects (the three "Palms," the World, Lulu Island, etc.).

Population and Expatriates

Population statistics for the UAE are somewhat unreliable given the large movement of both legal and illegal immigrants in and out of the UAE each day, rapidly developing cities, and the lack of an accurate ground census. They are somewhere between hype, hope, and that wonderful Arab perspective summarized in the saying, "God willing!" Some sources put the population at 2.6 million while others claim 4.7 million. However speculative, we're comfortable with the following country and city statistics:

United Arab Emirates	4.5 million
■ Dubai	1.4 million
■ Abu Dhabi	1.1 million
■ Sharjah	550,000

From a population perspective, this puts the UAE near the size of Singapore, Norway, Croatia, Eritrea, or Costa Rica.

The UAE's population is broken down into the following local (Emirati) and expatriate population groups:

■ Emiratis	18%
■ Arab/Iranian	23%
■ South Asian	51%
■ Other	8%

Annual population growth fluctuates widely, depending on how many expatriates the Emiratis permit to enter the country. At present the government annually issues over 500,000 visas for guest workers. This number will go up or down depending on the labor needs of the country.

Tourist figures also are unreliable—again, somewhere between hope and hype—since the government does not have an accurate system for gathering visitor statistics other than counting heads at hotels. Indeed, the arrival process is so pleasant and hassle-free that when you arrive in the UAE, no one bothers to have you fill out a standard immigration form indicating your country of origin or the purpose of your visit. That's left to the check-in process at hotels. Since the two of us stayed at six hotels and resorts during our last visit to the UAE, we probably were counted as 12 visitors! Depending on how you count, somewhere between 6 and 10 million visitors come to the UAE each year (approximately 400,000 Americans visit each year). Visitors who stay with friends or relatives miss being counted. How many visitors are leisure versus business versus guest workers is anybody's guess. It's a lot.

Religion

Islam is the official religion of the UAE, which is primarily practiced by the Emiratis (20 percent of the local population) and supported by the government. Approximately 85 percent of Emiratis are Sunni Muslims and 15 percent are Shi'a Muslims.

You will see many beautiful mosques throughout the UAE as well as experience the traditional daily call to prayers. The government

observes Muslim holidays, and most locals and expatriates are expected to respect Ramadan, the ninth month of the Muslim lunar calendar when Muslims are supposed to fast during the day and shops and restaurants observe abbreviated hours. For expatriates and tourists, alcohol consumption primarily becomes an evening activity centered in the restaurants, bars, pubs, and nightclubs of hotels and resorts.

The UAE is ostensibly tolerant of other peoples and religions, except for Jews and Judaism. The UAE government follows the anti-Israeli policies of fellow Arab countries by prohibiting Israeli citizens and anyone who has an Israeli visa stamp in their passport entry into the UAE.

The remaining 80 percent of the population practice a variety of religions, depending on their country of origin—Christianity, Buddhism, Hinduism, etc. Christian churches maintain a very low profile in the UAE, primarily found behind walls and with no signage. If you're a Christian in search of a church, you'll need to ask at your hotel about locations of churches and get directions written out to be given to taxi drivers who may not know where to find such inconspicuous places.

Cities

The UAE is primarily a desert country where nearly 75 percent of the population resides in three major cities: Dubai, Abu Dhabi, and Sharjah. Most of the remaining population resides in other urban areas, such as Al Ain which borders on Oman.

Both Dubai and Abu Dhabi are well planned cities adjusting to today's new economic and population realities. Dubai is noted for its wide boulevards, traffic congestion, and high-rise buildings. Abu Dhabi is also known for its broad boulevards and tall buildings as well as boasts many green parks and gardens. At present Abu Dhabi lacks Dubai's traffic congestion.

Online Traveler Feedback

Visit this interesting collection of websites, forums, and blogs to find out what other travelers are currently saying about the UAE, Dubai, Abu Dhabi, and Sharjah:

- www.virtualtourist.com
- www.tripadvisor.com
- http://thorntree.lonelyplanet.com
- www.travelblog.org
- www.travelblogs.com
- www.travelpod.com
- http://blogs.bootsnall.com
- http://blog.realtravel.com
- www.travbuddy.com
- www.globenotes.com
- http://blog.travelpost.com

While many of these sites represent the observations or "streams of consciousness" of young and inexperienced budget travelers who are still in the "Wow!" and "I don't miss home yet" stages of their lives, nonetheless, you may find some useful tips for planning your trip to the UAE.

Photos and Videos

For dramatic visual representations of the UAE, we recommend viewing the video clips and photos of the UAE on our travel website—www.ishoparoundtheworld.com. You'll find them under the second question about the UAE and in the separate photo gallery:

- http://www.ishoparoundtheworld.com/uae/destination_uae_2.html#photvid (video clips)
- http://www.ishoparoundtheworld.com/uae/uae_photoalbums.html (photo gallery)

The video clip section includes more than 45 one—to six-minute videos on various aspects of the UAE: country, people, women, construction, development projects, islands, hotels, shopping malls, labor force, horse racing, safety, architecture, and airport.

Our photo gallery, as well as links to over 25 other photo galleries, includes thousands of photos about all aspects of the United Arab Emirates.

You may also want to check on local and regional news by checking our the popular English-language Arab news network, Aljazeera, which can be viewed online:

www.aljazeera.net/english

You also may be able to access several excellent special features on the United Arab Emirates produced by Aljazeera but accessed through www.YouTube.com.

Safety Realities

When we first announced our plans to visit the United Arab Emirates, the usual response from fellow Americans was a hesitant warning about being so adventuresome to travel into ostensibly dangerous territory— *"Be careful!"* How little they know the world beyond U.S. news headlines about terrorism, the simmering Middle East, and unwelcome Americans! We already knew the UAE was an oasis of safety and security, and our on-the-ground experience confirmed that this is a very safe place to visit.

In fact, the UAE's booming real estate, investment, and tourist industries are largely in response to the "safe haven" reputation of the UAE. Indeed, the UAE has a stellar reputation as being *"everybody's friend, and nobody's enemy,"* which sometimes makes for strange bedfellows. And most people like to keep it that way, since they never know when they may need it! This is ostensibly an Arab country— never mind it's actually run by Asians—and you are welcome.

Safety and Security

The UAE is a very safe country to visit. Indeed, few places in the world can boast such a high degree of safety and security. You can walk and drive in most places without fear of encountering difficulties. While there is little theft in the UAE, it's always good to take sensible precautions with your valuables, especially in crowded shopping areas and when leaving valuables in cars and hotel rooms. Keep doors locked and valuables out of sight.

Whatever you do, at least for now, you need not worry about safety and security other than keeping a close eye on what can be at times threatening traffic. Even the water, which is produced through huge desalinization plants, is safe to drink in Dubai and Abu Dhabi. Crime is negligible, almost unheard of in this highly self-regulated society. Travelers should always remember that safety begins at home—you must take responsibility for your own personal safety. In other words, don't tempt others to take advantage of you.

As in many other countries, the biggest danger in the UAE is being involved in an automobile accident. So watch where you walk, drive defensively, wear seatbelts, and be very observant of your surroundings.

Some visitors may feel intimidated by a few enterprising South Asian hawkers of fake name-brand watches and handbags who hang around the souks of Deira (Old Dubai). While somewhat aggressive, we found them to be harmless and entertaining. Except for this group, you'll seldom be pestered by touts who prey on tourists. This is a tourist-friendly country where you will be left alone.

Violence and Terrorism

The UAE is a sea of tranquillity in what is generally viewed as a volatile region that witnesses numerous religious, sectarian, military, and terrorist activities. However, most violence tends to be confined to Afghanistan, Iraq, Lebanon, Palestine, and Israel. The UAE tends to attract wealthy refugees and financiers from those war-torn countries.

Although a great deal of money laundering and terrorist financing passes through the UAE's secretive banking channels, the UAE has not been a target for terrorist activities. It will most likely remain a safe haven for everyone who comes here. Indeed, this is a "hands off" country for everyone involved in conflicts within the region. It's simply too important for everyone concerned, including terrorist organizations and organized crime (Russian and Indian mafias), to be disrupted by terrorism. As a result, the powers that be in the UAE are friendly to everyone who makes financial sense.

Travel Warnings and Advisories

The U.S. Department of State (http://travel.state.gov) issues the following travel advisory for Americans traveling to the UAE:

> Americans in the United Arab Emirates should exercise a high level of
> security awareness. The Department of State remains concerned
> about the possibility of terrorist attacks against U.S. citizens and

interests throughout the world. Americans should maintain a low profile, vary routes and times for all required travel, and treat mail and packages from unfamiliar sources with caution. In addition, U.S. citizens are urged to avoid contact with any suspicious, unfamiliar objects, and to report the presence of the objects to local authorities. U.S. Government personnel overseas have been advised to take the same precautions. In addition, U.S. Government facilities may temporarily close or suspend public services from time to time as necessary to review their security posture and ensure its adequacy.

Taking photographs of potentially-sensitive UAE military and civilian sites, or foreign diplomatic missions, including the U.S. Embassy, may result in arrest, detention and/or prosecution by local authorities. In addition, engaging in mapping activities, especially mapping which includes the use of GPS equipment, without coordination with UAE authorities, may have the same consequences.

On several occasions in the past three years, small groups of expatriate recreational boaters were detained by the Iranian Coast Guard for alleged violation of Iranian territorial waters while fishing near the island of Abu Musa, approximately 20 miles from Dubai. The UAE and Iran have had a long-standing dispute concerning jurisdiction of Abu Musa. Fishing or sailing in these waters may result in seizure of vessels and detention of passengers and crew in Iran. Obtaining consular assistance in Iran is difficult and can only be done through the Swiss Embassy in Tehran, which acts as a Protecting Power, providing limited U.S. consular services.

Several countries issue useful travel warnings and advisories on the UAE:

- Australia: www.smarttraveller.gov.au
- Canada: http://www.voyage.gc.ca/dest/sos/warnings-en.asp
- New Zealand: www.safetravel.govt.nz
- United Kingdom: www.fco.gov.uk/travel

Women

Women generally feel safe traveling in the UAE. However, they should be sensitive to local customs by doing the following:

1. Dress conservatively—bare shoulders, midriffs, and legs (wearing shorts) should be avoided.

2. Avoid eye contact with staring males—many Middle Eastern males interpret eye contact with a Western female as an invitation to make sexual advances.

3. Avoid traveling alone; a male companion often deters unwelcome encounters.

Medical Facilities and Health

The UAE has a well-developed health care system, which includes public and private hospitals as well as health clinics and pharmacies. Nonetheless, you are well advised to travel with evacuation insurance should you encounter a serious medical problem.

For information on vaccinations and other health precautions, such as safe food and water and insect bite protection, call the U.S. Centers for Disease Control and Prevention's hotline for international travelers at 1-877-394-8747 or visit their website: http://www.cdc.gov/travel.

While travelers should be fine drinking tap water in major hotels and restaurants in Dubai and Abu Dhabi since the water supply comes from desalination plants, most such places offer bottled water. Tap water elsewhere may be of questionable quality. Food handling standards are generally good. Bottled water and drinks are readily available throughout the UAE.

Do you need any special medical services? Dubai has quickly become a major player in the world **medical tourism** movement, boasting world-class medical facilities and expertise to attract thousands of visitors to come here for inexpensive medical procedures. Combining duty-free shopping with medical procedures, visitors are urged to consider Dubai over other popular international medical tourism destinations. Throughout the upcoming decade Dubai should compete well with such noted medical tourism centers as Thailand, India, and Singapore. For more information on this movement and facilities, check out these websites:

www.dubaihealthnews.com
www.recoverdiscover.com
www.arabmedicare.com

Traffic Safety

Traffic safety is an important issue in the UAE. If you decide to rent a car, which we strongly recommend in this land of cars and superhighways, be sure to rent from a reputable company (Dollar, Avis, and Hertz are good choices), take out full insurance, get a good map, drive defensively, observe local travel laws (they are enforced), and learn to navigate traffic roundabouts.

The UAE has a high incidence of accidents, which is understandable given the multinational Third World composition of the population, which includes many bad driving habits imported from other countries. Drivers have a habit of abruptly cutting in front of other drivers. The old traffic adage that *"He who signals his intention loses the advantage"* is very applicable to driving habits in the UAE!

Be prepared to make lots of U-turns and navigate congested roundabouts. Indeed, this is the country of few left turns, ubiquitous U-turns, and lots of roundabouts! The U-turn areas are clearly marked, but it may take a few frustrating kilometers of driving before you come to such a turnaround area. Roundabouts are good alternatives to making U-turns. But be very careful when entering roundabouts. You may not encounter courteous drivers in these places, and many roundabouts are unable to handle heavy traffic flows—sure signs that such roundabouts have outlived their usefulness and thus require some re-engineering!

Roads and Borders

While the UAE shares borders with Qatar, Saudi Arabia, and Oman, the only one that concerns most visitors is the one with Oman. Indeed, many visitors to the UAE decide to visit neighboring Oman by road. You can easily rent a car in the UAE (be sure to do so with Dollar, Avis,

or Hertz, the only three companies that allow you to take a car into Oman and back) and drive to Muscat, the capital of Oman. Be sure to let the rental company know you plan to travel to Oman and purchase insurance for Oman. Since insurance is not available at the border, you will not be able to take a car into Oman without applicable insurance.

From UAE border crossing points, the drive to Muscat is a very pleasant six hours along good-surfaced and often well-lit roads. The major border crossings with Oman are at Hatta (east of Dubai) or Al Ain (southeast of Dubai or directly east of Abu Dhabi). We prefer the Al Ain crossing because it gives us an opportunity to visit one of the UAE's largest and most important inland cities. The border crossing into Oman may take an hour or more, depending on the work habits of Omani immigration officials. It's not an efficient bureaucratic operation. Returning to the UAE is relatively easy since you probably won't need a visa. You may choose to return by an alternate border crossing.

Taxes

The UAE has very few taxes. No departure taxes, no sales taxes, and no export taxes. However, both Dubai and Abu Dhabi charge a municipal tax—10 and 6 percent respectively—that is included in your hotel and restaurant bills.

The Dark Side

Like anywhere else in the world, there are a few dark sides to the UAE that you may or may not encounter. They are worth being aware of to put this place in clearer perspective.

The UAE, especially Dubai, is reputed to be the world's third major center for sex tourism—sharing this space with infamous Bangkok and Amsterdam. The dark side, which includes involuntary servitude, sexual exploitation, labor abuses, drug trafficking, and money-laundering, is perhaps best summarized in the CIA's World Fact Book section on the United Arab Emirates (www.cia.gov/cia/publications/factbook).

In fact, if you hang around Dubai International Airport long enough, you may see new crews of suspected hookers arriving from Russia, Europe, Asia, and Africa to service Dubai's lively nightlife and rapidly developing tourism industry. The Russian Mafia largely controls Dubai's prostitution trade, and both Russian and Chinese hookers are often found working the streets and beaches along Rolla Street and the Golden Sands  area (off Bank Street). The down-and-out hookers, including many HIV-positive types, are reputed to work the streets and sleazy clubs and hotels of less affluent Deira. The Indian Mafia is noted for its money-lending activities and role in handling inter-family trade feuds. Most tourists don't see this aspect of Dubai unless they ask taxi drivers about visiting such places.

In addition to prostitution, Dubai is reputed to be the region's crossroads for criminal activity. It's a center for drug and arms smuggling as well as for organized crime centering around Russian and Indian mobsters. Deira Creek, Dubai's traditional center for trade, is sometimes referred to as Smuggler's Creek. It's lined with many *dhows*—rickety wood boats laden with goods—from Iran engaged in this trade. *U.S. News & World Report* recently reported that some money actually gets laundered through the popular Gold Souk, in addition to Dubai's many banking and financial institutions. Iranian arms smugglers and  Arab jihadists also operate through Dubai. In fact, funds for the 9/11 hijackers and African embassy bombers were transferred through

Dubai. As one CIA operative has speculated, Iran is probably financing the development of its nuclear weapons industry through Dubai!

The UAE's human rights record has come under criticism in recent years because of the scandalous labor conditions (low pay, heavy indebtedness, long hours, hot environment, no rights, lack of safety, injuries, suicides, seized passports, squalid labor camps, questionable housing, abuse) surrounding the army of guest workers who construct all those fabulous buildings and operate the country's many services. Most of the construction workers are poor and illiterate indentured South Asians—primarily from India, Pakistan, Bangladesh, Nepal, Sri Lanka—who make from US$5 to US$7 a day, are indebted to labor contractors who arranged their jobs and passage, and live in awful conditions. Their plight has been the subject of several special human rights reports that have tarnished the image of the UAE because of its "dirty little secret." While some changes have been made in local laws and a few model labor camps have been constructed, nonetheless, the situation remains desperate for thousands of these workers who are at the mercy of predatory contract labor firms and local employers. In addition, recent labor unrest has resulted from the declining value of the U.S. dollar—laborers are paid in local currency, which is pegged to the U.S. dollar, but currencies in many of their home countries are pegged to the much stronger Euro. The result is the declining value of workers' wages and smaller remittances to families back home. For more information on this situation, view these investigative videos:

- http://video.news.sky.com/skynews/video
- http://youtube.com/watch?v=UUW9MWLIQYw
- http://www.youtube.com/watch?v=hMxbpsw_UTE
- http://www.youtube.com/watch?v=fOF97JrUej4

Local Laws You Need to Know About

Local law is a combination of secular and Islamic law. Religious courts enforce Islamic law which is known as Shariah. While no tourists have yet been stoned to death, on occasion a local or expatriate does get this form of death sentence, often for murder or sexual misconduct, such as raping daughters or relatives. However, few executions ever take place in the UAE, and all are done the old-fashioned way—by firing squad at Al-Wathba prison near the Abu Dhabi International Airport.

The UAE's legal system is in transition, especially given the importance of codifying foreign investment and property laws to acceptable international standards. While foreigners have been able to own property (freeholder rights only since 2002) in certain designated development areas, which is largely responsible for the UAE's tremendous property boom during the past five years, their long-term legal rights, such as inheritance, remain uncertain. In addition, there is some ambiguity as to who really owns the property—you or the developer. In other words, you may or may not be able to sell your property with ease. Also, UAE courts will apply Shariah law to property questions, which is a real problem if an owner dies. The courts may not allow the property to be transferred to a female spouse. There are also other questionable details of ownership that reinforce the old adage that *"The devil is always in the details."*

If you are tempted to buy a condo, apartment, or villa in the UAE, be sure you understand your rights and get legal advice from a local law firm that specializes in property rights. Property ownership rights are not the same as in your country. For starters, pick up a copy of Explorer's expatriate guidebook at any major bookstore in the UAE—***Dubai: The Complete Residents' Guide.*** You'll find a similar guide on Abu Dhabi.

Be especially careful about parking meters and traffic cameras. You will receive hefty fines for violating either. While many traffic cameras do not work, it's best to assume they are functional and thus may catch you for speeding. If you rent a car and violate the law, you may find an unwelcome legal charge appearing on your credit card once you return home!

Languages

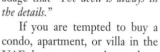

This is a bilingual country. The official language of the UAE is Arabic. However, English is widely spoken along with Hindi and Urdu, the languages of Indians. Since many taxi drivers are from India and Pakistan, their English may be difficult to understand at times. "Hinglish"—commonly referred to as Indian English—is a combination of Hindi or Urdu and heavily accented English.

Since 180 nationalities are represented in the UAE, you'll hear many other languages spoken throughout the country. When you visit the Spice Souk in Old Dubai, for example, you'll hear Farsi spoken since most of the merchants are from Iran; most speak some English and

Arabic. German, French, and Japanese tourists manage to navigate this place well in their own language as well as in English.

Since road signs and maps are in English, you'll have little difficulty driving in the UAE. Just make sure you have a good map with sufficient details (a good compass also will come in handy) to take you beyond the confines of the central business district of each city.

If you get lost, you can usually find someone who speaks English to help you get re-oriented. However, you may need to ask three different people the same question in order to get accurate information. It's not unusual to get faulty advice from well-meaning people. This problem has little to do with English-language skills and more to do with a sense of geography and directional intelligence.

As in many other countries, you'll seldom get lost for more than 15 minutes because of your lack of local language skills. Getting lost and found is often one of the joys of travel. Indeed, you'll probably meet some really nice people in process of getting lost and found!

Useful Arabic Words and Phrases

A few words spoken in the local language will go a long way in making friends and opening the doors for assistance and learning about the locals. The following phrases are a good starting point for introducing yourself to the locals:

- Hello   Marhaba
- Goodbye   Ma/a salameh
- My name is   Ismee
- What is your name?   Shoo ismak?
- Thank you   Shukran
- You're welcome   Afwan
- Please   Law samaht/min fadlak
- Excuse me   An iznak
- What time is it?   Edesh el sa'aa?
- Home much does this cost?   Bikaam hatha?
- One   Waahid
- Two   Tinain

- Three   Thalaateh
- Four   Arba'a
- Five   Khamseh
- Six   Sitteh
- Seven   Sab'a
- Eight   Tamenyeh
- Nine   Tis'a
- Ten   Ashra
- Where is the restroom?   Wen il hamaam?
- Left   Shmaal
- Right   Yameen
- Straight   Dughree
- Where?   Wain?
- Money   Masari

Climate and Seasons

When planning to visit the UAE, be sure to take into consideration the country's extreme climate as well as several special events and holidays that can negatively affect your plans.

The UAE boasts sunshine throughout the year. However, you'll probably want to avoid certain months, which can be very uncomfortable because of high heat and humidity.

The best time to visit the UAE is winter and early spring (November to April). These are the coolest months and also the best times for shopping, sports activities, and various festivals. From November to February, daytime temperatures are around 30°C (mid-80°F) and humidity is relatively low. During January and February desert evenings can be cool, requiring a sweater or lightweight jacket or jumper.

The summer months (May to September) can be extremely hot and humid, with daytime temperatures usually over 40°C (104°F). However, during this time of the year many hotels reduce prices by 30 to 50 percent.

The inland cities of Al Ain and Hatta, which are located at higher elevations than the coastal cities of Dubai, Abu Dhabi, and Sharjah, are cooler throughout the year.

What little rain that does fall (42mm per year) usually occurs between January and March. Sometimes rains can be torrential.

Activities

The UAE sponsors several activities throughout the year to attract international visitors, from world class golf, tennis, horse racing, and auto racing (Formula One Grand Prix Abu Dhabi for 2009) to shopping and cultural festivals.

Dubai's annual shopping festival, the Dubai Shopping Festival (DSF), usually runs for one month, during the months of January and February. However, you'll need to check on the exact dates for each year, since the times change from year to year: www.dubaishopping festival.com. Dubai also sponsors a summer shopping festival—Dubai Summer Surprises: www.mydsf.com.

The Dubai Shopping Festival is a very busy time of year, especially since three major sports events also take place during this time:

- Dubai Desert Classic (Professional Golf Association tournament)
- Dubai Open (ATP event)
- Dubai World Cup (world's richest horse race)

Ramadan

When planning your trip to the UAE or any other Middle Eastern country, keep in mind Ramadan, the holy month of fasting (no eating, drinking, smoking, or sexual activity during the day), which varies according to the Islamic lunar calendar. In 2008, for example, Ramadan ran from September 1st to October 1st. In 2009, Ramadan runs from August 21st to September 21st. During Ramadan, shops and restaurants outside the major hotels restrict hours to accommodate their staff members. Traffic is also lighter during the morning hours. And laws on indecent public behavior (hugging and kissing) may be strictly enforced.

Given such restricted hours and activities, you may want to plan your trip either before or after Ramadan. However, Ramadan in the UAE is much less restrictive than in other Muslim countries. At least know when Ramadan starts during the year you plan to travel to the UAE—then count 30 days to see if it might negatively affect your travel plans.

Useful Resources

You'll find numerous print and online resources to plan your trip to the UAE. And once you arrive, you'll find a wealth of additional resources to navigate this place with ease. In fact, you may feel overwhelmed with all the information available on Dubai!

Print

Some of the best English language travel guides on the UAE come from Lonely Planet, Time Out, Insight, Rough Guides, and Footprint. However, most of these books only focus on Dubai:

- *Dubai* (Lonely Planet)
- *Dubai* (Insight Pocket Guide)
- *Footprint Dubai* (Footprint)
- *Best of Dubai* (Lonely Planet)
- *Time Out Dubai, Abu Dhabi, and the UAE* (Time Out)
- *Dubai Encounter* (Lonely Planet)
- *Rough Guides' Dubai Directions* (Rough Guides)
- *Cool Restaurants Dubai*
- *Top 10 Dubai and Abu Ahabi*
- *Spectrum Guide to the United Arab Emirates*
- *Inside Dubai*
- *Travellers Dubai*

The most detailed information on Dubai and Abu Dhabi is found in the two essential expatriate guides published annually by Explorer Publishing (www.explorer-publishing.com):

- *Dubai: The Complete Residents' Guide*
- *Abu Dhabi: The Complete Residents' Guide*

These two books are difficult to find outside the UAE (try www.impact publications.com), but they are widely available at the airports and in bookstores and hotels within the country. Also available in bookstores in the UAE are several other useful annual guides:

- *The Good Food Guide: The UAE's Best Restaurants and Bars*
- *Shopping: Your Definitive Guide to Dubai's Malls, Stores, Souks and Boutiques*

Your hotel should have the latest issues of these two essential weekly Time Out publications on what's going on in both Dubai and Abu Dhabi:

- *Time Out Dubai*
- *Time Out Abu Dhabi*

Also, look for a variety of publications produced by the Government of Dubai's Department of Tourism and Commerce Marketing, such as:

- ***Dubai: Official Pocket Guide***
- ***Dubai At a Glance*** (the ubiquitous map of Dubai)

Also look for a few free tourist guides, such as *Discover Dubai* and *City Info*, which may be available at your hotel or in some shops and shopping centers.

While the free government map (*Dubai At a Glance*) is available everywhere and seems to be used by everyone, it has its limitations—small print is hard to read, only covers part of the city, and lacks sufficient detail. As a result, you may want to visit a bookstore to pick up some additional maps of the city. One of best maps is iMap's *Dubai*, which includes 2D and 3D maps of the Dubai Creek area (*Deira and Bur Dubai*).

Online

For online background information about the UAE, Dubai, Abu Dhabi, and Sharjah, go to these websites, which include a wealth of information on the history, economics, culture, geography, military, politics, transportation, education, and demographics of these places:

- **Wikipedia—UAE**
  http://en.wikipedia.org/wiki/United_Arab_Emirates
- **Wikipedia—Dubai**
  http://en.wikipedia.org/wiki/Dubai
- **Wikipedia—Abu Dhabi**
  http://en.wikipedia.org/wiki/Abu_Dhabi
- **Wikipedia—Sharjah**
  http://en.wikipedia.org/wiki/Sharjah
- **Wikitravel—UAE**
  http://wikitravel.org/en/United_Arab_Emirates
- **CIA's World Factbook**
  www.cia.gov/library/publications/the-world-factbook/geos/ae.html

Some of the best websites, with extensive coverage of travel in the UAE, include the following:

Travel Websites

Dubai
- www.timeoutdubai.com
- http://dubaitourism.co.ae

- www.dubailife.com
- www.dubaicityguide.com/main/index.asp?ref=vis
- www.wordtravels.com/Cities/United+Arab+ Emirates/Dubai
- www.world66.com/asia/middleeast/unitedarabemirates/dubai

Abu Dhabi
- www.timeoutabudhabi.com
- www.abudhabitourism.ae/Corp/en/default.aspx
- www.wordtravels.com/Cities/United+Arab+Emirates/ Abu+Dhabi
- www.executivetravelmagazine.com/page/Abu+Dhabi
- www.miceonline.net/abudhabi/introConvention.htm

Sharjah
- www.sharjah-welcome.com
- www.dubaicityguide.com/sharjah/index.asp
- www.expo-centre.co.ae/about/Sharjah.html

Also, check out our list of UAE **tour and tour group websites** (see pages 75-76) for useful information on various aspects of travel in the UAE.

UAE News Sites
- www.gulfnews.com
- www.uaenews.com
- www.khaleejtimes.com
- www.uaeinteract.com
- www.xpress4me.com/home
- www.godubai.com/gulftoday
- www.7days.ae

Anticipated Costs

When considering the costs of travel to the UAE, always keep in mind that you are visiting a land of plenty where you will be offered an incredible smorgasbord of tempting treasures and pleasures. Indeed, some critics say the UAE has too much of everything, especially on the luxury end of the travel spectrum. However, this is not an issue with visitors who enjoy an abundance of quality choices when they travel. Even budget travelers have options. This place dazzles even the most seasoned travelers who think they have seen and done everything.

If you enjoy the finer things in life and cost is not a major concern, the UAE will more than meet your expectations as a very special place worth visiting. If you are a budget traveler, you may want to recalculate your anticipated costs—take enough cash and credit card reserves for unanticipated expenses and temptations.

Budget Up

While many exotic places around the world were initially opened up to tourism by backpackers, budget travelers, and Lonely Planet devotees, the UAE was basically developed by wealthy oil sheikhs, businessmen, investors, traders, and five-star hoteliers. As a result, the UAE lacks a strong budget travel tradition as well as associated accommodations, restaurants, shopping, and transportation responsive to the needs of such travelers. Unlike nearby Morocco, Egypt, Ethiopia, Oman, Yemen, Jordan, Syria, Iran, Turkey, Pakistan, and India—where budget travelers have had a major impact on opening these countries to tourism and where the budget travel industry is alive and well—the UAE was pioneered by a different class of traveler with a decided emphasis on luxury travel. The UAE especially attracts high-end travelers who are not particularly sensitive to costs. And it has stayed that way over the past two decades and is likely to continue so in the foreseeable future.

However, budget travelers are still welcome in the UAE, but they should consider "budgeting up" in anticipation of additional travel costs. The least expensive accommodations, restaurants, and shopping appealing to such travel budgets are disproportionately found in the Deira area of Old Dubai and in Sharjah.

Five-Star Hotel-Centered Luxury

While you need not spend a fortune in the UAE, you most likely will spend a great deal of money here, more so than in many other places you have visited. An increasingly expensive place for local residents, above all the UAE is a luxury destination for independent travelers who confine many of their activities to five-star hotels and resorts, which are much more than just convenient places to sleep. Indeed, these multi-faceted properties are major centers for accommodations, restaurants, bars, pubs, nightclubs, spas, sports activities, meetings—and shopping.

The UAE is especially popular with affluent travelers from the Middle East, Asia, Russia, Europe, and the UK who are prepared to spend a great deal of money here enjoying the finer things in life— hotels, resorts, fine restaurants, nightclubs, shopping, sports activities, and desert safaris. Some will even purchase condos, apartments, or villas as they get caught up in the UAE's building and property investment frenzy. Many also have the advantage of traveling with a strong European currency, the Euro, which goes far in a country that pegs its currency to the sometimes weaker U.S. dollar.

Travel styles differ among various nationalities. Americans, for example, always seem to be on the move, staying in one location for only a few days. On the other hand, Germans are known to select one resort and then spend 7-10 days enjoying their stay in that single location. Even expatriates from nearby countries enjoy coming to Dubai on R&R to experience a luxurious sojourn. Regardless of costs, they are thrilled to just be here since they have nothing like it where they live!

Budget and cultural travelers may feel overwhelmed by all the conspicuous wealth that flows through the tourist industry, as well as lament the lack of authentic cultural opportunities in a land preoccupied with shaping the future.

Best Bargains

The best deals in the UAE are on transportation, parking, local foods, and some shopping.

Transportation and Parking

Taxis are very inexpensive, with most rides costing US$1-2. Rental cars also are a good deal, with many available for under US$35 a day. While some areas have parking meters, most parking in Dubai and Abu Dhabi is free. If you are in a ticketed area, be sure to faithfully feed the ticket machine and properly display your payment receipt on the dashboard of your car. The parking cops seem to quickly catch violators, who are then subject to a stiff fine (US$30).

Tours

You can select from a variety of package tours, independent tours, and local guides that can range from US$100 to US$500 a day per person. For prices and other details on such services, check out the websites we listed under tours and tour groups.

Accommodations

Accommodations can be a major expense when traveling in the UAE. Indeed, both Dubai and Abu Dhabi have a disproportionate number of four—and five-star hotels and resorts that go for US$300 to US$2,000 a night. Given the high occupancy rates of many properties during the November to March high season, little discounting takes place when hotel rooms are in such short supply. Even four-star hotels during the peak season go for over US$400 a night (some triple their prices during high season), if you can get in! With over 100 new hotels under construction, this situation may change during the next few years. If you visit the UAE during the off season, many hotels discount up to 50 percent off their normal rack rate.

You can find rooms for under US$100 a night (try the St. George Hotel Dubai in Deira) during the off season, but finding anything under US$80 a night may be difficult.

You can save substantially on the cost of accommodations by renting a one—or two-bedroom condo or apartment (frequently referred to as "vacation rentals," "vacation hotels," or "hotel apartments"). However, these places are not as convenient, nor do they have as many amenities (restaurants, bars, spas, sports facilities, personal services) available as the major hotels and resorts.

For pricing details on accommodations, including discounted hotels and resorts, check out our hotel and resort section.

Dining

The UAE offers a variety of dining options that appeal to all budgets and travel lifestyles. Outstanding restaurants in the top hotels, such as the Burj Al Arab (Dubai) and the Emirates Palace (Abu Dhabi), can be expensive (US$150-$200+ per person), especially if you order wine with your meal. Keep in mind that menu prices often include tax and service, which reflect 16 to 20 percent of your total bill.

Outside the top international hotels, you'll seldom pay more than US$20 for a meal. We identify many of the best places to dine in Dubai and Abu Dhabi in our restaurant section.

At the same time, you can find some excellent local restaurants and eateries that offer substantial meals for under US$10 per person. Many are ethnic eateries in the Deira and Bur Dubai areas. Your least expensive (also known as local fast-food) dining choices are shawarma food stalls, Indian restaurants in Old Dubai, and fast food restaurants and cafes in shopping malls and along major streets.

Shopping

You'll find some bargain shopping, especially in the Karama Centre area and in the souks of Deira. However, you usually get what you pay for in these areas—cheap goods. Duty-free shops advertise major savings, and stores periodically run sales, especially during the annual Dubai Shopping Festival. Depending on where you come from and your comparative shopping experience, savings can be substantial on many tax-free luxury items that also go on sale. However, you really need to know the comparable cost of products elsewhere before assuming you're getting good bargains in the UAE.

Planning and Serendipity

You can travel this country on US$100 or US$10,000 a day, depending on your preferences and travel style. Some budget travelers manage to get by comfortably for under US$100 a day. But most travelers can expect to spend from US$200 to US$500 a day per person, which includes accommodations, food, and transportation. Hotels, often the largest daily expense, will be most expensive during the annual Dubai Shopping Festival. Prices may be one-half to one-third as much during "slower" tourist seasons.

Shoppers find costs to be very unpredictable, depending on their shopping interests and sleuthing skills for bargains. For them, costs and serendipity go hand in hand!

Money Matters

The local monetary unit is the **dirham** (Dhs), which is divided into 100 fils and pegged to the U.S. dollar. It's also called the AED (Arab Emirate Dirham).

The exchange rate (2008) for US dollars is: US$1 = Dhs. 3.6740 (Dhs.1 = US$.27218). You can check current exchange rates by going to these online currency converters:

- www.oanda.com
- www.xe.com
- www.x-rates.com

Coins and bank notes are available in the following denominations:

- **Coins:** Silver-colored and available in three denominations: Dhs.1 (round), 50 fils (7-sided), and 25 fils (round).
- **Banknotes:** Printed in eight different colored denominations:
  Dhs.5—brown
  Dhs.10—green
  Dhs.20—light blue
  Dhs.50—purple
  Dhs.100—pink

Dhs.200—brown/green

Dhs.500—blue

Dhs.1000—brown/purple

You can **exchange money** at banks, hotels, and money changers (most deal with cash only). Banks tend to give the best exchange rates, although money changers outside the airport often give good rates on large denomination bills. Money changers are very convenient since they are found in shopping centers and near souks.

Banks are open Saturday through Thursday, 8am to 2pm or 3pm. Some banks keep longer hours.

Banks and some exchanges accept **traveler's checks**. It's most convenient to carry traveler's checks in denominations of US$100.

ATMs are widely available in Dubai and Abu Dhabi at banks, in shopping centers, and at some hotels.

Major credit cards (Visa, MasterCard, American Express, Diners Card) are widely accepted in hotels, restaurants, and shops in Dubai and Abu Dhabi. It's always a good idea to travel with at least two different credit cards, just in case you have any issues in using your credit card when traveling abroad. Also, keep in mind that most credit card companies will charge you an extra fee (1-2 percent) for using your credit cards when traveling abroad. Since shops in souks prefer cash, you're in a better position to bargain with cash than with credit cards.

Keep these tips in mind when using money in the UAE:

- Take sufficient cash—it always comes in handy, especially in souks and outside Dubai and Abu Dhabi.

- If using US dollars to exchange money, bring crisp new notes. US$100 notes usually get the best exchange rate; bring some smaller denominations for times you don't expect to spend US$100 before leaving the country.

- Use credit cards in places that readily accept them and where there is no advantage in using cash—major hotels, restaurants, and shops.

- Plan to use cash which shopping in the local souks and small street shops.

- Carry small change in local currency for taxis and small purchases—many taxi drivers are short of small change. Dhs.1 coins and Dhs.5 and Dhs.10 banknotes will come in handy with taxis.

- Be careful about adding tips to restaurant credit card slips in major restaurants. Since most of these places already include a

10-percent service charge in their prices, you're throwing away your money by adding a tip, which most likely will not go to your server.

Frequently Asked Questions

How safe are Dubai and the UAE?

About as safe as it gets these days for travelers. The biggest safety issues are traffic and accidents. For a discussion of this subject, see our section on safety and security (pages 26-28).

When's the best time to travel to the UAE?

It depends on your budget, interests, and tolerance for heat. In terms of weather, the UAE is very hot in the summer from May through September. This also is the off season when hotel and resort prices are a bargain—many at one-half to one-third of their peak season rates.

The winter months of December, January, and February can be very pleasant, but this also is the high season when hotels are full and their prices skyrocket—the US$120 a night hotel in September becomes a $420 a night hotel in January, and you may have difficulty getting in at any price! January, February, and March also are busy months for several international sports tournaments in Dubai and Abu Dhabi.

Shopping festivals are held annually during January and February and again in late June through August.

Will I get lost if I try to travel on my own?

It's difficult to get lost here since maps and signage are relatively good and English is widely spoken within Dubai and Abu Dhabi. With a compass and a map, and a willingness to ask questions, you shouldn't get lost for long even outside these cities. In the process, you'll probably have a good time finding your way around.

Our general travel rule of thumb is this: You probably won't get lost for more than 15 minutes anywhere you travel in the world. If you do, you'll most likely have a wonderful road story to tell once you get home. Indeed, getting lost may be one of the highlights of your trip!

What documents do I need to get into the UAE?

For most nationals from the Middle East, Europe, and the Americas arriving as tourists, all you need is a valid passport since visas are issued upon arrival. See our visa section on requirements and procedures. Evidence of vaccinations or an international health card is not required unless you come from a cholera-infected area of the world.

Is it okay to travel from Israel to the UAE?

Yes and no. It's okay as long as you know how to play the visa game. In solidarity with other Arab countries, the UAE has an anti-Israeli policy—you may not enter their country if you are an Israeli citizen or show evidence of having traveled to Israel. The most obvious evidence is a passport stamp. If you've been to Israel, make sure Israeli immigration officials do not put an Israeli stamp in your passport. They routinely give visitors a special stamped paper in lieu of the passport stamp since they know visitors have to play this visa game with Arab countries.

How should I pack for the UAE?

Remember that dress is relatively neat and conservative in the UAE. Confine beachwear, including shorts, to beaches, hotels, and resorts—they are not appropriately worn elsewhere. When packing clothes, take into consideration the UAE's hot and humid climate. Lightweight summer clothing is recommended for most of the year. Desert evenings can be cool even in the summer, but especially in the winter. You also would be wise to include a good pair of walking shoes, a hat, a compass (will really help with directions outside the cities), credit cards, and traveler's checks.

Don't forget to pack lots of film, flash cards, tapes, disks, and back-up batteries for your cameras since the UAE is of special interest to photographers wishing to document this incredible place—especially the many tall buildings and delightful desert scenes.

Shoppers should consider taking one empty suitcase filled with bubble wrap and a few packing items, such as tape, scissors, twine, black magic marker, and "FRAGILE" stickers. These items will come in handy when you get ready to leave the UAE with any treasures that could get damaged if not packed properly.

I only have a week. Where should I go?

Check out our sample itineraries, which will primarily take you to Dubai, Abu Dhabi, and Sharjah. We recommend a 10-day trip that also would include neighboring Oman. With an extra three to four days, you should seriously consider driving to Oman, which is only about two hours from Dubai or Abu Dhabi. This is one of the most interesting countries on the Arabian Peninsula, which also is undergoing a major building boom that is different from that of glitzy Dubai. If you have time, consider spending a few days in Yemen.

Where can I get a good map?

You should be able pick up the widely used government-issued map on Dubai—*Dubai At a Glance*—at the airport, hotels, and tourist offices.

It's a small fold-out map with a general overview of the city that also identifies many key locations (hotels, malls, sites). It doesn't provide much detail on particular areas, which at times can be frustrating, especially if you're driving through the city or looking for particular addresses.

You'll find a similar map, glossier and more detailed, for Abu Dhabi—Abu Dhabi City Map—at the Abu Dhabi airport and hotels.

Neither of these maps take you very far beyond the cities. The local bookstores also have maps of both Dubai and Abu Dhabi. Useful road maps of the UAE are difficult to find.

How careful do I need to be about the food and drinks in UAE?

While the local water should be safe—produced and treated through huge desalination plants—travelers are wise to stay with bottled water, which is plentiful and inexpensive. Food handling in major restaurants is considered good by international standards, including fresh salads. But it's always good to be careful in what you eat since you don't want to spend time recovering from an illness.

What's the best way to get around in Dubai and Abu Dhabi?

At least for now, Dubai and Abu Dhabi do not have public transportation systems other than a crowded bus service that primarily handles local residents who know where they are going. The most convenient way to get around is by metered taxis, which are relatively cheap. Self-drive cars also are inexpensive, and driving is not very difficult given the UAE's good road system. However, during certain times of the day driving in Dubai can be a challenge because of the extremely congested traffic in certain parts of the city. The Deira and Bur Dubai sections of Old Dubai are best covered on foot. If you have a self-drive car, you may still want to take a taxi into and out of these very congested areas.

What's the best way to get around the rest of the UAE?

Either a self-drive car or a car with driver. You may want to consider taking local tours. For details on these options, see our sections on transportation and tours.

What's best way to get my treasures home?

Most major shops that work with international visitors are experienced in arranging international shipments. Just make sure you feel confident that they can do the job. Some merchants may tell you that they can ship—"no problem"—but once you start probing the details, you discover they are engaging in wishful thinking.

Start by asking questions about the whole shipping process—whom they use, what paperwork you will need for receiving your shipment, how long it will take, who does the packing, and the total costs for packing and shipping from the store to your door. You may be surprised by their answers to these questions!

Make sure you pay particular attention to the quality of packing. Some merchants don't have a clue as to how best to pack delicate items—they wrap to disguise the identity of the item rather than secure it!

There's nothing worse than finding a unique treasure and then receiving it damaged, because someone did not know how to pack properly. This is when that recommended suitcase full of bubble wrap, along with packing tape, comes in handy as you re-pack items to your own standards.

Keep in mind that you will need to clear Customs at your end and pay additional fees for handling your shipment at the airport or shipping terminal and then arranging for it to be delivered to your home or office.

You may find the cost of receiving a shipment at your end is as expensive as the international transportation! Indeed, a US$500 shipping quote may turn out to cost you US$1,000 because of all the additional add-on fees and transportation charges at your end. International shipments by sea from the UAE should cost no more than US$250 per cubic meter.

You may find that shipping many items by air freight is more convenient and not much more expensive than shipping by sea. Be sure to check on the comparative costs of sea versus air shipments.

If you are considering air shipments, make sure you get a quote for air freight shipments, which can be arranged through a shipping broker. Shipping by FedEx, UPS, or DHL can be extremely expensive for large items—two to three times more than air freight. You pay for the convenience of delivery to your door. At present flights across the Atlantic allow two pieces of checked baggage per passenger. However, the recent charge for a second piece of buggage imposed on domestic U.S. flights may be extended to international fights in the future.

TIP: Whenever possible, take your treasures with you. If you travel with one suitcase, you can use your additional baggage allowance to transport your purchases in another suitcase or a special well-packed box.

Many shops will pack your items to airline specifications. Alternatively, many hotels can help you pack boxes or will direct you to good packers. Just ask the concierge or front desk for packing and shipping assistance.

Using your baggage allowance in this manner may save you a few hundred dollars in international shipping costs. But be sure to check with the airlines on specifications for such a box. Security regulations on some airlines may prohibit such packing.

What should I do about money?

Spending money is easy in the UAE. Credit cards are widely accepted, and you'll find ATM machines in major banks, shopping malls, and hotels. It's always good to carry cash and some traveler's checks, just in case you need to make large purchases where it's to your advantage to pay cash.

Where's the best place to shop?

It depends on your interests. Dubai is the UAE's shopping center. Its 40+ shopping malls are filled with the latest in designer labels, luxury goods, and arts and crafts. The famous Gold Souk and most major shopping centers and top hotels have numerous shops offering gold and jewelry. If you're interested in carpets, arts, and crafts, a trip to the Blue Souk in Sharjah should be on your list. See our shopping section for information on shopping in the UAE.

What else is there to do other than shop in the UAE?

The UAE offers a wide variety of activities, especially sports and recreation, from spectator sports (horse and camel races) to desert safaris and deep sea fishing. You'll probably find less than one day of sightseeing in Dubai. The museum and cultural center of the UAE is Sharjah, although Abu Dhabi will soon have a few world-class museums.

What's there to do at night?

Dubai is famous for its active nightlife. This includes everything from late night shopping to restaurants, dinner cruises, bars, pubs, nightclubs, and outdoor concerts, which include popular DJs, dancing, and live musical entertainment.

Should I consider buying property in the UAE?

Since 2002, the year expatriates could legally purchase property, the real estate market has been very hot in Dubai and Abu Dhabi. Be careful what you wish for since this could be an overheated market, and there are some important unresolved issues concerning ownership and transfer of property for foreign owners.

Is the UAE a good place for medical procedures?

All indications are that the UAE is becoming a big regional player for quality medical care, especially since opening the first phase of the Dubai Healthcare City in 2007. They also are marketing themselves as a new center for medical tourism, competing favorably with Thailand, Singapore, India, and South Africa. Given the UAE's money-is-no-object pattern of attracting top talent, developing first-class infrastructure, and acquiring the necessary technology to compete globally and with an eye on becoming the best in the world, we recommend taking a serious look at what the UAE has to offer for medical care. It will be special.

The UAE in Brief

Abu Dhabi: The capital city and largest emirate (87 percent of land area) in the UAE.

Airlines: The national carrier is Emirates, one of the world's top 10 airlines. The UAE is serviced by 113 airlines with direct links to more than 195 destinations around the world.

Al Ain: Known as the Garden City and spread over several kilometers, this modern desert oasis and university town with impressive wide boulevards is a major border entry point with Oman (Buraimi). It's located about 160 kilometers east of Abu Dhabi and southeast of Dubai.

Alcohol: Only available in licensed hotel restaurants, pubs, bars, and clubs. Non-Muslim locals must have an Alcohol License in order to purchase alcohol.

Area: 83,600 square kilometers or 32,278 square miles—slightly smaller than the U.S. state of Maine.

Banks: Most banks are open from 8am to 1pm Saturday through Wednesday, and from 8am to 12noon on Thursday. The HSBC is open 8am to 3pm. Some banks also are open from 4:30pm to 6:30pm.

Borders: 867 kilometers of borders shared with Oman (410 kilometers) and Saudi Arabia (457 kilometers).

Climate: The UAE has a subtropical arid climate. Winter temperatures range from 10°C (50°F) to 30°C (86°F); summer temperatures can hit a high of 48°C (118.4°F).

Credit cards: Major hotels, restaurants, shops, car rental firms, tour groups, and other tourism players usually accept Visa, MasterCard American Express, and Diners Card.

Cruise terminal: The state-of-the-art Dubai Cruise Terminal is located at Port Rashid, which lies at the mouth of Dubai Creek.

Currency: The Dirham (Dhs) is the UAE's monetary unit. At the time of writing, it was pegged to the U.S. dollar at the rate of US$1 = Dhs.3.675.

Desert safari: Usually a half-day, full-day, or overnight tour into the Arabian desert by four-wheel drive vehicle. Includes various desert activities, such as dune bashing (driving over hilly sand dunes), sand skiing, camel riding, exploring wadis (dry river valleys), visiting a Bedouin village, and dining in the desert (usually a moonlit barbecue buffet with traditional entertainment).

Dubai: The country's second largest emirate—about the size of the U.S. state of Rhode Island. The city of Dubai is the UAE's largest city and main commercial center.

Dubai Desert Classic: The UAE's most prestigious golfing tournament, which attracts many of the world's leading professional golfers, such as Tiger Woods, Vijay Singh, Ernie Els, and Colin Montgomerie.

Dubai Tennis Open: Held at the state-of-the-art Dubai Tennis Stadium, this annual event attracts many of the world's leading tennis professionals, including Roger Federer, Andre Agassi, Marat Safin, Lindsay Davenport, and the Williams sisters.

Dubai World Cup: One of the UAE's most important sports events and fashionable social gatherings. Indeed, this is the world's richest horse race (US$2 million+ purse) held annually at Nad Al Sheba Club.

Electricity: The electricity supply is 220/240 volts at 50 cycles. Electrical configurations take three-prong plugs.

Falconry: A popular traditional Bedouin activity, often included in a desert safari. Watch the different species of falcons do their flying routines.

GDP per capita: US$49,700 (2006).

Global Village: The major center for Dubai's annual festivals, especially the Dubai Shopping Festival. Various countries around the world showcase their products and offer live performances (music and dance) to the millions of visitors attracted to these expansive grounds. Includes an international food court.

Hatta: Located 105 kilometers east of Dubai, this is a popular weekend destination in the Hajar Mountains. Must cross into Oman to reach Hatta.

Hours: Beginning in September 2006, the UAE's official weekend (for government offices and schools) shifted from Thursday/Friday to Friday/Saturday in order to better align the UAE with business operations in other parts of the world. Friday remains the Muslim holy day. Government organizations are open Sunday through Thursday from 7:30am to 3pm (some from 8am to 2pm). Private companies are open from either 8am to 6pm or do a split shift, 8am-1pm and 4pm-7pm. Shopping hours vary. Shopping malls are usually open from Saturday through Thursday,10am to 10pm, and on Friday, 2pm-10pm. Many shops outside shopping malls are open from 9am until 1pm and from 4pm until 9pm. During shopping festivals shopping malls may stay open until 1am.

Independence day: December 2, 1971.

Labor force: 3 million workers in agriculture (7%), industry (15%), and services (78%).

Language: The national language is Arabic. English is widely spoken and used in business.

Local Time: The UAE is four hours ahead of Greenwich Mean Time. When it's 12noon in London, it's 4pm in the UAE; when it's 12noon in New York City (Standard Time), it's 9pm in the UAE.

Location: Stretches along the southern shore of the Arabian (Persian) Gulf in the southeastern section of the Arabian Peninsula. Strategically located along the southern approach to the Strait of Hormuz—one of the world's most vital transit points for crude oil.

Mall of the Emirates: The ultimate shopping mall, which is also the world's first shopping resort. A massive hotel and shopping complex complete with over 420 stores, a 14-screen cineplex, a two-level family entertainment zone with indoor roller coasters, over 70 cafes and restaurants, and the world-famous Ski Dubai, an Alpine-themed snow resort where you can literally ski on the day's freshly produced coat of snow.

Medical care: First-rate in Dubai's many private hospitals and clinics.

Medical tourism: One of Dubai's growing attractions for international visitors. World-class medical facilities and service developed by private medical groups and centered in the recently opened Dubai Healthcare City.

Money changers: Money exchanges are found in shopping malls and elsewhere in the cities. They are normally open daily 8am-1pm and 4:30pm-7pm.

Natural hazards: Frequent sand and dust storms.

Natural resources: Primarily petroleum and natural gas, which are centered in Abu Dhabi.

Newspapers: You'll find two English-language newspapers in Dubai—*Gulf News* and *Khaleej Times*. You'll also find online versions of these publications: www.gulfnews.com and www.khaleejtimes.com.

Photography: Locals, especially women, and others in their national dress, do not appreciate having their photos taken. If you want a personal photo, ask permission.

Population: Approximately 4.5 million (19% Emirati, 23% other Arab and Iranian, 50% South Asians, and 8% other expatriates).

Religion: Islam is the official religion of the UAE. Approximately 85 percent of Emirates are Sunni Muslims and 15 percent are Shi'a Muslims. The expat population (79 percent) practice a variety of religions, depending on their country of origin—Christianity, Buddhism, Hinduism, etc. Christian churches maintain a very low profile in the UAE—primarily found behind walls and with no signage.

Sharjah: Located immediately to the northeast of Dubai, this is the UAE's cultural capital with its many museums and heritage sites. It's also a major center of carpets (visit the Blue Souk).

Shopping festivals: Each year Dubai organizes three shopping festivals. The most popular and heavily promoted one is the annual Dubai Shopping Festival (since 1996), which takes place for 32 days during January and February (check www.mydsf.com for exact dates, as these change from year to year) and is promoted as a "world-class shopping and family entertainment" extravaganza. Its main venue is the Global Village followed by the various shopping malls and the airport duty-free area. The Dubai Summer Surprises shopping festival (since 1998) takes place in the heat of the summer, from late June through September, and is mainly centered in the cool shopping malls. Dubai the City That Cares shopping festival (since 1998) is promoted during the holy month of Ramadan (dates vary from year to year, depending on the lunar calendar). Emphasizing the spirit of charity, this festival results in lively shopping malls and souks after Iftar (fast-breaking) and late night shopping until 1am!

Souk: A term referring to a traditional market or bazaar area (a complex or a street), which can include anything from household goods and fresh foods to clothes, handicrafts, antiques, and souvenirs. Every city has one or more souks. Some have been upgraded to become modern air-conditioned souks.

Sports: The UAE offers dozens of spectator and participant sports activities. See our sports and recreation section for related information.

Taxes: The UAE is a tax-free country, except for tourist taxes that are added to hotel and restaurant bills: 10% in Dubai and 6% in Abu Dhabi

Temperatures: see Climate

Terrain: A relatively flat, barren coastal plain that merges into rolling sand dunes punctuated by a vast desert wasteland. Mountains located in the east.

Tipping: Many restaurants add a 10% service charge to menu prices. When no service charge is indicated, it's customary to leave a 10% tip.

Visas: Most visitors, except AGCC nationals, need a visa to visit the UAE. These are issued upon arrival for most nationals and are good for either 14 days (transit visa) or 30 days (renewable Visit Visa or non-renewable Tourist Visa).

Wadi: Dry river valley cut through rocky hills or mountains.

Water: Most tap water in Dubai and Abu Dhabi is produced through huge desalination plants. It's considered safe to drink, but most tourists and residents prefer bottled mineral water which is readily available.

Weekend holiday: Friday and Saturday (changed in September 2006 from Thursday and Friday).

Wildlife: Look for Arabian oryx and gazelle, which populate the 225-square-kilometer Dubai Desert Conservation Reserve (DDCR) operated by the Dubai government and Emirates Al Maha Desert Resort and Spa. To view this exquisite wildlife, which was first released into the Reserve from Al Maha in 2004, stay at the fabulous Al Maha Desert Resort and Spa—where you can also enjoy camel trekking, horse riding, falconry, and archery—or contact one of the four approved safari operators who have access to this area: Arabian Adventures, Alpha Tours, Travco, and Lama Tours.

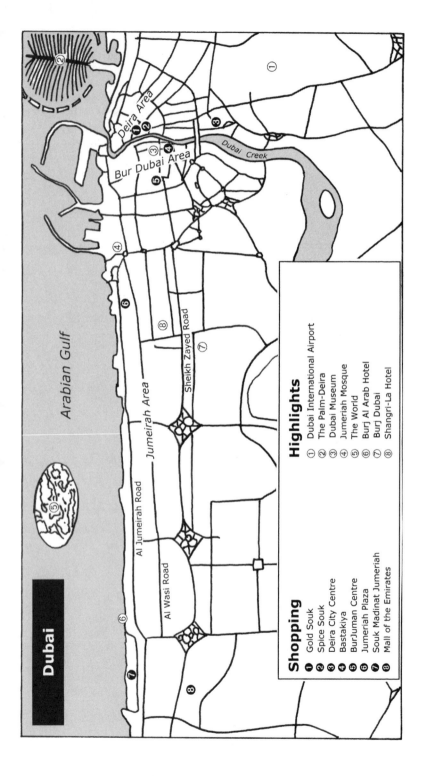

Dubai

Arabian Gulf

Deira Area

Bur Dubai Area

Dubai Creek

Jumeirah Area

Al Jumeirah Road

Al Wasi Road

Sheikh Zayed Road

Highlights
1. Dubai International Airport
2. The Palm-Deira
3. Dubai Museum
4. Jumeriah Mosque
5. The World
6. Burj Al Arab Hotel
7. Burj Dubai
8. Shangri-La Hotel

Shopping
1. Gold Souk
2. Spice Souk
3. Deira City Centre
4. Bastakiya
5. BurJuman Centre
6. Jumeriah Plaza
7. Souk Madinat Jumeriah
8. Mall of the Emirates

Navigating the UAE

GETTING AROUND and enjoying your stay in the UAE requires some basic knowledge about distances, transportation, major areas, alternative activities, and tour options. The UAE has a great deal to offer visitors who know how to navigate this place on their own or with the assistance of local tour groups. If you have limited time, you'll want to plan well each day of your stay.

Size and Distances

Remember, this is a relatively small country—about the size of the U.S. states of South Carolina, Maine, or Indiana, or the country of Austria. Since roads are excellent and distances between major cities are minimal, you can reach most places within a 30-minute to two-hour drive from Dubai. In fact, you may want to make Dubai your base from which to visit other areas of the country.

If you are based in Dubai or Abu Dhabi, this is how long it should take to go between major locations by self-drive car or taxi:

Dubai to Abu Dhabi	$1\frac{1}{2}$ - 2 hours
Dubai to Sharjah	45 minutes
Dubai to Al Ain	$1\frac{1}{2}$ - 2 hours
Dubai to Hatta	$1\frac{1}{2}$ - 2 hours
Abu Dhabi to Al Ain	$1\frac{1}{2}$ - 2 hours

Since Dubai is very spread out from north to south, going from the northern end of the city (Dubai International Airport or Deira area) to the southern end (Dubai Marina or Jebel Ali Port) may take 45 minutes to an hour, depending on traffic. Major bottleneck points are the overworked and poorly engineered Maktoum Bridge spanning Dubai Creek, the congested streets of Old Dubai (Deira and Bur Dubai), and traffic-choked Sheikh Zayed Road. Driving through any of these areas during the city's three daily rush-hour periods will significantly slow down your travel plans to get across the city.

Sample Itineraries

Visitors should spend a minimum of three days in the UAE to see the highlights of Dubai and Abu Dhabi. Seven days here would be sufficient to cover the major cities as well as key outlying areas, including the interior city of Al Ain and a desert safari. Most visitors, however, focus on Dubai, which seems to have it all—hotels, restaurants, shopping malls, souks, entertainment, cruises, and outdoor activities.

We suggest the following three-, five-, and seven-day itineraries for the UAE:

Days	Area/Activity
1	Old Dubai: Deira and Bur Dubai areas
2	New Dubai: Sheikh Zayed Road and Jumeirah area
3	Abu Dhabi

Days	Area/Activity
1	Old Dubai: Deira and Bur Dubai areas
2	New Dubai: Sheikh Zayed Road and Jumeirah area
3	Abu Dhabi
4	Sharjah
5	Desert safari

1	Old Dubai: Deira and Bur Dubai areas
2	New Dubai: Sheikh Zayed Road and Jumeirah area
3	Abu Dhabi
4	Sharjah
5	Al Ain
6	Desert safari
7	Dubai (The Palms, Dubailand, Deira)

Laid-back **Abu Dhabi** primarily appeals to local residents and businessmen who enjoy its less frantic lifestyle. While you can easily cover the highlights of Abu Dhabi in one day, you may want to stay overnight in Abu Dhabi. Two days here may be too much, unless you plan to attend sporting events, enjoy the beaches, or explore beyond the city—do a desert safari and/or visit Al Ain.

Sharjah, which is a 45-minute drive north of Dubai, is a rapidly developing city, which boasts several interesting museums, cultural sites, art galleries, and souks/shopping malls. You can easily cover this city in a day trip from Dubai. It's not necessary to stay overnight in Sharjah.

Dubai

Dubai is a sprawling city that is constantly growing up and out, metamorphosing into an even Greater Dubai. However, it won't take you long to figure out this city and decide what you like and dislike about it. Dubai currently has four major sections, which we recommend visiting in this order:

Deira Creek Area

Located just west of the airport and north of other major sections of the city, Deira Creek is basically a waterway that divides the two oldest sections of the city—**Deira** on the north side and **Bur Dubai** on the south side of the creek. Until just a few years ago, this whole area was Dubai's central business and residential district. But today, if you look farther south from the banks of Deira, you'll see, in the horizon, numerous high-rise buildings that define the city's new business district and our second major area in Dubai—**Sheikh Zayed Road**.

Sometimes aptly referred to as Smuggler's Creek, Dubai Creek is the center of this emirate's trading heritage. It's a very **busy and picturesque waterway** lined with traditional dhow (Arabic wooden boats), crossed by abra (water taxi), and navigated by small boats and cruise ships that operate day and night. Both areas are noted for their boats, docks, narrow streets, congested traffic, a few architecturally interesting high-rise office buildings, some major hotels, a few historic buildings, residential areas, and traditional souks and street shops that cater to Dubai's large immigrant community as well as attract many tourists in search of a cultural experience. Tourists especially enjoy browsing through the souks, taking the water taxi, and joining an evening dhow dinner cruise. These two areas also are linked by two bridges, a tunnel, and numerous water taxis. Both areas are relatively easy to walk during the cool season. If you have a rental car, you may want to leave it at your hotel and take a taxi into these two areas.

> **TIP:** Take a camera when you visit the Dubai Creek area. You'll have numerous opportunities to take some of the most interesting photos of Dubai in this area.

Deira Section

On the **Deira side** (north) of the creek, ask the taxi to take you to either the **Gold Souk** or **Spice Souk**—two of the city's major destinations for tourists. Either place will put you in the heart of the most interesting sections of Deira. You also may want to visit the nearby **Covered Souk**, with its cheap household items, and the **Fish Souk**—primarily cultural rather than potential shopping experiences.

The favorite area of Dubai for many visitors who shun the city's boring shopping malls, Deira has the largest number of traditional

souks that wind around numerous narrow alleys, tiny lanes, and convoluted streets. Usually crowded with people and chaotic with cars, delivery trucks, and pushcarts transporting goods by foot to various shops, much of this area has the look and feel of a colorful Third World market out of Iran, India, Pakistan, or Sri Lanka—countries of origin for many of the local merchants and laborers. You'll also pass by hundreds of small shops and restaurants, primarily catering to the clothing, luggage, and household needs of expatriate Indians and Pakistanis. You can easily cover this area in two to four hours, unless you get carried away shopping in the Gold Souk or waste too much time following touts who attempt to sell you knock-off watches and designer handbags from small rooms tucked away in the hallways of buildings in the Covered Souk.

The long and narrow **Spice Souk**—operated by Iranian merchants who offer a fascinating selection of traditionally displayed spices (in bags and bins), and who attempt to persuade tourists that they have powerful natural Viagra, which is often displayed next to a product appropriately labeled "Iranian Snake Oil"—is especially interesting. You may want to pick up some souvenirs here, such as frankincense, an incense burner, saffron, cinnamon, or other spices.

Remember, the souks are closed from 1 to 4pm each day, so plan your day accordingly. You may, for example, want to have a long lunch at one of the major hotels in this area—Sheraton Dubai Creek, Taj Palace, Hyatt Regency, JW Marriott, Traders, Hilton Dubai Creek, Park Hyatt, SAS Radisson (formerly the Inter-Continental Dubai), Sofitel. This also is a good time to explore other interesting parts of Deira. For example, walk along the shoreline and observe the numerous dhow from Iran loading and unloading their cargos the old fashioned way—by hand and crane—and take pictures of the green, black, and white painted ceramic camels in front of the municipal building as well as marvel at several interesting buildings. Indeed, Deira is still home to several architecturally imaginative commercial build-  ings, such as the **Etisalat Telecommunications Building** with a huge golf ball-like structure at the top and the gleaming green-windowed Rolex Building and award-winning **National Bank of Dubai** building (The Pregnant Lady) next to the Sheraton Dubai Creek Hotel as well as the Dubai Creek Golf & Yacht Club with its iconic white dhow sails stretching over the water.

This area also boasts one of Dubai's largest and most popular shopping centers with locals, the 280+ shop family-oriented **Deira City Centre** (www.deiracitycentre.com), although by no means one of our favorites since we find it very "average" as far as shopping malls go (major tenants include Ikea and Carrefour). You may want to return to the Deira area, after you've had a chance to experience the rest of Dubai and the UAE. It's the closest you'll get to a traditional local experience. Compared to this area, other areas in Dubai seem modern and futuristic.

> **TIP: Both begin and end your visit to Dubai in the Deira area.** By so doing, you'll be reminded that there is more to this place than lots of redundant shopping malls, high-rise commercial buildings, fast-food restaurants, food courts, and Disneyland-like re-creations and demonstrations. Still standing with lots of character, this unique area confirms the fact that Dubai has a soul of its own. There are traditional enclaves after all!

But major changes are on the way for this area. For example, a new bridge is being completed to alleviate the terrible traffic congestion of the overworked and poorly engineered Maktoum Bridge. Immediately to the west, and extending into the Arabian Gulf, is one of Dubai's three Palm island reclamation projects—**The Palm Deira** (www.the palm.ae/deira). When completed, this huge residential area, complete with hotels and restaurants, will feed into the Deira area. At the eastern end of Deira, immediately to the south of Dubai International Airport and along the banks of Dubai Creek, is one of Dubai's most ambitious community development projects—**Dubai Festival City** (www.dubai festivalcity.com). This will literally become a city within the city with upscale residential areas, hotels, restaurants, shops, and commercial buildings. Dubai Creek is about to get a major face lift, and new waterfront buildings and activities will soon transform the eastern end of Dubai Creek.

Whatever you do, don't overlook congested Deira. It has its own unique character and secrets, and it's coming back in a very big way with two massive development projects that will transform this area forever! You'll soon be welcoming the "New Deira."

Bur Dubai Section

Directly across the creek from Deira is one of the city's most popular expatriate residential and festive entertainment areas as well as home to several historical sites that make up the city's heritage area—**Bur Dubai**. Laced with narrow streets and an attractive waterfront corniche, this can be a very crowded area, especially at night when the streets often come to a nightmarish halt. Crammed into this area are lots of nondescript apartment buildings, supermarkets, shopping malls, small street shops, restaurants, cafes, bars, and nightclubs. When standing along the corniche or in front of the Textile Souk, you'll find this is a great area from which to take photos of Dubai Creek and the old and new architecture dotting the skyline of Deira.

Bur Dubai is divided into two sections—**Bastakiya** in the east and **Shindagha** in the west. Major shopping is found to the west and south. To get to the most convenient sections, ask the taxi driver to take you to **Al Fahidi Street**. A somewhat busy and disorienting area, this whole area deserves to be walked. Start your walking tour at the Basta Art Café, Sheik Mohammed Center for Cultural Understanding (they have metered parking if you're driving), or the Bastakiah Nights Restaurant (just around the corner and a good place for lunch or dinner with its attractive courtyard and rooftop views of the city). You'll see numerous reconstructed **wind-tower houses** in this area—a symbol of old Dubai and its Iranian merchants who settled this area, the **Bastakiya Quarter**. From these starting places you can easily walk the old section of the city via Al Fahidi Street, which will take you to the Dubai Museum, the Ruler's Court, Grand Mosque, and the covered Bur Dubai Souk (Textile Souk), a newly renovated textile and shoe souk along the creek and next to the water taxi stand. If you continue west and north, you'll be in the **Shindagha area**. Here you'll be able to visit a few old houses of Sheikhs (Sheikh Juma al-Maktoum House, Sheikh Saeed bin Thani House, and Sheikh Obaid bin Thani House) as well as the interesting Heritage Village and Diving Village.

Visiting these two sections of Bur Dubai will be the closest you'll get to a historical experience in Dubai! Expect to spend three to five hours covering this area, depending on how long you linger at the intriguing underground **Dubai Museum**. This area also boasts one of the city's most upscale shopping malls—**BurJuman Centre** (www.bur juman.com) along Trade Centre Road.

The remaining sections of Dubai—to the west and south—are most conveniently reached by car. If you've rented a car, it's time to hit the road to visit the rest of the city—areas that have only recently come to life as the "New Dubai" with its architectural wonders and iconic structures that have quickly left the Dubai Creek area behind.

Sheikh Zayed Road

Located approximately four kilometers directly west of Bur Dubai is Dubai's major financial and hotel district, or what many people consider to be Dubai's new commercial center. Largely created within the past five years, the northern end of this often congested eight-lane Sheikh Zayed Road includes some of the country's tallest buildings and most impressive, although not particularly creative, architecture. Lining both sides of this road for about four kilometers is a high concentration of commercial buildings—the **Dubai World Trade Centre** (built in 1979 and soon to be torn down), **Dubai International Financial Centre**, and what will soon become the world's tallest building and largest shopping center—**Burj Dubai** (www.bur dubai.com). Four of Dubai's major

five-star hotels also are located in this area—**Shangri-La**, **Fairmont**, **Dusit**, and **Emirates Towers**. Most of the major office buildings and hotels have small upscale shopping centers or a few interesting shops.

If you love modern architecture and tall buildings, as well as terrific views of the city, this section of Sheikh Zayed Road is a "must visit" destination. If nothing else, you should at least see what all this talk about the "New Dubai" and its financial power center is all about. And while you're at it, try some of the fine restaurants at the Shangri-La Hotel!

> **TIP:** Avoid crossing Sheikh Zayed Road on foot. It's often a nightmare of speeding traffic.

Continue farther west along this road for another 13 kilometers and you'll come to the sprawling **Mall of the Emirates** (Exit 39, Interchange 4), which is attached to the Kempinski Hotel and boasts the world's largest indoor ski dome, complete with chair lifts and spectators' restaurants. Here the road nearly joins the parallel Al Jumeirah Road with its numerous iconic structures—the self-proclaimed seven-star Burj Al Arab Hotel, The Palm Jumeirah Islands, and Dubai Marina. If you continue south along Sheikh Zayed Road for another 150 kilometers, you'll come to the UAE's capital—Abu Dhabi.

Jumeirah

The upscale residential and resort area of Jumeirah hugs the Arabian Gulf for nearly 20 kilometers and feeds into Jebel Ali Port and one of Dubai's most ambitious projects, the massive Dubai Waterfront city. Running south of Port Rashid at Dubai Creek, starting near the beautiful Jumeirah Mosque, this beachfront area is bordered by the six-lane **Al Jumeirah Road**, which includes four interchanges that connect to Sheikh Zayed Road one to two kilometers to the east. Jumeirah is Dubai's pleasure center with a fabulous collection of beaches, marinas, resorts, shopping centers, and housing complexes. The most distinctive structure, the iconic image of Dubai, is the tall seven-star **Burj Al Arab Hotel** (www.burj-al-arab.com)—reputed to be the world's tallest and best hotel—with its distinctive modernistic *dhow* architecture and colorful interior, a monument to the marriage of extraordinary money, engineering, and flamboyant taste. Flanked on each side next door is the Jumeirah Beach Hotel and the Madinat Jumeirah hotel and shopping complexes. Also in this area you'll find some of Dubai's most ambitious reclamation projects that are being turned into pricey residential islands—The World and The Palm Jumeirah. The Marina Towers complex, located at the Dubai Marina, includes numerous high-rise condominiums and apartments as well as some of Dubai's top hotels: Ritz-Carlton, Hilton Dubai Jumeirah, Habtoor Grand Resort &

Spa, Grosvenor House Dubai, Le Royal Meridien Beach Resort & Spa, and Sheraton Jumeirah Beach Resort & Towers. Two of our favorite arts and antiques shops—Showcase Antiques and Creative Arts Centre—can be found along this road. If you explore the total length of this area, as well as continue south into the new Jebel Ali area with its new Palm Jebel Ali island complex (even larger than The Palms Jumeirah) and Dubai Waterfront development, you may begin asking yourself *"Where are all the people with all the money coming from? Is this a new bubble economy?"* Never mind. This is where a great deal of questionable money ends up invested in pricey real estate purchased by absentee and anonymous owners. Much of this area, especially the villa and condo residential quarters, looks like a ghost town.

Dubailand and International City

Our fourth area is found in the southern and eastern sections of the city—a continuous band of development that sweeps the eastern inland area from north to south. Here, numerous mega projects are either just completed, partially completed, under construction, or still on the drawing board. Directly east of Deira and along the banks of Dubai Creek will be **Dubai Festival City**. Farther east along the road to Hatta will be the new **International City**. Immediately to the south, and on the road to Al Ain, are several huge projects—**Dubailand**, **Global Village**, **Living Legends**, **Dubai Autodrome**, and **Jumeirah Golf Estate**.

The **Global Village** (www.globalvillage.ae) is especially popular with shoppers during the annual **Dubai Shopping Festival** (www.mydsf.com). In fact, the Global Village is now the central focus of this festival. Located within Dubailand, it's laid out as a global souk with 67 country pavilions offering souvenirs and other products. During the festival, this place is packed with visitors who wander around more than 3,000 stalls that sell items from all over the world. Indeed, it attracts over 3 million visitors each year who come here to shop, browse exhibitions, and attend daily concerts.

Upcoming Projects With More Bragging Rights

Each year Dubai announces some new grandiose projects that give them bragging rights to having the biggest and best of something in the world—a sort of self-proclaimed Guinness Book of Records contest with itself, Abu Dhabi, and other cities of the world. Many follow a familiar pattern—the creation of iconic structures. At present the following major projects are underway or in the process of being completed. Several of our video clips on www.ishoparoundthe world.com feature these projects. Most will be completed during 2008 and 2009.

1. **The Palm Islands** (www.thepalm.ae): These creative and ambitious reclamation projects are the world's largest man-made islands. Connected to the mainland by long causeways and developed in the shape of a stylized palm tree, they include three Palm island projects: The Palm Deira, The Palm Jumeirah, and The Palm Jebel Ali. These are integrated residential (villas and apartments) and commercial projects that include hotels, resorts, restaurants, and shops. Developed by Nakheel, the UAE's premier iconic property development company closely connected to the ruler of Dubai, Sheikh Mohammad.

2. **The World** (www.theworld.ae): Situated about three kilometers offshore from the Jumeirah area (opposite the Dubai Offshore Sailing Club), this extremely ambitious project consists of 300 private islands in the shape of the world map. Another iconic property development project of Nakheel, it is designed to attract wealthy residents who want to experience the ultimate in exclusive island living and privacy. It also has attracted property developers who will build some exclusive island resorts, such as the Coral Island Resort, among the islands.

3. **Burj Dubai** (www.burjdubai.com): Located at the southern end of the Sheikh Zayed Road commercial section, this will become the world's tallest building (800+ meters tall) when it's finished in 2008. It will also house the world's largest shopping mall (Dubai Mall) as well as residential, commercial, leisure, and hotel sections along with parks and a lake.

4. **Dubailand** (www.dubailand.ae): Designed to be the region's major tourist and leisure center, Dubailand is essentially a family-oriented theme park complete with a sports city, roller coaster, water park, manmade volcano, theme parks, hotels, golf village, the Global Village, and what may also become the world's largest shopping center, the Mall of Arabia. Twice as big as Disneyworld in Florida, it consists of six huge leisure areas. It's literally a cross between Las Vegas and Disneyworld.

5. **Dubai Festival City** (www.dubaifestivalcity.com): Located immediately south of the Dubai International Airport and east of Deira along the banks of Dubai Creek, this huge waterfront development will be a city within a city. It will include shops, restaurants, hotels, corporate offices, a park, a nursery, residential areas, and schools. At the heart of the City will be the Festival Centre, which will include more than 400 shops, 70 restaurants and cafes, a marina, and a festival square.

6. **Dubai Waterfront** (www.dubaiwaterfront.ae): Located south of the Jumeirah area and adjacent to the Jebel Ali Port and The

Palm Jebel Ali, this massive development project will be bigger than Manhattan and Beirut with its more than 250 master-planned communities. It will include a new downtown with a harbor and a mix of commercial, residential, and resort areas.

7. **Dubai Marina** (http://en.wikipedia.org/wiki/Dubai_Marina): Nearing completion, this massive residential, hotel, and commercial complex lies immediately to the south of The Palm Jumeirah island project. It includes dozens of high-rise condominiums and apartment buildings which are densely packed into a self-contained community.

8. **Hydropolis** (www.hydropolis.com): This is the world's first underwater hotel, which is adjacent to Dubai Marina.

9. **New airport terminal** (www.dubaiairport.com): This new terminal will increase airport capacity from handling 24 million visitors to 70 million visitors a year.

Other projects nearing completion include Dubai Internet City, Dubai Silicon Oasis, Tropical Forest, and Zabeel Park.

The scope and scale of these projects is simply breathtaking. As the bulldozers move the sand and the towering cranes lift tons of steel and glass to complete hundreds of high-rise structures, one constantly asks the question: *"And where are all the people with all the money coming from?"* We could never get a good answer, except that they have been coming and more will be coming soon. Indeed, this is more than just a field of dreams.

There is an important message here for visitors: You will have more and more hotel, restaurant, shopping, and entertainment opportunities in the months and years ahead. If, as officials project, tourist arrivals increase from 6 million in 2006 to 15 million in 2010 and the number of hotel rooms increase from 40,000 to 90,000 by 2009, this city should be well prepared to handle its newfound tourist riches.

Abu Dhabi

Abu Dhabi is the capital of the UAE and the center of the country's great oil riches. This is oil country that has its own story to tell. The center for government and bureaucracy, here's where the big deals are made with the UAE's power elite. Abu Dhabi begs comparison to more glamorous, glitzy, and frenetic Dubai.

Money and Competition

When Dubai disingenuously claims its economy no longer depends on oil, it only tells part of a much larger story about who finances what from where. The oil money from Abu Dhabi continues to pour into

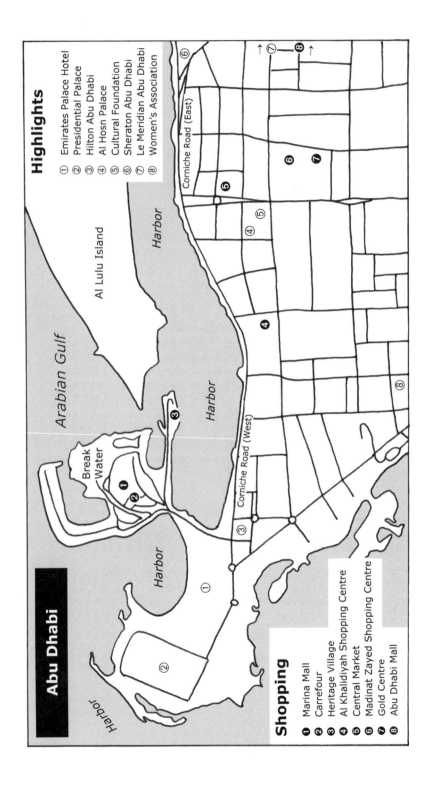

Abu Dhabi

Arabian Gulf

Al Lulu Island

Harbor

Break Water

Corniche Road (West)

Corniche Road (East)

Highlights

1. Emirates Palace Hotel
2. Presidential Palace
3. Hilton Abu Dhabi
4. Al Hosn Palace
5. Cultural Foundation
6. Sheraton Abu Dhabi
7. Le Meridian Abu Dhabi
8. Women's Association

Shopping

1. Marina Mall
2. Carrefour
3. Heritage Village
4. Al Khalidiyah Shopping Centre
5. Central Market
6. Madinat Zayed Shopping Centre
7. Gold Centre
8. Abu Dhabi Mall

Dubai. The real local money is centered in Abu Dhabi, but it invests a great deal of its wealth in Dubai. At the same time, this money crowd prefers living in Abu Dhabi but gambles on Dubai's future.

A city of tall commercial buildings, wide boulevards, green parks, manicured gardens, an attractive corniche, and shopping malls, family-friendly Abu Dhabi is much less hectic than Dubai. Indeed, this is a relatively quiet and conservative city that lacks the go-go tenor of Dubai. The hype and nightlife here are very sedate compared to Dubai. Abu Dhabi also is very aware that it lives in the shadow of Dubai, an awareness that leads to competition between the cities for celebrities, special events, and business. Abu Dhabi has nothing to compare to Dubai's shopping opportunities and complexes. However, times are changing as this city attempts to improve its cultural I.Q. with the acquisition of a Guggenheim Museum and other arts venues—an off-the-shelf approach to cultural development. Abu Dhabi also is the center for major international sports events and is developing its own residential areas and resorts in anticipation of tremendous growth in the years ahead.

Abu Dhabi's showcase property is the **Emirates Palace** (www.emiratespalace.com), an opulent self-proclaimed seven-star hotel/resort and icon that rivals Dubai's Burj Al Arab Hotel. While an over-the-top

government property (owned by the Emirates Group) with reputedly more than US$2 billion invested, the Emirates Palace is a class operation that may well overshadow the Burj Al Arab, depending on your tastes. This is the closest you will get to a

sheikh's palace that also doubles as a public hotel and resort with top restaurants, meeting areas, and sports facilities. If you visit only one major hotel in the UAE, make sure it's the Emirates Palace. If you've already visited the Burj Al Arab, you must compare it to the Emirates Palace—a very different experience. Visiting this place alone is worth the trip to Abu Dhabi!

When there are no special events taking place in Abu Dhabi, there's not a great deal to do there that would take more than one day of shopping, sightseeing, and entertainment. Since the demise of the popular Iranian souk, most of the city's major shopping is confined to two aging shopping malls—**Abu Dhabi Mall** (www.abudhabi-mall.com, north end of Ninth Street) and **Marina Mall** (www.marinamall.ae, The Breakwater)—which offer the same goods and services as found in the much better shopping malls of Dubai. Not surprisingly, these shopping malls primarily cater to the needs of local residents. Visitors may find them to be interesting cultural experiences where locals and expatriates bring their families to do a lot of window shopping, coffee drinking, and eating.

Sightseeing primarily focuses on the Cultural Foundation, Dhow Harbour, Heritage Village, and Petroleum Exhibition—all of which underwhelm many visitors.

Entertainment, which is usually in the form of live music, is primarily found in the bars and nightclubs of major hotels, such as the Sheraton (Zenith), Le Meridian (Captain's Arm), Hilton (Hemingways), and Novotel Centre Hotel (Mood Indigo).

Sports enthusiasts will find many opportunities for golf, tennis, sailing, fishing, scuba diving, snorkeling, and water skiing.

Desert safaris, which include camel riding, desert drives, horseback riding, dune bashing, sand boarding, and dining and sleeping under the stars, are sponsored by several tour operators in Abu Dhabi.

For a good summary of what's going on in Abu Dhabi, visit the Time Out website on this city:

www.timeoutabudhabi.com

Sharjah

Located just north of Dubai, Sharjah is a rapidly developing city that offers some interesting cultural and shopping opportunities for visitors. In fact, Sharjah is the UAE's cultural capital (UNESCO has called it the cultural capital of the Arab world) because of its 15 museums and many art galleries.

Since many people who work in Dubai commute from homes in Sharjah, traffic congestion to and from Dubai can be very heavy in early

morning and late afternoon. Consequently, the best time to visit Sharjah is in the morning when traffic is headed in the opposite direction.

Plan to visit Sharjah as a day trip from Dubai. It's a 45-minute drive from the Deira area of Dubai. In fact, you may be able to cover most of Sharjah's highlights within four to five hours and thus return to Dubai sometime in the afternoon. However, many visitors end up with a full day in Sharjah after they unexpectedly discover the city's many museums, art galleries, and shopping opportunities. Our recommendation: get to Sharjah early and keep your plans flexible. You just might stay until 11pm, which is the closing time for the Blue Souk! Since this is a very conservative community, which prohibits alcohol even in hotels, there's not much to do in the evening for those in search of Western-style entertainment. Shopping remains the most entertaining evening activity.

Sharjah's major attractions center around culture and shopping. Major **museums** include:

- Archaeological Museum

- Art Museum

- Desert Park and Arabian Wildlife Centre

- Heritage Museum

- Al Hisn Fort

- Sharjah Islamic Museum

- Museum for Arabic Calligraphy and Ornamentation

Be sure to visit the newly revitalized pedestrian-free **Heritage and Arts** section of downtown Sharjah, which runs parallel to the Corniche Road. This area includes several **art galleries** (Sharjah Art Galleries,

Emirates Fine Arts Society, Sharjah Art Centre, Very Special Arts Centre), **historic buildings** (Al-Hism Fort, Al-Midfa House, Bait Al Naboodah), **museums** (Islamic, Arabic Calligraphy and Ornamentation), and the old charming **Souq Al-Arsa**.

Shopping is centered in five areas:

- Blue Souk
- Sahara Centre
- Sharjah City Centre
- Souq Al-Arsa
- Souq Al Majarrah

If you're planning to shop in Sharjah, be sure to do so early or late in the day. Most shops close between 1pm and 4pm. If you have limited time, limit your shopping adventure to the huge **Blue Souk** (also known as the Central Souk or Souk Al Markazi), which boasts nearly 600 shops under two roofs, as well as explore the old **Souq Al-Arsa**, which is part of the city's Heritage and Arts section. Both shopping centers cater to locals and tourists. The Blue Souk alone may take a couple of hours to cover.

Transportation

 While it's not always easy to get around Dubai, your best bets are to take taxis, hire a car and driver, or drive your own rental car. We prefer taking taxis to some parts of the city and driving our own car to other parts of the city and beyond. These choices will become apparent as we discuss various areas of the city. Dubai does have a cheap bus system, but it's not worth the trouble since buses are crowded, routes are incomplete or inconvenient, and taxis are very inexpensive and convenient. Plans are underway to construct a light rail system, and an additional bridge is being constructed across Deira Creek—two projects that should help alleviate some of the city's traffic problems. In the meantime, you'll have to be patient with the slow progress of the traffic.

Buses

While both Dubai and Abu Dhabi have public bus systems, few tourists ever use them since they are crowded and not particularly convenient.

Taxis

Most visitors use the relatively convenient and inexpensive metered taxis to get around in Dubai and Abu Dhabi. They can be easily hailed along most major streets or found at hotels and shopping malls. However, taxis can be very difficult to find when major meetings and conventions are held in these cities. In the city, the flag drops at Dhs.3 (about US$.80) and short rides cost around Dhs.3 to Dhs.6. At the Dubai International Airport, the flag drops at Dhs.20 and the ride to your hotel may cost anywhere from Dhs.30 to Dhs.80, depending on the distance.

In the case of Dubai, plan to use taxis to get around the most congested sections of the city—primarily the Dubai Creek (Deira and Bur Dubai) area. You may want to rent a car to drive to other areas of the city.

Rental Cars

The best way to get around the UAE, including within the cities of Dubai, Abu Dhabi, and Sharjah, is to rent a car. Over 100 international and local rental car agencies are found in Dubai and Abu Dhabi. Several of them have desks in the arrival hall of the Dubai International Airport and many have representatives at the major hotels. You can easily arrange for a car once you arrive in the UAE.

Weekly car rentals are relatively inexpensive—running as little as US$30 a day, with full insurance and unlimited miles. If you plan to rent a car, it's best to arrive with an international driver's license and your country driver's license. While many car rental agencies will accept a foreign driver's license for driving within the UAE, they will not accept such licenses if you plan to drive into neighboring Oman. In fact, if you plan to drive to Oman, you will need to rethink your car rental plans. Only a few car rental companies—mainly Avis, Hertz, and Dollar—will permit their cars to be driven into Oman. In addition, they charge an extra insurance fee—one week minimum—for Oman. In 2007 this fee varied by company as follows:

- **Hertz**   Dhs.550 (US$152.78)
- **Avis**   Dhs.350 (US$97.22)
- **Dollar**   Dhs.150 (US$41.67)

Overall, we found Dollar Rent A Car to be the least expensive car rental company both within the UAE and between UAE and Oman. If you are planning to drive into Oman and usually arrange for a rental car online, be sure you select one of these three rental companies. Otherwise you may be stuck with a car that can only be driven within the UAE.

You also may want to delay renting a car in Dubai. Since Dubai is so spread out and parking is very convenient and free in many parts of the city, you'll want to drive to those parts of the city where it is convenient to drive. However, driving into certain areas of the city should be avoided, especially in the older sections of Deira and Bur Dubai where traffic congestion and parking can be horrendous. Save these areas for taxis. In fact, you may want to spend your first two days visiting these areas by taxis and then arrange for a rental car to drive to other more car-friendly areas of the city and beyond.

Driving Tips

If you decide to drive a car, you need to do the following:

1. **Observe the posted speed limits** because cameras are widely used to catch speeders. An unexpected speeding fine, which can be substantial, could be added to your car rental bill after you get home.

2. **Carry plenty of coins for the parking meters** that appear in several sections of the city. Feeding one of the large orange meters results in a printed parking time receipt that must be placed on the front right dashboard. Parking is cheap but fines are substantial—US$30.

3. **Drive defensively and carry extra insurance.** The UAE has a high incidence of accidents, which is understandable given the multinational Third World composition of the population, which includes many bad driving habits from other countries. Drivers have a habit of quickly cutting in front of other drivers. The old traffic adage that "He who signals his intention loses the advantage" is very applicable to driving habits in the UAE!

4. **Be prepared to make lots of U-turns and navigate congested roundabouts.** Indeed, this is the country of few left turns, ubiquitous U-turns, and lots of roundabouts! The U-turn areas are clearly marked, but it may take a few frustrating kilometers of driving before you come to such a turnaround area. Roundabouts are good alternatives to making U-turns. But be very careful when entering roundabouts. You may not meet courteous drivers in these places, and many roundabouts are unable to handle heavy traffic flows—sure signs that such roundabouts have outlived their usefulness!

5. **Ask for directions whenever necessary.** Maps are often incomplete or inaccurate, signage can be frustrating, and making turns often prohibited. You may have to drive a long distance before you can turn around and head in the right direction. But you may need to ask three different people the same question in order to get correct directions.

6. **Expect to get stuck in numerous traffic jams** in several areas of Dubai. Road engineering, especially around bridges, leaves much to be desired, and you'll seldom see a traffic cop work a traffic bottleneck. They at best watch the mess go by and then motorcycle down the road in search of accidents, coffee, conversation, and/or more observations. They appear next to useless for people stuck in traffic.

7. **Avoid driving in Dubai's highly congested Deira and Bur Dubai sections.** You're best served by navigating these areas by taxi or on foot.

Tours and Tour Groups

While you can navigate most of the UAE on your own with a good guidebook and map—especially the shopping malls, souks, museums, historic buildings, hotels, and restaurants—you are well advised to use the services of local tour groups for certain types of activities, such as city tours, dhow dinner cruises, deep sea fishing, hot air ballooning, mountain tours, stable tours, helicopter safaris, rock climbing, sand boarding, dune buggy safaris, dune dinner safaris, and overnight desert safaris. Visit the websites of the following tour groups for information on their services:

■ Arabian Adventures	www.arabian-adventures.com
■ Arabian Desert Tours	www.arabiandesert-dubai.com
■ Arabianlink Tours	www.arabianlinktours.com
■ Balloon Adventures Dubai	www.ballooning.ae
■ Big Bus Tours	www.bigbustours.com
■ Desert Rangers	www.desertrangers.com
■ Dubai Tourist & Travel Services	www.dxbtravels.com
■ East Adventure Tours	www.holidayindubai.com
■ Good Times Tourism	www.goodtimesdubai.com
■ Gulf Ventures	www.gulfventures.org
■ Hormuz Tourism	www.hormuztourism.com
■ Khasab Travel & Tours	www.khasabtours.com
■ Lama Desert Tours	www.lamadubai.com
■ Mountain High	www.mountainhighme.com
■ Net Tours	www.netgroupdubai.com www.nettoursdubai.com

- Oasis Palm Tourism   www.opdubai.com
- Off-Road Adventure   www.arabiantours.com
- Orient Tours   www.orienttours.ae
- Quality Tours   www.quality-tour.com
- SNTTA Travel & Tours   www.sntta.com
- Sunflower Tours   www.sunflowerdubai.com
- Sunshine Tours   www.adnh.com
- Voyagers Xtreme   www.turnertraveldubai.com

For more information on specialty tour groups, be sure to pick up a copy of the weekly *Time Out Dubai* and *Time Out Abu Dhabi* magazines or visit their respective websites:

www.timeoutdubai.com
www.timeoutabudhabi.com

Great Destinations

As noted under our sample itinerary section, there are lots of things to see and do in the UAE to occupy three to seven days, or even more. While most of your time will probably be spent in Dubai, try to include these places during your visit to the UAE:

- Dubai
- Abu Dhabi
- Sharjah
- Al Ain
- Hatta

What to Do

The UAE offers a wide variety of activities for all types of visitors, from shopping to participant and spectator sports. You can easily do the following on your own:

- Shop at souks, shopping malls, airport duty-free shops, and independent shops
- Visit museums
- Tour special buildings

- Cross Dubai Creek by abra (water taxi)
- Tour local development projects (The Palms, The World, Burj Dubai, Dubailand, Dubai Marina)
- Sample hotel nightlife
- Visit top restaurants and hotels
- Engage in sports (golf, tennis, horse racing, snorkeling, skiing)
- Photograph the new and old sections of Dubai

Several tour groups will assist you with these more specialized activities:

- Desert safaris
- Deep sea fishing
- Scuba diving
- City tours
- Dhow dinner cruise
- Hot air ballooning
- Mountain tour
- Helicopter safaris
- Rock climbing
- Sand boarding
- Dune buggy safaris
- Dune dinner safaris
- Overnight desert safaris
- Horseback riding
- Camel trekking
- Falconry
- Bird watching

Travel in the UAE primarily focuses on these activities:

1. **Shopping:** Souks, shopping malls, airport duty-free shops, and independent shops for everything from antiques, jewelry, art, and crafts to spices, perfumes, luggage, carpets, and designer clothes and accessories.

2. **Sightseeing:** Viewing new and old architecture, mosques, museums, and old buildings.

3. **Outdoor activities:** Primarily participant (golf, tennis) and spectator (horse racing) sports, desert safaris, scuba diving, deep sea fishing, hot air ballooning, camel trekking, horseback (fast Arabian) riding. Includes many international tournaments— horse racing, golf, tennis, sailing, power boating, auto racing, and rugby.

4. **Dining:** Restaurants offering excellent international cuisines, desert dune dining, ethnic foods, and fast foods (from hamburgers and tacos to shawarma) for all tastes and budgets.

5. **Entertainment:** Primarily socializing and musical entertainment (DJs, karaoke, live performances, dancing) at restaurants, cafes, bars, pubs, and clubs in major hotels in Dubai, and to some extent in Abu Dhabi. Includes large entertainment venues for live performances of international celebrities as well as offers cinemas and theaters.

6. **Conferences and exhibitions:** Dubai is a very popular meeting, incentive, and exhibition destination. Hundreds of international and regional groups come to Dubai each year for meetings and conferences, which are held at the Dubai International Exhibition Centre, World Trade Centre, Airport Expo Dubai, or hotels and resorts.

Top 10 Destinations and Activities

Dubai's top 10 attractions, which are on the "must see and do" lists of many visitors, include the following:

1. Souks (Gold, Spice, Covered) in Deira area (Dubai)

2. Historical and cultural sites in Bastakiya Quarter and Shindagha area of Bur Dubai (Dubai)

3. Mall of the Emirates (Dubai)

4. Burj Al Arab Hotel (Dubai)

5. The Palm Islands (Dubai)

6. Dhow dinner cruise (Dubai)

7. Jumeirah Mosque (Dubai)

8. Emirates Palace (Abu Dhabi)

9. Desert safari (Abu Dhabi)

10. Museums in Sharjah

Best Places to Stay

DESPITE ALL THE cheap oil and labor to build the UAE, this is a very expensive place to operate, especially for visitors with five-star and iconic tastes. Once you try to book a hotel or resort, you'll realize one important fact of travel life about this place—you don't come to the UAE to save money! You come here to indulge yourself.

Properties

Both Dubai and Abu Dhabi have an abundance of five-star hotels and resorts, which also are major centers for dining, entertainment, and recreation. In addition, these cities also boast what their property developers proclaim to be the world's first seven-star hotels—the iconic, opulent, and over-the-top **Burj Al Arab** in Dubai and the **Emirates Palace** in Abu Dhabi. Dubai will soon be the home of an extravagant underwater hotel, the Hydropolis, as well as many other properties competing for new iconic status.

Both cities lack many inexpensive hotels and budget-friendly accommodations, although you can find places for less than US$100 a night during the off season.

Just be prepared to pay a lot to stay in the UAE—perhaps double what you might expect.

At the same time, you may not feel you're getting good value for your travel dollar when it comes to accommodations, especially if you primarily use a hotel for sleeping and arrive during the high season.

Many of the best hotels are operated by **international hotel chains** (Ritz-Carlton, Four Seasons, Jumeirah, Sheraton, Shangri-la, Kempinski, Moevenpick, InterContinental, Hilton, Le Meridian, Grand Hyatt, JW Marriott, Fairmont, Ramada, Novotel, Holiday Inn, Ibis), which also boast some of the best international restaurants and enter-

tainment venues. Dubai's and Abu Dhabi's two seven-star hotels are operated by Jumeirah (Burj Al Arab) and Kempinski (Emirates Palace).

Except during the low season (June through September), when it is blistering hot and properties offer discounted rates and special promotions, hotel and resort prices are generally high compared to many other cities in the world. Think London, Paris, and Moscow—not Cairo, Amman, Damascus, or Istanbul.

Very little discounting takes place during the high season, which tends to run from November through April, with January being an especially busy month. For example, expect to pay US$500 a night and up for an

average five-star hotel room—twice the monthly salary of most guest workers who are constructing all the buildings in Dubai and Abu Dhabi. At that time even four-star hotels will go for US$350 to US$450 a night. What ostensible savings you may acquire on shopping during the much publicized annual Dubai Shopping Festival will probably go to over-priced accommodations.

With the UAE's visitors increasing at an annual rate of 15 to 20 percent, more and more hotels and resorts are being built to accommodate this strong growth in tourism. Indeed, during 2007 at least 40 new hotels—most being five-star properties including the iconic Trump International Hotel and Tower, The Palm Atlantis, and Kempinski Emerald—were simultaneously under construction on Dubai's new Palm Jumeirah.

By 2009 the hotel and resort situation in the UAE will dramatically change as dozens of new properties open their doors to compete with the best of the best. This also means many more new restaurants, bars, pubs, clubs, spas, shops, and resort-type activities will be available to travelers. However, we don't expect to see prices fall or the availability of more budget accommodations. Both Dubai and Abu Dhabi continue to be a boom cities appealing to five-star tastes and budgets.

Condo and Apartment Rentals

One of the UAE's best kept travel secrets is the availability of reason-ably priced accommodations found in its many new housing develop-ments. If you want to save a great deal on housing, especially during the high season when hotel prices are high and availability is limited, you may want to consider renting a one- to three-bedroom condo, apartment, or villa for several days. These fully furnished private resi-dences, complete with cooking facilities, are especially attractive for families or couples traveling together. Many of these properties rent for under US$120 a day.

Dubai, for example, has thousands of empty condos, especially in the massive Dubai Marina development section of the southern Jumeirah area, where many absentee expatriates have purchased properties. Several property management groups rent these condos to visitors. Variously called "vacation rentals," "vacation hotels," or "hotel apartments," these properties can be reviewed by contacting a variety of management groups online:

- www.dubaishortstay.com
- www.d-vh.com
- www.dubaivacationrentals.com
- www.dubaifurnishedapartments.com
- www.vacationrentals.com

If you decide to rent a condo, it's best that you rent a car to get in and out of the housing developments, which are not conveniently located in reference to taxis.

Hotels and Resorts

Here is a sampling of the best hotels and resorts in Dubai, Abu Dhabi, and Al Ain:

Dubai

Over-the-Top

- Burj Al Arab

Five-Star

- Al Bustan Rotana Hotel
- Al Qasr Madinet Jumeirah
- Coral Deira Dubai
- Crowne Plaza Dubai
- Dhow Palace Hotel
- Dubai Marine Beach Resort & Spa
- Dusit Dubai
- Fairmont Dubai
- Grand Hyatt Dubai
- Grosvenor West Marina Beach
- Habtoor Grand Resort & Spa
- Hilton Dubai Creek
- Hilton Fujairah
- Hilton Dubai Jumeirah
- Hyatt Regency Dubai & Galleria
- InterContinental Hotel Dubai—Festival City
- Jumeirah Beach Hotel
- Jumeirah Emirates Towers
- Jumeirah Beach Club and Resort Spa
- JW Marriott Hotel Dubai
- Jebel Ali Golf Resort & Spa
- Kempinski Mall of the Emirates
- Le Meridien Royal Beach Resort & Spa
- Le Meridien Dubai
- Le Meridien Fairway
- Le Meridien Mina Seyahi Resort
- Le Royal Meridien Dubai
- Metropolitan Palace Dubai
- Moevenpick Hotel Bur Dubai
- The Palace At One and Only Royal Mirage
- Park Hyatt Dubai
- Radisson SAS Hotel Dubai Media City
- Ritz-Carlton Dubai

- Shangri-La Hotel Dubai
- Sheraton Deira Hotel and Towers
- Sheraton Dubai Creek Hotel and Towers
- Sheraton Jumeirah Beach Resort
- Sofitel Dubai City Centre
- Taj Palace Dubai

Four-Star
- Al Bustan Residence Hotel
- Al Khaleej Palace Hotel
- Al Khaleej Suites
- Al Manzil Hotel
- Arabian Courtyard Bur Dubai
- Burjuman Rotana Suites
- Chelsea Hotel
- Chelsea Tower Hotel
- Coral Boutique Hotel Apartments
- Courtyard Dubai Green Community
- Dar Al Sondos by Le Meridien
- Dubai Metropolitan Hotel
- Flora Grand
- Holiday Inn Downtown
- Jumeira Rotana Hotel
- Landmark Plaza
- Le Meridien Residence Baniyas Square
- Le Meridien Residence Deira
- Le Meridien al Sondos Hotel Apartments
- Marriott Executive Apartments
- Marriott Executive Apartments Dubai
- Millennium Airport Hotel
- Oasis Beach Hotel Dubai
- Qamardeen Hotel
- Radisson SAS Hotel Dubai Deira Creek
- Regent Beach Resort
- Regent Palace Hotel

- Rihab Rotana Suites Hotel
- Rimal Rotana Suites
- Renaissance Dubai
- Savoy Suites Hotel
- Somerset Jadaf
- Traders Hotel
- Villa Rotana Suites

Three-Star

- Arabian Court
- Arabian Park Hotel
- Golden Sands Hotel Apartments Dubai
- Grand Moov Hotel
- Four Points Bur Dubai
- Hallmark Hotel Dubai
- K-porte Inn Dubai
- Seashell Inn
- St. George Hotel
- York International

Abu Dhabi

Over the Top

- Emirates Palace
- Al Maha Desert Resort

Five-Star

- Al Raha Beach Hotel
- Beach Rotana Hotel & Towers
- Crowne Plaza Abu Dhabi
- Hilton Abu Dhabi
- InterContinental Abu Dhabi
- Le Meridien Abu Dhabi
- Le Royal Meridien Abu Dhabi
- Millennium Hotel Abu Dhabi
- Sands Hotel

- Shangri-La Hotel Abu Dhabi
- Sheraton Abu Dhabi Resort & Towers

Four-Star

- Al Maha Rotana Suites
- Golden Tulip Al Jazira
- Golden Tulip Dalma Suites
- Hilton Baynunah
- Novotel Abu Dhabi Centre Hotel
- Sheraton Khalidiya Hotel Abu Dhabi

Three-Star

- Al Rawda Rotana Suites
- Hilton Corniche Residence
- International Rotana Inn Hotel

Al Ain

- Al Ain InterContinental
- Al Ain Rotana Hotel
- Hilton Al Ain
- Mercure Grand Jebel Hafeet

Our Recommendations

The UAE abounds with excellent properties. We especially found the following hotels and resorts to be outstanding.

Dubai

❑ **Shangri-La Hotel Dubai:** *Sheikh Zayed Road, Dubai, U.A.E. (P.O. Box 75880), Tel. 971-4-343-8888, Fax 971-4-343-8886. E-mail: sldb@shangri-la.com. Website: www.shangri-la.com.* This award-winning 43-story hotel is situated among a bevy of high-rise towers which form the ever changing Dubai skyline. Centrally located on Sheikh Zayed Road, it is 15 minutes from the airport, 5 minutes from the World Trade Center and Dubai Convention Center, and close to shopping malls, golf courses, and beaches.

The 301 guestrooms and suites offer luxurious touches, all the conveniences guests expect from a five-star hotel, and the legendary hospitality Shangri-La is known for. The tasteful decor blends light woods with neutral furnishings that have a clean-cut contemporary look, yet are comfortable and luxurious. Some amenities include an in-room locker which will store and charge a laptop computer, a work desk area with IDD telephone with voice mail and complimentary dataport access, interactive television with satellite movie channels, and complimentary tea and coffee-making facilities. The Horizon Club guestrooms and suites offer an exclusive retreat where guests can experience a higher standard of accommodation and personalized service with additional privileges and facilities, Breakfast is served each morning in the Club Lounge, and throughout the day complimentary juices, tea and coffee are served, with cocktails and canapés in the early evening. A dedicated health club, sundeck and indoor swimming pool for the exclusive use of Club guests is located on level 42.

Nine restaurants and bars offer a fusion of global tastes accentuated by stylish interiors. Cuisines range from an international buffet and seafood to Vietnamese at _Hoi An_ and authentic Moroccan at _Marrakesh_. Cantonese cuisine is available at _Shang Palace_, the signature restaurant of Shangri-La Hotels.

Business Center open 24/7; fully equipped Health Club & Spa; complimentary shuttle and access to a private beach facility is available; Conference/Banquet Facilities.

❏ **The Fairmont Dubai:** _Sheikh Zayed Road, Dubai, U.A.E. (P.O. Box 97555), Tel. 971-4-332-5555, Fax 971-4-332-4555. E-mail: dubai. reservations@fairmont.com. Website: www.fairmont.com._ Located in the midst of the business district on the Sheikh Zayed Road and connected by a covered walkway to the Convention Center, The Fairmont is 20 minutes from the airport, Dubai Media City and Dubai Internet City. The 394 guestrooms and suites offer comfortable luxury accommodations, tastefully decorated and offering the amenities expected from a five-star property. An entire floor is devoted to specialty guestrooms and suites from minimalist Japanese rooms to sumptuous Arabian rooms. Fairmont Gold floors offer a dedicated lounge and benefits including airport transfers, daily breakfast, and in-room Internet access.

A vast range of food and beverage options are offered by ten dining and entertainment venues, from _Spectrum on One_, the award-winning signature restuarant, the intimate _Exchange Grill_ for relaxed dining, or _Bacchus_ for casual Italian dining with pool-side views.

Business Center; Health Club & Spa; Conference/Banquet Facilities.

❑ **Burj Al Arab:** *P.O. Box 74147, Dubai, U.A.E., Tel: 971-4-301-7777, Fax 971-4-301-7000. E-mail: BAAfeedback@jumeirah.com. Website: www.jumeirah.com.* Burj Al Arab, is the iconic landmark and symbol of Dubai. Shaped like the sail of an Arabian dhow, Burj Al Arab is to Dubai what the Eiffel Tower is to Paris. Located on a man-made island 280 meters offshore, it is about 30 minutes from the airport (unless you arrive by helicopter) and not far from the Emirates Mall. If one plans to leave the hotel often for sightseeing or shopping excursions, a car is highly desirable as this property is out along the beach farther from many of the shopping venues than the hotels along Sheik Zayed Road.

An all-suite hotel, Burj Al Arab offers 202 duplex suites. The highly personalized service is epitomized by reception desks on every floor, in-suite check-in, and exclusive butlers that provide around-the-clock assistance for each guest. All suites feature floor-to-ceiling windows framing a view of the sea. Much has been written about the "over the top"decor and although restraint may not be the decorators' major strength, we found the decor to be tamer than we expected. Suites are equipped with the latest technology, laptop computers and Internet access.

Two of the restaurants have engendered much press as well. *Al Muntaha Sky View Restaurant*, which means the ultimate or highest, is suspended 200 meters above the Arabian Gulf offering great views of Dubai and the coastline. Here Mediterranean cuisine is served in a sophisticated setting with scenic windows to the world. *Al Mahara Seafood Restaurant* features a three-minute simulated submarine voyage from the hotel to the restaurant during which "passengers" view sights from beneath the sea on plasma screens fitted into the windows of the submarine. In the restaurant, diners can enjoy a selection of seafood while watching a variety of fish from small angel fish to the blacktip reef shark circling the waters in the large aquarium. There are seven restaurants to choose from.

Health Club & Spa: Conference/Banquet Facilities.

> **TIP:** If you decide, as many visitors to Dubai do, that though you are not a guest you want to visit Burj Al Arab for a first-hand look, be forewarned that there is a check-point that must be passed before gaining access to the island and the hotel. You must have an access number to gain entry. Since there are two restaurants within the hotel that are attractions in themselves, make a reservation to dine (reservations are required) at the Al Mahara or Al Muntaha—see mention made of these restaurants in the hotel section above or for more detail check our restaurant section. You will be rewarded with a memorable dining experience and have the opportunity to gawk at the interior of the hotel as well. Note your reservation number as you will need it to gain access to the property.

❑ **Madinat Jumeirah:** *P.O. Box 75157, Dubai, UAE, Tel. 971-4-366-8888, Fax 971-4-366-7788. E-mail: Mjinfo@jumeirah.com. Website: www.madinatjumeirah.com.* The name, 'Madinat Jumeirah', translates as the 'city of Jumeirah' which describes this property rather well. The complex is comprised of two hotels, Mina A'Salam, designed with authentic style Arabian architecture, and Al Qasr, designed to reflect a sheikh's summer residence. The wind towers, a feature of local architecture, are lighted at night and can be seen from the Jumeirah Beach Road. Along with Dar Al Masyaf, made up of 29 two-story courtyard summer houses, Madinat Jumeirah offers 867 guestrooms and suites. Its 45 restaurants, cafes, and bars offer an eclectic array of international cuisines. A kilometer of private beach connects Madinat Jumeirah with neighboring Burj Al Arab, Jumeirah Beach Hotel, and Wild Wadi Water Park. Although not far from the huge shopping complex, Mall of the Emirates, this property is a bit "out of town." Without a car, guests will have moderately long taxi rides to visit most of the city centers.

A unique feature within the complex of waterways and walkways is Souk Madinat Jumeirah which provides a bazaar atmosphere for 75 open-fronted shops and galleries which sell a variety of home decorative accessories, furniture, carpets, and other items. It doesn't provide the experience of an authentic souk and we found the range of products offered to be a bit limited; nonetheless for a hotel guest who prefers not to leave the cocoon of the resort and who doesn't want to bother with bargaining, this venue does provide a convenient shopping opportunity. Spa/ Fitness Facilities; Conference/Banquet Facilities.

❑ **One & Only Royal Mirage Residence & Spa:** *P.O. Box 37252, Dubai, U.A.E., Tel. 971-4-399-9999, Fax 971-4-399-9998. E-mail: residence@royalmiragedubai.com. Website: www.lhw.com/royalmirage dubai.* A member of the Leading Hotels of the World, nestled within 60 acres of beachfront overlooking The Palm Island Bay, One & Only Royal Mirage is a boutique resort designed in Arabian style architecture. It is comprised of 28 prestige guestrooms, 20 suites, and one garden villa linked to a private reception lounge. The *Dining Room* and its outdoor terrace serves breakfast, lunch, and dinner. The *Library* serves afternoon tea, refreshments, and specialty cocktails. Located within a larger resort complex which also features the Palace and the Arabian Court, guests of the Residence & Spa can enjoy any one of the six additional restaurants—each serving its own unique cuisine. Fitness facilities and Spa.

❏ **Traders Hotel:** *Corner of Abu Baker Al Siddique & Salah Al Din Roads, (P.O. Box 81877), Dubai, U.A.E., Tel. 971-4-265-9888, Fax 971-4-265-9777. E-mail: thdb@shangri-la.com. Website: www.shan gri-la.com.* Traders Hotel is one of Dubai's leading four-star deluxe hotels providing travelers with well-appointed guest rooms, comprehensive facilities, excellent service standards, and value for the money. The hotel is located in the heart of Deira, Dubai's traditional commercial/shopping district, and near to the Gold Souk, Spice Market, Dubai City Center, and Abra stations—to cross the Dubai Creek to Bur Dubai. There are 250 guestrooms and suites available, and 34 Traders Club rooms. Guestrooms feature cream-colored walls, earth-tone carpeting and dark-wood furnishings, and include interactive TV with satellite channels, dataport or broadband Internet access, work desk, IDD telephone with voice mail, electronic in-room locker, mini-bar/refrigerator, iron/ironing board, and tea/coffee making facilities. Guests on Traders Club floors enjoy additional services, some of which include: private club floor check-in/check-out, lounge facilities with refreshments throughout the day, complimentary buffet breakfast, and two-way airport transfer.

Traders Hotel features three food and beverage outlets. The *Junction*, the main dining restaurant, is decorated with Omani artwork—beautiful old wooden doors and smaller antique pieces showcased in niche areas. The dishes are inspired by the restaurant's international multi-cuisine concept. The *Chameleon Bar* serves cocktails and snacks, and the *Lobby Lounge* serves light refreshments.

24-hour Business Center; Health Club, Conference/Banquet Facilities.

❏ **Al Maha Desert Resort:** *Al Maha Head Office, 3rd Floor, Emirates Holidays Building, Sheikh Zayed Road (P.O. Box 7631), Dubai, U.A.E., Tel. 971-4-303-4222, Fax 971-4-343-9696. Website: www.al-maha.com.* This is Arabia as you imagined it to be—wrapped up in first-class luxury—and within a 45-60 minute drive from Dubai. After being surrounded by the skyscrapers of Sheik Al Zayed Road and the highest, tallest, biggest syndrome that seemingly drives building in Dubai, get out to the desert for an entirely different experience. Designed to reflect a Bedouin encampment, Al Maha is set within 225 square kilometers of desert landscape. Views of the Hajar Mountains and surrounding dunes are interrupted only by the appearance of the gazelle-like oryx or one of the other animals that graze at the scrub or may even venture to take a drink from your private plunge/infinity pool. An oryx was grazing contentedly one evening as we took the buggy back to our Bedouin Suite after dinner, and the next morning there was one near our pool.

The 37 Bedouin Suites are each comprised of a separate tented area that includes a generous sized sleeping/sitting area, large bathroom with double sinks, large tub and separate walk-in shower, and an enclosed toilet. Each suite has a private temperature-controlled pool (for those cool desert evenings) surrounded by a wooden deck with chaise lounges and a table with chairs. Each suite has handcrafted furnishings, antiques, and artifacts of the area. There are two Royal Suites and two Emirates Suites; each has two bedrooms and baths. The Presidential Suite has three bedrooms—two with custom super-sized king beds and the third with twin beds.

Three meals a day are included. Breakfast and lunch are served buffet style with a wide range of selections provided. Dinner is a served affair rather than buffet. Diners may chose from the menu or make requests of the chef in advance of the meal. Guests are also entitled to two complimentary on-site activities each day during their stay at Al Maha. Chose from traditional desert pursuits such as falconry, camel treks, horse riding, archery, or dune bashing (an outing in a rugged four-wheel drive vehicle over the dunes.) The horses are pure-bred Arabians and, we were told, "provide the thrill of a lifetime for an experienced rider, but a novice will be on the ground and on his back in less than two minutes."

In addition to the private plunge pools with each suite, there is a larger pool, a spa with exercise equipment for those who wish to be active and treatment rooms for those who want to be pampered. There are conference facilities that can accommodate up to 40 guests in boardroom style, 60 in conference style, and 90 in theater style seating. Banquet facilities available. Business center & services. There is a small, but very nice shopping boutique.

Book a jeep transfer from Dubai to the hotel, or if you are self-driving you can park your car inside the entrance gate (24-hour guard and within a fenced area) and transfer by jeep—about a ten-minute drive to the guest quarters. No private vehicles are permitted on the grounds.

Al Ain

❑ **Intercontinental Al Ain Resort:** *P.O. Box 16031, Al Ain, U.A.E., Tel. 971-3-768-6686, Fax 971-3-768-6766, Website: www.ichotels group.com.* Located at the edge of the city of Al Ain (across the border from Burami in Oman), the Intercontinental provides 216 guestrooms and suites. Suites are quite large and include a small kitchen area, large combination dining/living space, and a separate dressing area off the bedroom. The bathroom is the same as what one would expect in a regular room—one sink, combination tub/shower, and toilet. Four restaurants: *Arabesque* provides a large international buffet as well as a la carte for breakfast, lunch, and dinner; The *Wok* includes a sushi bar and serves Thai food as well as a seafood buffet two nights a week; *Tanjore* serves a wide variety of Indian cuisine as well as vegetarian selections; *Luce Ristorante Italiano & Club* serves Italian food and a live band entertains the dinner crowd. *Oasis Pool Bar* serves snacks and refreshments.

Health & Fitness Center; Business Center; Conference/ Banquet Facilities.

❑ **Hilton Al Ain:** *Al Sarooj District, Hilton Street, Al Ain, U.A.E., Tel. 971-3-768-6666, Fax 971-3-768-6888.* Located at the edge of the city of Al Ain, near the Intercontinental, the Hilton provides 202 guestrooms and suites. Eight food and beverage outlets include: *Flavours* for Oriental dishes; *Al Khayam Persian Restaurant* serves traditional Iranian dishes; choose Tex-Mex dishes at *Paco's Bar*; *Casa Romana Restaurant* serves Italian specialties; or order light fare at the *Palm Court Coffee Shop* or *Hiltonia Club House/ Sports Bar*.

Health & Fitness Center; Business Center; Conference/ Banquet Facilities.

Abu Dhabi

❑ **Emirates Palace:** *P.O. Box 39999, Abu Dhabi, U.A.E., Tel. 971-2-690-9000, Fax 971-2-690-9999, E-mail: reservations.emirates palace@kempinski.com. Website: www.emiratespalace.com.* In a country where every sheik tries to outdo the next sheik by building the biggest, the tallest, or the most luxurious in nearly everything, Emirates Palace stands out. It is grand in its scope and ambition, yet for the most part taste has not been tossed to the wayside. The hotel design incorporates traditional Arabian elements such as the grand dome—claimed to be larger than the dome in St. Peter's in Rome—and 114 smaller domes spread over the building. The colors of the building reflect the different shades of sand found in the Arabian desert. The 302 deluxe luxury rooms feature 755 plasma screens—at least one in each guestroom and multiple screens in the 92 suites. The guestrooms are tastefully decorated in brocaded fabrics and have a definite European flair. A collection of 1,002 Swarovski crystal chandeliers especially commissioned for the Emirates Palace adorn the hotel. There are two landscaped pools and two spas—one in each wing. There are two helicopter pads, 140 elevators, 7,000 doors, 128 kitchens and pantries, and if you decide to take a stroll around the building, plan on a 2.5-km walk. The setting is lovely along a 1.3-km sandy beach. With a total of 30 Welcome Ambassadors representing 17 nationalities ready to greet guests in the main lobby, how can you not feel at home?

The hotel boasts some fine dining venues: *Mezzaluna* serves Italian selections; try *Sayad* for seafood; *Le Vendôme* for Oriental specialties; or select from a number of other restaurants from poolside dining next to the pool in either wing or try one of the many restaurants that are regularly being added to this hotel that was only just opened in 2005.

There are shops offering a selection of exclusive brands in luxury jewelry and fashion.

Everything is truly first class. You will want for nothing, except perhaps money!

Business Center; Fitness Center and Spa located in both the East and West wings; Conference/Banquet Facilities.

❑ **Hilton Abu Dhabi Hotel:** *P.O. Box 877, Abu Dhabi, U.A.E., Tel. 971-2-681-1900, Fax 971-2-681-1696.* Located on the Corniche Road, close to the financial district and within walking distance of several shopping malls, all the guestrooms have a view of either the Arabian Gulf or the hotel's landscaped gardens. Contemporary guestrooms and suites with marble bathrooms provide expected amenities. Suites offer access to the executive lounge and complimentary breakfast. Some suites have a full kitchen. Several restaurants include *Bice Restaurant and Bar* for traditional and modern Italian cuisine; *La Terrazza Restaurant*, with Mediterranean fare, serves both buffet and a la carte meals; *Hemingways*, is a casual spot with live music, beers on tap and margaritas by the jug to go with the food; *Vienna Plaza* is an Austrian styled coffee house and is a popular meeting place for locals; *Mawal Restaurant* is known for its authentic Lebanese cuisine. Parking, run by the hotel, is free for hotel guests. To reach the hotel beach, there is access via a pedestrian tunnel that goes under the Corniche Road.

Health and Fitness Center; Business Center; Conference/Banquet Facilities.

❑ **Hilton Baynunah:** *P.O. Box 30877, Abu Dhabi, U.A.E., Tel. 971-2-632-7777, Fax 971-2-621-6777.* Located across the Corniche Road and with some yet to be developed land between the hotel and the sea, the higher floors afford a view of the Arabian Gulf. The city center is only a few minutes away, and so too are the major shopping districts of Marina Mall, Abu Dhabi Mall, and the Gold Souk—which is actually a modern shopping mall filled with jewelry stores rather than a traditional souk! The Hilton Baynunah has fewer of the extra services offered by the larger Hilton Abu Dhabi, but it has become popular for business travelers who appreciate the kitchenette, executive lounge access with complimentary breakfast, 21-inch TV, and high-speed Internet access. The white tile bathrooms are bright and roomy. The bottom line is the Baynunah is considered good value. The *Abu Dhabi Restaurant's* menu offers a blending of Oriental and Mediterranean flavors. Outdoor parking is available free of charge in front of the hotel (spaces not always available) or there is a covered car park available at a nominal charge. Business Center; Skyline Health Club; Indoor Pool; Meeting Rooms.

5

Shopping the UAE

THIS Q&A EXCHANGE between a local and a visitor says volumes about traveling and shopping the UAE:

Question: How do you like Dubai?
Answer: It should be nice when it's finished!

A Work in Progress

Being finished is not in the cards for Dubai. It's a work in progress, which you'll quickly see as you navigate its incredible shopping and real estate complexes and understand what we call **desert retailing** in the land of amazing **shopping resorts** and property developments.

But first let's examine some important shopping rules before you hit the ground running with your shopping lists and credit cards. These rules are tied to two major economic dynamics in Dubai—**real estate** and **tourism**.

You've probably heard it all—the UAE, and especially Dubai, is one of the world's great shopping paradises, a fabulous tax-free shopping destination offering great buys, where mall-hopping is another form of sport for escaping a sometimes harsh desert environment. You can even own a lovely piece of property (condo, apartment, villa, island) as well as take a five-star resort holiday while getting affordable medical procedures!

While this is all true, let's put this in perspective so we don't go overboard and make some errors along the way.

Desert Retailing and Mall-Hopping

When it comes to shopping, the UAE and Dubai are synonymous. While much of Dubai looks and feels new, one should never forget that this place has long been a successful **trading entrepot** (evidence is clearly presented in the souks and heritage areas of Old Dubai), a home for many talented traders within the Gulf region.

Today, these are well financed (oil) traders who have gone global with a diversified portfolio of airlines, banks, investment houses,

 communication systems, and real estate. At their home base, they literally redefine what tourism and shopping are all about—we call it **desert retailing**—as Dubai's menus and schemes constantly expand to include more locations, products, services, and themes for attracting a record number of visitors to its shores and sands. One day it's the three Palm Islands (Jumeirah, Jebel Ali, and Deira) and The World—four of the world's largest and most innovative residential and commercial reclamation projects. The next day it's Dubailand, Festival City, Bawadi, Hydropolis (a luxury underwater hotel), and the Global Village. And next month it will be the world's tallest building and largest shopping centers. And the following month the government may reveal even more ambitious development plans for this desert city of the future—innovative residential (revolving penthouses) and shopping complexes, museums, sports venues, and celebrity events.

Whatever you may say about this place, it's all about business and shopping—and attracting more tourists to its showcase shores.

Here's the essence of desert retailing for visitors: When it's a scorching 43°C (109°F) outdoors or when a sandstorm clouds this pale desert wasteland, Dubai's more then 40 colorful shopping malls offer air-conditioned shelter and comfort—including the world's largest indoor snow play area, where you can literally ski downhill and build a snowman while surrounded by a hotel, alpine restaurant with a blazing fireplace, cafes, retail shops, a traditional souk, salons, and cinemas (Mall of the Emirates—www.mall oftheemirates.com).

The UAE's shiny new desert fortresses beckon you to forget Mother Nature and instead shop 'til you drop from 10am until 10pm, or sometimes even until midnight and beyond! Above all, this most unlikely place is a magical desert kingdom that speaks your language and welcomes your credit cards.

Dubai's retail centers, which are quickly becoming shopping resorts, are the 21st-century version of a princely desert oasis. Visitors soon learn the art of **mall-hopping**—a power walking sport along marble corridors to be added to the UAE's already long list of appealing sports activities.

Great buys? Well, yes and no. It's your call based on your comparative shopping expertise. In the end, the notion of getting bargains may not be as important as participating in a **unique UAE travel-shopping experience**—a cultural tour de force in how to pleasantly part with your money. It depends on where you come from, your budget, and how carefully you watch your spending. If you're a tightwad shopper, you've probably come to the wrong place.

Indeed, there are a lot of shopping opportunities in Dubai tied to huge real estate and development complexes. In fact, by the year 2009, Dubai hopes to boast five of the world's seven largest shopping malls to further accommodate the nearly 15 million projected tourists! A planned US$54 billion hospitality and tourism project—Bawadi—will include over 50 new hotels and several shopping malls. The annual Dubai Shopping Festival, centered in the airport, shopping malls, and the Global Village, draws thousands of additional visitors to its shores and sometimes overloads the airport with extra bags, boxes, and even crated refrigerators destined for such places as Moscow and Mumbai.

Shopping also extends to two other important sectors—real estate and health care. Much of the booming property market is focused on enticing foreign buyers to invest in **real estate**. And Dubai's private hospitals, clinics, and health centers are gearing up for an expected boom in **medical tourism**, which would compete with the popular world-class medical facilities in Thailand, India, and Singapore—countries that offer everything from sex change operations (Dubai is not into this) and cosmetic surgery to hip replacements or heart bypasses (Dubai should compete well in these surgical areas).

Shopping Resorts

When it comes to shopping, big doesn't necessarily mean the best or most appealing. Above all, it means lots of once inhospitable desert square footage being transformed into massive air-conditioned shopping malls that also function as food and entertainment centers for local residents in search of things to see and do in their spare time.

Especially for tourists, Dubai continues to pioneer the notion of a **shopping resort**—an iconic post-shopping mall concept that is likely to spread to many other countries attempting to build much of their tourist infrastructure around shopping, dining, and entertainment.

The Taste(s) of New Money

As might be expected from new money—much of it coming to this safe haven from Russia, Eastern Europe, Syria, Lebanon, Iraq, and Iran—chasing big dreams that mingle with money managers, roving expatriates, shady international characters, and soldiers of fortune, there's a certain amount of glitzy Las Vegas—and Disneyland-style that goes with this territory. Indeed, for those who value quality and good taste, Dubai's attempt to construct the biggest and grandest often results in buildings of questionable taste.

Just step into and be initially wowed by the iconic and over-the-top Burj Al Arab Hotel—a self-proclaimed seven-star hotel and a photographer's and engineer's delight—and you'll see lots of in-your-face bright and colorful designs that meet the palatial expectations of the driving force behind this one-of-a-kind opulent hotel—Sheikh Mohammad. It definitely makes a statement about the use of colors and materials.

Much of what gets built here doesn't make immediate economic sense, but it does make statements about money management for those who have decided to park their wealth in real estate—what now appears to be a long-term commitment to the UAE. At least for now, many dreams have come true as the UAE continues to embark on some of the world's most ambitious development projects tied to hospitality, tourism, real estate, trade, and investment. Dubai alone is expected to treble its gross domestic product (GDP) to $108 billion by 2015.

22 Shopping Realities

Call it shopping, but buyers from shopping-rich countries (North America and parts of Asia) may discover this is not the shopping mecca they expected it would be. When you hear about tax-free and bargain shopping in the UAE, always remember that **real estate** is the number one business in Dubai. When you go retail shopping in the desert, you encounter some very expensive real estate and high overhead costs, which get passed on to visitors at five-star hotels and shopping malls. And these costs will continue to get higher as more ambitious projects, such as the three Palm Islands, become operational with even more hotels, resorts, and shopping complexes.

Be careful what you wish for when shopping in Dubai. Don't believe you are getting good shopping deals just because advertisements, sale signs, and press articles claim it is so. In fact, Dubai has a habit of "saying it is so," which confuses reality for many first-time visitors who are not accustomed to the local art of bravado. One's perceptions of value of the sales vary depending on where one comes from. For example, our judgments are based in part on the discount and luxury we experience daily in metropolitan Washington, DC, tempered by our many shopping experiences around the world.

Keeping these caveats in mind, you'll most likely discover that shopping in Dubai is an incredible experience, even for those who say they usually hate shopping. Here are 22 shopping realities we found on the ground when we shopped the UAE:

1. **The most appealing shopping for many visitors is centered on Dubai.** While Abu Dhabi and Sharjah offer some shopping opportunities, they pale in comparison to Dubai. Shopping in those cities primarily focuses on the needs of local residents rather than tourists. You probably won't find many things in Abu Dhabi that you can't find in Dubai. Sharjah is a different story, especially its massive Blue Souk, that emphasizes regional arts, crafts, and antiques, and especially hand-woven carpets. By all means plan to visit Abu Dhabi and Sharjah for special events, outdoor sports activities, meetings, museums, art, culture, and some handicraft shopping, but keep your credit cards focused on the shops and shopping malls of Dubai—and maybe Sharjah's Blue Souk. Not surprisingly, most of our remaining 21 shopping rules address shopping in Dubai.

2. **Shopping is very spread out and thus requires a good transportation strategy.** Since Dubai lacks a public transportation system, you'll need to take taxis, which are relatively inexpensive, hire a car with driver, or rent a self-drive car to get around from one shopping area to another. Going from one shopping mall or souk to another may take from 15 to 45 minutes by car, depending on the traffic. You can minimize such traveling by booking a room in the hotel (Kempinski) attached to the Mall of the Emirates and then spend most of your time under one shopping and entertainment roof! While convenient, such an approach would mean missing out on another 95 percent of Dubai's shopping.

3. **Shopping hours tend to be very shopper—and family enter-tainment-friendly.** Most shops in shopping malls are open 12 hours a day, from 10am to 10pm. However, many street shops and shops in souks, which defer to more traditional Middle Eastern work and family routines, close from 1 to 4pm each day. During the annual shopping festival and the Muslim holy month of Ramadan, shopping hours of some malls are extended to midnight and 1am—proving once again that shopping is an all-day form of entertainment.

4. **While you'll find lots of shopping in the UAE, you may or may not buy much.** Unless you come from a heavily taxed country that offers a paucity of goods or a culture that emphasizes gold and jewelry, the simple truth is that many visitors can probably find the same products back home at comparable or even better prices—but without the resort setting. Wealthy Russians, Middle Easterners, and Africans especially like to shop in the UAE, because they can buy products here that are not available back home, or they get good buys on things that may be heavily taxed in their home country.

5. **Shopping in the UAE is convenient and viewed as a form of entertainment.** Many visitors like to shop in the UAE because of convenience—shopping is in abundance everywhere you go and it's often under one air-conditioned roof, accented with food courts, restaurants, cafes, and entertainment and recreation centers. Shopping in and of itself is **entertaining**—it gives both locals and visitors something to do during the heat of the day as well as until 10pm or later with their families. The fact that many people are found in a shopping mall doesn't necessarily mean they are actually shopping—many are simply killing time by window shopping and cruising for food and friendship. Mall shopping is a local and more culturally acceptable entertainment alternative to highly Westernized hotel-based nightlife centered around bars, pubs, nightclubs, music, dancing, alcohol, and sex. In fact, during the annual Dubai Shopping Festival, shopping and entertainment are formally linked—numerous entertainment events take place in the midst of all the shopping. When families "go out" at night, they frequently decide to focus on activities in shopping malls. If you normally don't spend much time shopping at home, you'll probably find time to go shopping and become engaged in the process during your stay in the UAE. Not surprisingly, many visitors get caught up in the UAE's shopping frenzy simply because shopping is so convenient. It's also a great way to kill time in airports. Whether shopping in the UAE is a good deal or not is another question altogether!

6. **Shopping is often over-rated and redundant—less than what meets the eye.** After visiting three or four major shopping centers (for starters, try the Mall of the Emirates, BurJuman Centre, Wafi City, and Ibn Battuta Mall—by 2009 look for the new Mall of Arabia, Dubai Mall, and five other mega-malls), it begins to look the same. Indeed, you may be underwhelmed in a place that would lead you to think that shopping is an overwhelming experience. Similar shops, often under the same ownership, using different names, and offering the same products, are found everywhere you go. **Shopping mall fatigue** may soon set in! Welcome to the land of redundant shopping known for its expansive air-conditioned family-friendly shopping malls with popular food courts and entertainment centers.

7. **Most everything is imported and declared duty-free.** As an entrepot and tax-free trading center, the UAE produces very little of interest to visitors. Most everything found in the souks and shopping malls is produced abroad and is shipped or flown in from other countries. Therefore, prices of goods reflect the costs of international shipping, local handling, and shop rents, which are considerable.

8. **The UAE offers an over-abundance of expensive European designer goods,** which are easily found elsewhere in the world. Even during sale periods, deep discounts may not appeal to you. For example, a men's US$800 shirt reduced to US$400 during the shopping festival has little appeal to visitors who would never think of ever buying a $400 shirt. But you can save $400 on a shirt, which is definitely a huge savings. The same is true for the US$2,000 handbag that goes on sale for US$1,200. You really have to be part of the very expensive **designer-brand shopping culture** to fully appreciate much of what passes for shopping in the UAE. If, on the other hand, you're looking for good value and bargains, you're probably shopping in the wrong place. Those US$10 shirts, US$20 knock-off watches, and US$30 jackets are best found in the bargain basement markets of Delhi, Bangkok, Saigon, Shanghai, and Hong Kong rather than in the shopping malls of Dubai—although you might try the shops at the **Karama Centre** (Kuwait Street) for such bargain shopping, including some ostensibly counterfeit merchandise without the obvious fake labels.

9. **Unique arts and antiques are primarily produced by local or commuting expatriates, imported from neighboring Oman, or presented in hotel lobbies as part of international art road shows.** Only a couple of shops in Dubai and a few galleries in Sharjah are worth visiting for authentic arts and antiques. The rest tend to be souvenir shops with lots of imported stuff from

India and Pakistan. However, the UAE art scene is about to dramatically change as the UAE's deal makers build new world-class art museums (Guggenheim and Louvre for starters) in Abu Dhabi and take on the international art scene, especially New York City and London, as a global center for serious art. Shops and auction houses (Christie's is already functioning in Abu Dhabi) offering quality international art, primarily paintings and sculpture, will soon follow.

10. **Locally produced handicrafts are not particularly well designed nor appealing to visitors who have difficulty knowing what to do with them!** From color, design, and utilitarian perspectives, locally produced handicrafts are generally disappointing. For a sampling of these, visit the handicraft center of the Women's Union in Abu Dhabi. However difficult to make, these products cannot compete with better designed and less expensive imported handicrafts or designer goods.

11. **Dubai is one of the world's major gold trading centers.** Visit the large Gold Souk in Deira, which offers lots of traditional 22k gold jewelry, and you'll see why. This area especially appeals to visitors from the Middle East and Asia who appreciate bright shiny gold jewelry crafted in traditional designs. Most of the shops here also offer varying qualities of jewelry made with diamonds, precious stones, 18k gold, and silver. The newer Gold and Diamond Park (Sheikh Zayed Road, Al Quoz), which is a modern version of the traditional Gold Souk, also showcases many jewelry stores. The really good stuff, which is very expensive and produced by exclusive jewelry houses in Europe and America, is found in a few shops of top hotels (Burj Al Arab in Dubai and Emirates Palace in Abu Dhabi) and in Dubai's major shopping malls (especially Wafi City, Emirates Towers, Deira City Centre, BurJuman, Ibn Battuta Mall, and Mall of the Emirates).

12. **Most shopping is centered in dozens of boring, although sometimes exciting, air-conditioned shopping malls, which may remind you of shopping back home.** You may want to concentrate on Dubai's largest and most luxurious shopping centers—for now (2008) it's the Mall of the Emirates and BurJurman Centre—because they offer unusual architecture and indoor activities, such as snow skiing and surfing, as well as expansive food courts and entertainment centers. More and more new luxurious shopping malls—several following the "shopping resort" concept pioneered by the Mall of the Emirates—will be opening in the months ahead. If nothing else, these are great

places to go cruising in the heat of the day and for doing something into the late evening.

13. **The larger shopping centers are very family—and stomach-friendly.** Many shopping malls are family entertainment centers complete with children's play areas, high-tech cinemas, and food courts. At least with local residents, many shopping centers function as relatively inexpensive and comfortable family social centers where food and entertainment tend to be more popular than products in the stores. A weekly outing to a shopping mall is family entertainment!

14. **The most fun shopping for many visitors is found in the traditional souks of Old Dubai—spice, gold, textile, food, and covered—and the arts and crafts sections of the Blue Souk in Sharjah.** While these exotic places may not offer much to the visitor beyond a few souvenirs, they are usually more interesting than the air-conditioned shopping malls. The souks are definitely cultural experiences where you can practice your bargaining skills and meet local merchants from Iran, India, and elsewhere. Especially around the gold, covered, and spice souks in Dubai, you'll even encounter a few roving touts who attempt to hawk knock-off watches and poor-quality designer goods. Visit the spice market to buy crystals of frankincense and myrrh. These spices are even packaged along with a small incense burner to make interesting gifts for folks back home.

15. **Be sure to check out airport shopping both upon arrival and departure.** Both Dubai and Abu Dhabi offer extensive duty-free airport shopping. Consequently, you may want to arrive at the airport an hour or two early in order to browse the shops. Don't forget to explore this shopping scene upon arrival. Since this is a tax-free destination, you can shop the airport duty-free shops upon arrival and departure. In fact, over 20 percent of all airport duty-free revenue is generated from inbound passengers.

16. **Expect to be pestered on the streets of Deira (Dubai) by young South Asian men peddling knock-off watches and designer handbags at inflated prices.** While the UAE has a reputation for being a tout-free country, you will encounter the ubiquitous Third World tout in and around the souks of Deira. These are the only people who pester shoppers in the UAE. While you may want to visit the tiny back lanes and upstairs hideouts (usually a small room jam-packed with products) to see their counterfeit goods, don't waste your money on such items. These products suffer from two great shopping evils—overpriced (before bargaining) and dreadful quality. If you decide to risk buying from these touts, don't pay more than 30 percent of the

initial asking prices. US$80-100 for a knock-off watch is simply ridiculous—US$20-30 should be the street price.

17. **Despite its duty-free reputation and annual shopping festival with advertised 30 to 70% discounts, you may or may not save much money on shopping in the UAE.** It depends on your country of origin. Americans, for example, are the world's most spoiled shoppers, since they come from a highly competitive retail and wholesale environment (think Wal-Mart, Costco, Amazon.com) that stresses discounts, sales, and the lowest prices, including the concept of "loss leader" (selling at or below cost to get you into the door so you'll buy other above-cost items). Not surprisingly, so-called bargain duty-free shopping in the UAE is not a bargain for many Americans, who may pay 10 percent more in the UAE for comparable goods back home. They are used to getting great shopping deals online (for examples, see our own online shopping mall at www.ishop aroundtheworld.com), at warehouse clubs and outlet malls, and during numerous seasonal and holiday sales. Even high-end designer goods are sold during seasonal sales at mark-down prices. But if you come from Russia, Africa, and parts of Europe and Asia, shopping here may look very good—10-30 percent below retail!

18. **Most shops take major credit cards.** The exception are small shops in souks that prefer cash. Some shops may try to add on a 3—to 5-percent commission to cover their credit card processing charges. Cash is still the preferred method of transaction.

19. **Don't be afraid to bargain.** Bargain whenever and wherever you can, even in a shopping mall where shops ostensibly don't allow bargaining and put up sales or "fixed prices" signs to keep away bargainers. Savvy shoppers aren't deterred by such wishful retail thinking! Shop owners and some sales personnel may be authorized to give instant discounts, but only if you ask if they can do better on the price—especially if you indicate interest in purchasing several items. On the other hand, bargaining is a way of life in souks, where you can expect to get 10 to 50% discounts, depending on the merchant and your ability to bargain. Check out our bargaining tips in preparation for such shopping by visiting www.ishoparoundtheworld.com.

20. **The best time to shop in Dubai is reputedly during the annual Dubai Shopping Festival, which usually takes place for 32 days during January and February.** This festival is advertised as a "world-class shopping and family entertainment" extravaganza. During this festival many shops advertise 30 to 70% discounts on select items as well as many giveaways of cash, luxury

cars, and gold bars. However, winning a luxury car may require buying raffle tickets for US$200 to US$300 each—something you can also do online. Since this also is a busy time of the year for international sporting events, hotels tend to be full and thus charge full rack rate. In other words, everything except shopping may cost you top dollar during this so-called bargain period. At the same time, only certain items tend to be put on sale. When it relates to clothes, shoes, and fashion accessories, many items that go on sale are from the previous season's merchandise—similar to sales at Macy's and Saks Fifth Avenue in the United States. Some shops are known to inflate their suggested retail prices so that their so-called big discounts are not really as big as advertised— was that US$800 shirt reduced by 50% to US$400 really US$800 before the sale or is this just clever desert retailing? This January/February shopping event is complemented by a late June through August celebration—**Dubai Summer Surprises**—an attempt in the heat of the summer to keep the international spotlight on Dubai's shopping as more and more mega-malls come on line to further saturate this city's already extensive shopping complexes. Even the holy month of Ramadan, which varies each year with the lunar calendar, is a shopping festival month (Dubai the City That Cares), when shopping malls stay open until 1am. As Dubai moves into its next phase of shopping—the cannibalization of existing shopping malls with more mega shopping resorts—we expect to see more such shopping promotions and celebrations take place throughout the year. The future of today's many popular shopping malls may be in question within the next few years!

21. **Be careful in buying big ticket items such as a piece of pretty waterfront or oceanview property.** The post-2002 gold rush for foreigners to buy condos, apartments, and villas in the UAE has added billions of dollars to the local economy. However, foreigners have yet to fully understand what they are getting into, especially when it comes to such key issues as who owns what, inheritance, and Shariah courts. The UAE's legal system is in transition, especially given the importance of codifying foreign investment and property laws to acceptable international standards. While foreigners can now (since 2002) own property (freeholder rights only) in certain designated development areas, which is largely responsible for the UAE's tremendous property boom during the past five years, their long-term legal rights, such as inheritance, remain uncertain. In addition, there is some ambiguity as to who really owns the property—you or the developer. In other words, you may or may not be able to sell your property with ease. Also, UAE courts will apply Shariah law to property questions, which is a real problem if an owner

dies. The courts may not allow the property to be transferred to a female spouse. There are also other questionable details of ownership that reinforce the old adage that "*The devil is always in the details.*" If you are tempted to buy a condo, apartment, or villa in the UAE, be sure you understand your rights and get legal advice from a reputable local law firm that specializes in property rights rather than reassuring ("no problem") advice from a seller. Property ownership rights are not the same as in your country. For starters, pick up a copy of Explorer's expatriate guidebook at any major bookstore in the UAE—***Dubai: The Complete Residents' Guide***. You'll find a similar guide on Abu Dhabi in the bookstores of Dubai and Abu Dhabi and online through www.impactpublications.com.

22. **If you're in the market for medical procedures, consider shopping Dubai's growing medical market.** Dubai continues to develop world-class private medical facilities (hospitals, clinics, and wellness centers) to service international visitors. In fact, it may soon become the world's center for medical tourism as its new medical cities near completion. The recently opened first phase of the Dubai Healthcare City (DHCC), a 4-million square foot complex attracting top medical and management talent, is quickly becoming an important regional center for medical services, education, research, and development as well as an international medical tourism center.

Shopping Psychology 101

You'll quickly discover that Dubai and the rest of the UAE produce few products that are uniquely local in origin. This place is all about desert retailing—a trading psychology that tempts visitors to shop 'til they drop in traditional mall-based retail settings. Except for a few local handicrafts, most everything is imported into the UAE. So, after adding transportation costs and displaying goods in high-cost shopping malls linked by cheap taxi rides, what advantage is there in shopping here versus in other countries?

The UAE's main drawing cards for shopping are fourfold:

1. **Everything is presented as tax—or duty-free.** In other words, no import duties have been added to the cost of goods—only shipping and local handling charges, which can be substantial given the high costs of operating desert retail space in upscale air-conditioned shopping malls.

2. **Shopping is concentrated within several large and entertaining shopping centers with many appealing shops and selections.** While many travelers may not be serious shoppers back

home, once in Dubai they are presented with high-density shopping for a wide range of products they might not look for back home. As such, Dubai offers a smorgasbord of shopping alternatives and a collective "let's buy" psychology. Entertainment plays an important role in promoting Dubai's shopping.

3. **Dubai exudes a mega-mania approach to everything—the biggest and the best—and then tries to wrap it in the notion of offering "good buys."** So far, having it both ways has worked, as visitors continue to stream into Dubai to take advantage of its perceived treasures and pleasures. Indeed, Dubai continues to stretch the limits of traditional mall-based shopping by transforming shopping centers into shopping resorts and entertainment centers rather than encouraging serious competition through discount warehouses, name-brand outlet malls, or online discount shopping.

4. **Dubai sponsors an annual shopping festival during January and February and further promotes itself throughout the year as a shopping mecca.** During the annual shopping festival, shoppers receive additional savings (30-70%) on many items that are specially priced for this event. The June-August Dubai Summer Surprises offers similar shopping promotions.

New World of Shopping Resorts

Dubai increasingly refers to its huge multi-faceted shopping complexes as "shopping resorts" rather than just shopping malls or centers, which tend to lack imagination and the entrepreneurial spirit of UAE developers. These resorts are especially attractive for people who normally hate shopping! Indeed, Dubai's largest complexes, such as the **Mall of the Emirates**, includes a major five-star hotel (Kempinski) along with an indoor snow ski operation (Ski Dubai), day spas, cinemas, theater and art center (Dubai Community Theatre and Arts Centre—DUCTAC, www.ductac.org), children's play areas, restaurants, and coffee shops. These are one-stop shopping, dining, sleeping, education, cultural, sports, fitness, rejuvenation, and entertainment centers—literally a city within a city. From 10am to 10pm, and sometimes until midnight, you can enjoy the many treasures and pleasures of an indoor air-conditioned city within a city.

The Mall of the Emirates is only one of many such shopping resorts, which will soon make international headlines as the largest shopping mall in the world. Two new shopping resorts that were built in 2008—**Mall of Arabia** and **Dubai Mall**—will be competing for the title of the largest shopping mall in the world, along with three others coming on board by 2009!

What to Buy

With so many souks, shopping malls, hotel shops, and street shops, you can find just about everything here. The product range is staggering and shopping interests will vary with different national groups. For example, Russians and Indians are known to air-freight refrigerators from Dubai to Moscow and New Delhi, because they are such a good buy at Dubai's Carrefour store compared to what they find back home. But if you're from a shopping-rich country, chances are you won't come to Dubai to buy refrigerators, washing machines, air-conditioners, televisions, and computers—things you can readily get back home at decent prices. Indians, the predominant expatriate group, are especially interested in traditional clothes, such as saris for women, as well as inexpensive garments, such as the US$4 men's shirt found in the 24-hour hypermarkets. These products stand in sharp contrast to European designer clothes and accessories, such as the US$2,000 handbag and the US$800 men's shirt that appeal to upscale travelers who ostensibly come here to search for shopping bargains!

Arts and Antiques

Dubai offers few local arts and antiques. Most art, usually paintings and sculptures, is either produced by Western expatriates or imported from abroad. Most all antiques, especially Omani doors, furniture, accessory pieces, lanterns, frankincense pots, Arabian coffee pots, and Bedouin jewelry, are imported from Oman and India. They often share floor and shelf space with a wide assortment of handicrafts, souvenirs, and gift items.

Serious international art is just beginning to appear in the UAE. It's partly fueled by the building boom and decorators who need to incorporate art into UAE's many new spaces. It's also a sign that the UAE is a serious place for art and culture rather than just offshore business and desert tourism.

But art and culture are business of a different kind. Indeed, Sheikh Mohammed bin Rashid Al Maktoum has visions of making Dubai a global art center on par with New York City and London. And, as with most such dreams, they can be turned into reality if you throw enough money in the right direction—hire top talent and spend millions of dollars to create great museums. Welcome, again, to Instant UAE and Dubai, where money is often no object and where art and culture are just a few more extravagant buildings away!

Signs of the of emergence of serious international art can be found at special hotel exhibitions (international art road shows) and auctions in Abu Dhabi, a city that is currently planning to spend billions of dollars on two new branches of world-class art museums—the Guggenheim Abu Dhabi Museum and the Louvre Abu Dhabi—which will further enhance the foothold Christie's auction house already has in generating US$8-10 million in sales during its initial (2006 and 2007) fine art auctions in Abu Dhabi. Indeed, the UAE hopes to soon become a major art center in the Middle East—another crossroads or hub—for serious international collectors of modern and contemporary Arab, Iranian, Indian, Asian, and Western art.

At present you won't find many arts and antiques in the souks and shopping malls, which primarily offer less appealing handicrafts and souvenirs. In fact, Dubai's two best shops for arts and antiques are actually independent galleries operated by knowledgeable expatriates who also are talented artists and antique collectors: **Creative Arts Centre** and **Showcase Antiques, Art, and Frame** (see "Best of the Best" below for contact information). Given Dubai's commercial and residential property boom, there is currently a high demand for art and antiques to grace the lobbies of commercial buildings, hotels, resorts, condos, and homes. These two top shops are extremely busy procuring art and providing expert framing services to businesses and individuals. Indeed, as you will quickly discover when visiting these two top art and antique shops, **art framing** is one of the hottest businesses in Dubai!

Fashion and Accessories

You won't lack for fashion and accessories in Dubai's many shopping malls and hotel shopping arcades—they are everywhere! You'll find the latest in European fashion and accessories in Dubai's most exclusive shopping malls—BurJuman, Ibu Battuta, Mall of the Emirates, Emirates Towers, Wafi City, Mercato Mall, and Deira City Centre— along with attractive traditional clothes and accessories for Arabs and Indians. In fact, if you shopped only these seven shopping malls, plus Dubai's top hotels and resorts and the airport duty-free shopping area, you would find the best design selection of clothing and accessories for both men and women.

Jewelry

You'll find a wide range of jewelry in the UAE, from traditional Asian and Middle Eastern gold and Bedouin silver jewelry to modern Western designs from leading European and American jewelers. The **Gold Souk** in Deira is the largest center for jewelry. It's also the center for more traditional jewelry, whereas the most exclusive shopping malls (BurJuman Centre, Ibn Battuta Mall, Wafi City) and hotels (Burj Al Arab, Ritz-Carlton, Jumeirah Beach) are centers for exclusive international designer jewelry, such as Cartier (Emirates Towers), Graff (Wafi City), and Tiffany & Co. (Deira City Centre). The relatively new **Gold and Diamond Park** (Sheikh Zayad Road, Al Quoz)—a modern version of the Gold Souk—conveniently showcases many jewelry stores in an air-conditioned mall setting.

Handicrafts

Many of the ubiquitous handicrafts found in the UAE come from India as well as several countries in Asia, the Middle East, and North Africa. Look for lots of bronze, brass, and copper items along with ceramics, woven baskets, glassware, daggers, and textiles. While you'll find many stores offering a combination of handicrafts, souvenirs, and gift items in shopping malls (look for the **Arabian Souk** on the first floor, Yellow Zone, of the Mall of the Emirates), some of the best quality handicrafts will be found in a few arts and crafts shops in the **Bastakiah** area of Bur Dubai, such as the **XVA Gallery** and **The Majlis Gallery**, as well as at **Creative Arts Centre** and at **Showcase Antiques, Art, and Frame**.

Souvenirs and Gifts

Shops in shopping malls and the airport abound with varying quality and appealing souvenir and gift items. You can find everything from inexpensive and kitschy stuffed animals, Burj Al Arab paperweights, shisha pipes, daggers, and packaged teas, spices, and foodstuffs to unique handcrafted art objects and expensive Mont Blanc pen sets and glassware. Several shopping malls and department stores have separate sections devoted to international souvenirs and gifts. Be sure to check out the arts and crafts shops in the Bastakiah area of Bur Dubai for good quality one-of-a-kind handcrafted gift items.

Carpets and Textiles

Several shops in Dubai and Abu Dhabi offer a wide selection of handmade and machine-made carpets of varying quality and selection from throughout the region, especially from neighboring Iran. Given Dubai's building boom, carpets are in great demand there. However, connoisseurs of collectible carpets may be disappointed with the limited carpet shopping opportunities in Dubai.

Most major shopping malls (Ibn Battuta Mall, Deira City Centre, Mall of the Emirates) in Dubai have at least one shop devoted to carpets. One of the best selections of collectible hand-woven carpets can be found at this somewhat difficult-to-find small shop located near the Iranian Hospital—**Al Madaen** (Pagoda House, Satwa, Tel. 345-4488).

You may want to visit the many carpet shops on the second level of the huge Blue Souk in Sharjah, where selections and prices may be more agreeable with your needs and budget. At least check out this place before making any carpet purchases in Dubai or Abu Dhabi.

Spices and Teas

The **Spice Market** in Deira offers a good selection of traditional spices and teas in an exotic setting where you can bargain for your purchases. Many of the items come from neighboring Iran. You'll also find good selections of spices and teas in various hypermarkets. Look for packages of frankincense and myrrh—some even come with a small incense burner—in the spice and covered markets of Deira.

Electronics

The airport duty-free shops, shopping malls, department stores, and numerous shops in Bur Dubai are filled with the latest electronic gadgets, from computers and printers to digital cameras. Savvy shoppers for electronic goods tend to head for the many electronic shops lining Computer Street—Khalid Bin Al Waleed Road (intersects with Mankhool Road)—in Bur Dubai.

Real Estate

Dubai and, to a lesser extent, Abu Dhabi are well known for a booming real estate market, which is especially aimed at expatriate investors, corporations, and seasonal visitors. You'll have no problem finding companies willing to offer you space in the latest innovative condo or villa development project. The Palm Islands (www.thepalm.ae), The World (www.theworld.ae), Dubai Marina (www.dubaimarina.ae), and Dubai Festival City (www.dubaifestivalcity.com) are just four of many high-end property development projects that have put Dubai on the global property development map and justified its claims to having created the Eighth Wonder of the World (see video clips of these unique property developments on our website, www.ishoparound theworld.com)!

As noted earlier, just make sure you understand what you're getting into with the local legal system. Buying property in the UAE could become a very expensive lesson in buying high in what may well become a bubble real estate economy. Indeed, Dubai is well into the process of overbuilding residential properties for absentee homeowners/investors, most of whom come from neighboring Arab countries as well as from the United Kingdom, Russia, and several Eastern European countries. However, Dubai has an excellent track record in transforming dreams into reality—build it and they will come—as millions of new visitors come to Dubai each year to further fuel its booming property market.

Medical Tourism and Health Procedures

Have you ever considered shopping for reasonably priced quality health services and medical procedures, such as a face lift, dental work, knee or hip replacement, eye surgery, or even heart surgery? You may have heard the praises of medical tourism in Thailand, Singapore, India, Taiwan, South Africa, Mexico, and Brazil, but what about the UAE, which prides itself on new infrastructure, top talent, and being a global center for so many important things in life?

Where to Shop in Dubai

Your traditional shopping choices in Dubai are somewhat staggering, from the very moment you step off the airplane or cruise ship to when you board once again. Just click onto the websites of Dubai's top souks and shopping malls (see below) and you'll discover that shopping here is a very serious—and competitive—business. Asterisks (*) indicate the best of the best:

Airport duty-free shops—both inbound and outbound

- Dubai*
- Abu Dhabi
- Sharjah

Traditional Souks (Old Dubai)

- Covered (Deira)
- Food (Deira)
- Gold (Deira)*   www.dubaigoldsouk.com
- Spice (Deira)*
- Textile (Bur Dubai)

Modern Souks

- Global Village   www.globalvillage.ae
- Gold & Diamond Park   www.goldanddiamondpark.com
- Karama Centre
- Souk Madinat Jumeriah*   www.madinatjumeirah.com/
  shopping

Shopping Malls

- BurJuman Centre**   www.burjuman.com
- Deira City Centre*   www.deiracitycentre.com
- Dragonmart
- Dubai Festival City*   www.dubaifestivalcity.com
- Dubai Mall
  (world's largest in 2008)* www.thedubaimall.com
- Emirates Towers*   www.jumeirahemiratestowers
  com/lifestyle
- Hamarain Centre

As might be expected, Dubai is well positioned to be a major player in the world health tourism movement by offering a variety of medical procedures to visitors in search of quality health care at reasonable prices. It already offers high quality medical services in both public and private facilities, although private hospitals, health centers, and clinics (the most popular being American Hospital www.ahdubai.com, Al Zahra Hospital www.alzahra.com, and Welcare Hospital www.welcarehospital.com) play the most important role in medical tourism. With tourism increasing by nearly 15 percent a year, the number of annual visitors projected to be over 11 million by 2010, and a first-class tourist and health care infrastructure, including health spas and resorts for recuperating patients, medical tourism makes a great deal of sense in Dubai.

You'll find many qualified doctors, including American Board Certified, in Dubai offering cosmetic surgery through hospitals and clinics. For starters, visit these websites:

- Al Rustom's Skin & Laser Clinic   www.skin-and-laser.com
- American Hospital   www.ahdubai.com
- Belhoul European Hospital   www.belhouleuropean.com
- Cosmesurge   www.dubaicosmeticsurgery.com
- Emirates Hospital   www.emirateshospital.ae
- Gulf American Clinic   www.groupgmc.com/gulf-american-index.htlm
- Manchester Clinic   www.manchester-clinic.com
- Welcare Hospital   www.welcarehospital.com

But Dubai's health tourism plans include a full range of health procedures and services, even more grandiose than those offered by the pioneering hospitals and clinics in Bangkok and Singapore. These plans center on the new Dubai Healthcare City (www.dhcc.ae), which will be fully operational by 2010. Including branches of the Harvard Medical School, Mayo Clinic, and the Boston University Dental Health Center (to open in 2008), the Dubai Healthcare City will be the largest international medical center located between Europe and Southeast Asia. It, along with the Khalefa HealthCare City, will offer a wide range of medical services for visitors as well as world-class medical education and research. The government expects that medical tourism will add nearly US$2 billion to the UAE economy by 2010.

For an excellent directory to Dubai's health complex, be sure to get a copy of **Dubai: The Complete Residents' Guide**, which is available in major bookstores in Dubai (www.Explorer-Publishing.com). The companion **Abu Dhabi: A Complete Residents' Guide** includes similar information on Abu Dhabi.

- Ibn Battuta Mall**   www.ibnbattutamall.com
- Jumeirah Centre
- Jumeirah Plaza
- Karama Centre
- Al Khaleej Centre   www.alkhaleejcentre.com
- Mall of Arabia
  (world's largest in 2008)* www.mallofarabia.ae
- Mall of the Emirates**   www.malloftheemirates.com
- Mazaya Centre   www.mazayacentre.com/
                            index2.asp
- Mercato Mall*   www.mercatotowncentre.com
- Souk Madinat Jumeirah*   www.madinatjumeirah.com/
                            shopping
- The Village Shopping Mall www.thevillagedubai.com
- Wafi City**   www.waficity.com

Department Stores (all within shopping malls)

- Bhs (BurJuman)
- Debenhams (Mall of the Emirates)
- Harvey Nichols (Mall of the Emirates)
- Jashanal (Wafi City Mall)
- Marks & Spencer (Wafi City Mall)
- Saks Fifth Avenue (BurJuman)
- Salam (Wafi City Mall)

Special Events (www.mydsf.com)

- Dubai Shopping Festival
- Dubai Summer Surprises

Since many hotels are located next to or near shopping malls, hotel shopping in Dubai is limited to a few jewelry and clothing/accessory shops. Major hotels, such as the Burj Al Arab, include very exclusive jewelry stores (Aiyad Jewelry, Bulgari, Chopard, Diamoor).

Shipping With Ease

You'll have no problem shipping items from the UAE by either air or sea. In fact, since shipping is the life blood of this country, you should have no problem shipping your purchases from the UAE. Most shops are experienced in both packing and shipping. If you purchase a large item requiring packing and shipping services, be sure to inquire about such costs before making the purchase. You may find it's cheaper to buy a similar item back home than to go to the trouble and expense of shipping from the UAE.

If a shop says they can arrange shipping, make sure you feel confident that they can do the job. Start by asking questions about the whole shipping process—whom they use, what paperwork you will need for receiving your shipment, how long it will take, who does the packing, and the total costs for packing and shipping from the store to your door.

Make sure you pay particular attention to the quality of **packing**. There's nothing worse than purchasing a unique treasure and then receiving it damaged because someone did not know how to pack properly.

Keep in mind that you will need to clear Customs at your end and pay additional fees for handling your shipment at the airport or shipping terminal and then arrange for it to be delivered to your home or office. You may find the cost of receiving a shipment at your end is as expensive as the international transportation! Indeed, a US$500 shipping quote may turn out to cost twice as much because of the additional fees at the point of entry and transportation to your home.

You may find that shipping many items by air freight is more convenient and not much more expensive than shipping by sea. Be sure to check on the comparative costs of sea versus air shipments. If you are considering air shipments, make sure you get a quote from air freight shippers, which can be arranged through a shipping broker. Shipping by FedEx, UPS, or DHL can be extremely expensive for large items—two to three times more than air freight.

> **TIP: Whenever possible, take your treasures with you.** If you travel with one suitcase, you can use your additional baggage allowance to transport your purchases in another suitcase or a special well-packed box. Many shops will pack your items to airline specifications. Alternatively, many hotels can help you pack boxes or will direct you to good packers. Just ask the concierge or front desk for packing and shipping assistance. Using your baggage allowance in this manner may save you a few hundred dollars in international shipping costs. For example, we bought an antique Omani chest in Dubai, placed other items inside, including an old lantern from India, and the shop packed the chest well. We checked the box as part of our luggage, which went as cargo under the plane and it arrived home with us at no additional charge. In essence, we were able to ship the chest and additional items free because of this packing and shipping strategy, which we've frequently done when shopping in other countries.

Best of the Best Treasure Hunting

The following places should be of special interest to treasure hunters in Dubai:

Arts, Antiques, and Furniture

- **Al Jaber Gallery** (near Gold Souk and in Deira City Centre)
- **Creative Arts Centre** (Al Jumeirah Road/Beach Road, Jumeirah, Tel. 344-4394)
- **Showcase Antiques, Art, and Frame** (Beach Road, Tel. 348-8794, www.showcasedubai.com)*
- **XVA Gallery** (Bastakiya, Tel. 353-5383, www.xvagallery.com)
- **The Majlis Gallery** (Bastakiya, Tel. 353-6233, www.majlis gallery.com)

Jewelry

- **Aiyad Jewelry** (Burj Al Arab Hotel)
- **Azza Fahmy Jewellery** (Emirates Towers)
- **Cartier** (Emirates Towers and BurJuman)
- **Damas** (Deira City Centre and Ibn Battuta Mall)
- **Graff** (Wafi City)
- **Tiffany & Co.** (Deira City Centre and BurJuman)

Carpets and Textiles

- **Al Madaen** (near Iranian Hospital, Pagoda House, Satwa)
- **Carpetland** (Pyramid Building, Bur Dubai)
- **Pride of Kashmir** (Deira City Centre)
- **Toshkhana Trading** (near Gold Souk)

Fashion and Accessories

- **BurJuman Centre**
  - Bossini
  - Bugatti Fashion
  - Burberry
  - Calvin Klein
  - Celine
  - Christina Lacroix
  - DKNY

- Dolce & Gabbana
- Donna Karan
- Escada
- GF Ferre
- Giordano
- Hermes
- Kenneth Cole
- Kenzo
- MaxMara
- Polo Ralph Lauren
- Saks Fifth Avenue
- Whistles

■ **Wafi City Mall**

- Celine
- Oasis Fashion (hats)

■ **Ibn Battuta Mall**

- Oasis
- Pierre Cardin

■ **Mall of the Emirates**

- Gucci
- Reiss
- Versace
- Whistles
- Yves Saint Laurent

■ **Emirates Towers**

- Emporio Armani
- Jimmy Choo
- Villa Moda

■ **Mercato Mall**

- Cerruti
- Diesel
- Hugo Boss

■ **City Centre**

- Stephanel
- Women'Secret
- Zara

Shopping Abu Dhabi

While Abu Dhabi is the largest (87 percent of land area) and richest emirate in the UAE, it's very different from Dubai when it comes to

tourism, shopping, hotels, restaurants, entertainment, and property development. Abu Dhabi continues to build its reputation around its major strengths—government, sports, meetings, business deals, and resorts rather than on shopping and evening entertainment that attract so many visitors to Dubai. However, this may soon change as Abu Dhabi begins to more aggressively develop its tourism sector.

Abu Dhabi is now expanding its reputation to include art and culture with the development of new mega-museums and sponsoring art auctions. It's also becoming a center for communications and entertainment with new movie production facilities in partnership with Warner Brothers.

While Abu Dhabi, too, is into ambitious real estate and reclamation projects, it still lives in the shadow of Dubai, and for good reason. Wealthy local investors, who are very active in Dubai's property and investment markets, primarily live in Abu Dhabi. Their oil wealth fuels a great deal of Dubai's economy, especially the booming real estate market. And they prefer it that way.

Like the rest of the city, Abu Dhabi's shopping is much more laid back than Dubai's in-your-face shopping. It especially appeals to local residents who prefer shopping in the air-conditioned comfort of shopping malls, which also function as food and entertainment centers. Marina Mall, for example, is anchored by two

popular stores primarily frequented by locals—Ikea and Carrefour. The city does promote an annual Abu Dhabi shopping festival in March.

Abu Dhabi has two large modern shopping malls complete with food courts and entertainment venues:

- **Abu Dhabi Mall**
  www.abudhabi-mall.com
  http://en.wikipedia.org/wiki/Abu_Dhabi_Mall
- **Marina Mal**
  lhttp://en.wikipedia.org/wiki/Marina_Mall,_Abu_Dhabi

It also has a large **Gold Souk** and **Central Souk**—both essentially modern shopping centers—as well as a **Heritage Village** for buying local handicrafts and viewing demonstrations. Abu Dhabi's **Carpet Market** is an interesting cultural experience (merchants chase after your car as you arrive!) where selections are best termed "local carpet kitsch" (really ugly stuff!). Don't waste your time looking for this place, since it has nothing of interest to most visitors. You would never ship any of it home. You'll find a few carpet shops in Abu Dhabi, such as the **Persian Carpets and Antiques Exhibition**, but nothing special to recommend.

You'll also find a few shopping opportunities in the major hotels, such as the Emirates Palace, with its exclusive jewelry stores that appeal to its wealthy locals and international guests.

Shopping Sharjah

Sharjah, famous for its long trading history and culture, is an up-and-coming shopping destination that hopes to increasingly emphasize art and culture. It's not a place for shoppers interested in the latest designer goods from abroad, which is Dubai's specialty. In Sharjah, the focus is on art, antiques, and handicrafts from around the region. Visitors enjoy visiting the art galleries as well as the city's traditional and modern souks. However, after shopping in Dubai, you may feel a bit underwhelmed by the shopping choices in Sharjah. Nonetheless, a few hours in the galleries and souks will be sufficient for an interesting day trip to Sharjah.

If you're planning to shop in Sharjah, be sure to do so early or late in the day. Most shops close between 1pm and 4pm.

Since most visitors to Sharjah have limited time, we recommend confining your shopping to the huge Blue Souk and the old Souk Al-Arsa. Both offer an air of local authenticity largely absent in the shopping malls of Dubai and Abu Dhabi:

- **Blue Souk:** *Al Majaz, Corniche Road, next to lagoon. Open Saturday through Thursday, 9am - 1pm and 4-11pm, and Friday, 9am - 12noon and 4-11pm.* Also known as the Sharjah Central Souk or Souk Al Markazi, these two long two-story air-conditioned buildings—adjoined by foot bridges at the second level but parallel to each other and divided by a busy

street—from the outside look like an opulent train station embellished with intricate Islamic designs. Housing over 600 shops, it's reputed to be the largest wholesale and retail market in Arabia for handicrafts and textiles. The ground floor is dominated by jewelry, gold, clothing, and furniture shops offering a wide range of household goods. The second level, with its narrow walkways and crowded shops, especially appeals to tourists and collectors who sense they are shopping in a souk. Here you'll find many handicraft, souvenir, and carpet shops, interspersed with some antiques, offering products from all over the region, but with special emphasis on India, Pakistan, Afghanistan, Iran, Iraq, Yemen, and Morocco. If you're interested in handwoven carpets, be sure to explore the many rug shops on the second level. Some of our favorite shops include **Al Mutathkir Gems Nor Trading** for silver and **Azer Baijan Carpets House** for carpets, antiques, and tribal jewelry. Many visitors plan to make a brief stop here but end up spending a few hours here. Unlike shopping in the glitzy malls of Dubai, visitors to Sharjah's Blue Souk get a sense of authentic Arabian shopping.

- **Souk Al-Arsa:** Located in the city's Heritage and Arts section, this traditional covered souk is especially popular with tourists. Its wandering lanes are lined with arts, crafts, jewelry, and carpet shops as well as a few antique and collectible shops. Overall, an interesting but limited shopping stop in Sharjah.

Other shopping areas, which are of primary interest to local residents, include the **Sahara Centre** (Al Nahda Street), **Sharjah City Centre** (Al Wahda Street), and **Souq Al Majarrah** (Corniche Road).

6

Food and Entertainment

S IMILAR TO SHOPPING, dining and entertainment in the UAE are synonymous with Dubai. This non-stop city offers just about every cuisine you can think of and served in attractive hotel and club settings, shopping malls, and market areas. Evening entertainment involves everything from popular dinner cruises along Dubai Creek, cinemas, and concerts to live music, drinking, and dancing in bars, pubs, and nightclubs. Most private clubs stay open until 3am.

Keep in mind that the dining and entertainment scenes are very competitive and fluid in the UAE as more and more restaurants, bars, pubs, and nightclubs open in response to the continuing growth of tourism. Restaurants and nightclubs that are "hot" this year, including the ones we identify in this chapter, may become "average" or go out of business next year. Always check with your hotel concierge and other local resources on what are deemed to be the best of the best in dining and entertainment.

Food

Shopping and food seem to go together well in the UAE. Indeed, shoppers are often on the lookout for good restaurants for lunch and dinner—something they need to do during, between, and after their shopping sojourns.

The UAE is a unique culinary melting pot. Being a major international destination with a large expatriate community, many five-star hotels with top restaurants, and numerous mall-based food courts, the UAE offers all types of cuisines and dining venues for a wide range of budgets. All the major American-based fast-food and chain restaurants and coffee outlets (KFC, McDonald's, Starbucks, Dunkin Donuts, Burger King, Subway, Cinnabon, Baskin Robbins, Pizza Hut, Applebee's, Chili's, Hard Rock Café, Planet Hollywood) are here—as well as those of other countries (Costa Coffee, Black Canyon Thai Cuisine), including inexpensive Middle Eastern shawarma (shaved chicken kebab) stalls along the narrow but throbbing streets of Old Dubai.

You'll also find numerous cafes and bars that offer both food and drinks.

Your choices of cuisines run the gamut from Chinese to Indian to Mexican and Japanese. Italian, Mediterranean, Lebanese, and seafood restaurants are especially popular with visitors.

The UAE's top hotels (Burj Al Arab, Shangri-La, Grand Hyatt, JW Marriott, Jumeirah Beach Hotel, Le Meridien, Emirates Towers, Sheraton, Hilton, and InterContinental) also attract some of the world's top chefs. Consequently, dining out in Dubai often means dining in a world-class restaurant with fine cuisine and outstanding service. It also can mean a very unique dining experience, such as the Al Mahara restaurant at the Burj Al Arab hotel. Not surprisingly, dining in restaurants also can be an expensive adventure, especially when you order wine or other alcoholic beverages with your meal (basic wine can easily run US$10 to US$20 a glass).

At the same time, you can dine relatively inexpensively by frequenting the many small ethnic restaurants in Bur Dubai and Deira or fast-food restaurants and food courts found in shopping malls and along major streets. Since alcohol is not available in these places, you'll probably save a great deal on your dining bill!

Reservations

Most major restaurants recommend reservations for dinner. If you visit Dubai during the high season, be sure to make reservations well in advance. Many of Dubai's top restaurants, especially in the Burj Al Arab Hotel, are fully booked weeks in advance. If you plan to visit Dubai during the high season, you may want to e-mail, telephone, or fax your favorite restaurants for reservations prior to arriving in Dubai. Alternatively, if you're in town without reservations and a restaurant may be fully booked, you may want to inquire about dining very early (7:30pm) or very late (after 10:30pm)—times that could still be open.

Dining Hours

Many restaurants are open for both lunch and dinner, seven days a week. Others may only open for dinner, and some close one day a week, usually on Saturday.

Restaurants serving lunch are usually open between 12noon and 3pm, although some open at 12:30 and close at 3:30pm. Restaurants serving dinner usually open their doors around 7:30pm and close around 11pm or 12 midnight. Some stay open until 1 or 2am. Seasoned diners at Middle Eastern (Arabic and Lebanese) restaurants tend to dine late—10pm to 1-2am.

Food courts and cafes in shopping malls tend to follow the hours of the shopping malls—10am to 10pm.

During the fasting month of Ramadan, some restaurants may alter their daytime dining hours in deference to this Muslim custom, which may affect many of their employees.

Dress Codes

Dress in Dubai is generally casual but neat. While most major restaurants request business casual attire, a few restaurants in the top hotels have strict dress codes for men—a jacket and shirt with collar. If you arrive in the UAE without a jacket, all is not lost. You can often get a "loaner" jacket. When making a restaurant reservation, ask about the dress code. If the restaurant requires a jacket, tell them that you forgot to bring one and would appreciate it if they could loan you one for the evening. Most such restaurants keep extra jackets in stock just for such

 situations. As long as you call ahead with such a request, you should be able to pass the dress code, although your newly acquired jacket may not fit perfectly! Even if you don't make this request, chances are restaurant personnel will find you a jacket when you arrive in violation

of their dress code. Just be nice—apologize for this oversight and ask if they might have an extra jacket available for your use.

Similar to the discriminating "Members Only" signs at the entrance of many bars and nightclubs, restaurant dress codes are often flexible, depending on who you are, how you look, and what you say. A smile and kind words will often get you in!

Tips and Taxes

Many first-time visitors to the UAE are uncertain about tipping. Don't assume you should be leaving a tip, even though your credit card slip may include a tip line suggesting that you fill it in at your discretion. In fact, you are not expected to tip in most hotel restaurants. The reason is simple but little understood by most visitors: a 10% service charge is already included in the menu prices—along with a 10% (Dubai) or 6% (Abu Dhabi) municipality tax! Those who add a tip are actually double-tipping.

However, many restaurants outside hotels may not include the service charge and tax in the food prices. Instead, they may print this statement at the bottom of the menu: "Prices are subject to 10% service charge and 10% (or 6%) municipality tax." In these cases, both the service charge and tax are added to your restaurant bill.

At the same time, the service charge usually goes to the house rather than to the serving staff. Therefore, if you want to reward a server with a tip, give it directly to him or her in cash. Don't add it to your credit card charge slip since your add-on will usually go directly to the house rather than to the server. Tips are always appreciated, especially when given in cash.

Dining Resources

Food is like shopping in the UAE—an attractive form of entertainment. As might be expected, the dining scene in Dubai is constantly changing with new restaurants, pubs, and bars opening and new chefs changing menus. Many new restaurants open each year in response to Dubai's rapidly expanding business and tourist population.

Given the importance of food in this city, you'll find many books, magazines, and websites focused on dissecting the city's many cuisines and dining venues. For information on the best in dining in the UAE, be sure to pick up the latest issues of the weekly *Time Out* magazines for Dubai and Abu Dhabi, which are available through most hotels:

- *Time Out Dubai*
- *Time Out Abu Dhabi*

Serious diners purchase (Dhs.10) a copy of the definitive annual dining guide to the UAE, which reviews more than 400 great places to dine and drink:

- *The Good Food Guide: The UAE's Best Restaurants and Bars*

Also look for the *Time Out Guide to Eating and Drinking in Dubai* and *Posh Nosh, Cheap Eats and Star Bars*, which are available in most of the city's major bookstores. *Dubai: The Complete Residents' Guide*, which we recommended earlier, includes more than 300 restaurant reviews.

You also can review several Dubai restaurants by visiting these restaurant websites:

- www.timeoutdubai.com/dubai/restaurants
- www.10best.com/Dubai/Restaurants
- www.dubaicityguide.com/goingout/restaurants.asp
- www.dubai-eating.com

When you consider selecting a restaurant, keep in mind that Dubai's many hotel bars and pubs, such as Aussie Legends and Irish Village, also serve excellent food. They also are a popular venue for drinking and entertainment. For a listing of such combination dining, drinking, and entertainment establishments, survey our entertainment section below.

Since most of the major restaurants are located in hotels, you can often get a sneak preview of a restaurant by visiting the restaurant or dining section of the hotel's website. For example, if you are interested in dining at what many critics consider to be Dubai's best, and most unique and expensive, restaurant—the Al Mahara—visit the "dining" section of the Burj Al Arab Hotel website for information on this fabulous iconic seafood restaurant:

www.burj-al-arab.com/dining/al_mahara

Alcohol

The UAE's laws on alcohol greatly influence the location and popularity of restaurants with visitors. Remember, this is officially a Muslim country, which restricts the sale and consumption of alcohol to non-Muslim foreign visitors and locals with special permits. Because alcohol, with few exceptions, can only be sold in hotels and private clubs, most restaurants, bars, pubs, and entertainment venues are found in hotels and clubs. Since Dubai has over 300 hotels, and most of the five—and four-star hotels have six to eight restaurants, you'll find numerous dining and drinking choices throughout the city.

If you must have wine, beer, or other alcoholic beverages with your meals, plan to dine at hotels and clubs rather than on the streets of Dubai. However, in so doing, you'll miss out on some special restaurants that do not serve alcohol.

Dubai's Best Dining

Some of Dubai's best restaurants, including our exceptional "must visit" (*), include:

- **Al Mahara*** *Seafood/International*
  www.burj-al-arab.com/dining/al_mahara
  Burj Al Arab, Jumeirah
  12:30pm-3pm and 7pm-12 midnight
  Tel. 301-7600

- **Al Nafoorah*** *Arabic/Lebanese*
  Emirates Towers Hotel
  Sheikh Zayed Road
  Tel. 319-8088

- **Al Qasr** *Arabic/Lebanese*
  Dubai Marine Beach Resort & Spa
  12:30-3:30pm and 7:30pm-2am, Fri-Wed
  12:30-3:30pm and 7:30pm-3am, Thursday
  Tel. 346-1111

- **Amwaj** *Seafood*
  Shangri-La Hotel
  Sheikh Zayed Road
  12noon-3pm and 7pm-12midnight, Sun-Fri
  Closed Saturday
  Tel. 343-8888

- **Antique Bazaar**   *Indian*
  Four Points Sheraton
  Bank Street, Bur Dubai
  12:30-3pm and 7:30pm-3am, Sat-Thu
  7:30pm-3am, Friday
  Tel. 397-7444

- **Awtar**   *Arabic/Lebanese*
  Grand Hyatt Dubai
  Oud Metha
  12:30-3pm and 7:30pm-2am, Sun-Fri
  Closed Saturday
  Tel. 316-1234

- **Bastakia Nights***   *Arabic/Lebanese*
  Near Al-Faheidi Street
  (No alcohol but has shopping)
  Bastakia, Bur Dubai
  12:30pm-midnight, Sat-Thur
  2pm-midnight, Friday
  Tel. 353-7772

- **Benjarong**   *Thai*
  Dusit Hotel
  7:30pm-midnight
  Tel. 343-3333

- **Blue Elephant***   *Thai*
  Al-Bustan Rotana Hotel
  Casablanca Road
  Al-Garhoud
  12noon-3pm and 7-11:30pm
  Tel. 705-4660

- **Café Chic**   *French*
  Le Meridien Dubai
  Airport Road, Al-Garhoud
  12:30-2:45pm and 8-11:45pm
  Tel. 282-4040

- **China Club**   *Chinese*
  Radisson SAS Deira Creek Hotel
  12:30-3pm and 7:30-11pm, Sat-Thu
  11:30am-3pm and 7:30-11pm, Friday
  Tel. 205-7333

- **Eau Zone**   *European/Fusion*
  Royal Mirage
  12noon-3:30pm and 7-11:30pm
  Tel. 399-9999

- **Handi**   *Indian*
  Taj Palace Hotel, Deira
  12noon-3:30pm and 7-11:30pm
  Tel. 223-2222

- **Indego**   *Indian*
  Grosvenor House Dubai
  Dubai Marina
  7:30pm-12 midnight, Fri-Wed
  7:30pm-1am, Thursday
  Tel. 399-8888

- **JW's Steakhouse**   *Steakhouse*
  JW Marriott Hotel, Deira
  12:30-3:30pm and 7:30-11pm
  Tel. 262-4444

- **Kiku**   *Japanese*
  Le Meridien Dubai
  12:30-2:45pm and 7-11pm
  Tel. 282-4040

- **Latino House**   *Latin American*
  Al Murooj Rotana Hotel & Suites
  Sheikh Zayed Road
  12noon-3pm and 7pm-12midnight
  Tel. 321-1111

- **Marrakech***   *Moroccan*
  Shangri-La Hotel
  Sheikh Zayed Road
  6:30pm-1am, Sat-Thu
  Tel. 343-8888

- **Medzo**   *Italian*
  Pyramids, Wafi City
  Al-Qataiyat Road
  12:30-3pm and 7:30-11:30pm
  Tel. 324-0000

- **Mezzanine**   *European*
  Grosvenor House Dubai
  7:30pm-12 midnight, Fri-Wed
  7:30pm-1am, Thursday
  Tel. 399-8888

- **Mosaico**   *Italian*
  Emirates Towers Hotel
  24 hours a day
  Tel. 319-8088

- **Peppercrab***   *Singaporean*
  Grant Hyatt Dubai
  Al-Qataiyat Road
  7-11:30pm, Mon-Sat
  7pm-1am, Wed and Thu
  Tel. 317-222

- **Shabestan**   *Persian*
  Radisson SAS Hotel
  Deira Creek
  12:15-3:15pm and 7:15-11:15pm
  Tel. 222-7171

- **Sarband**   *Persian*
  Century Village
  Garhoud
  11am-2am
  Tel. 282-3891

- **Spectrum on One**   *International*
  Fairmont Hotel
  6pm-1am
  Tel. 311-8316

- **Verre***   *French*
  Hilton Dubai Creek
  Baniyas Road
  7pm-11pm
  Tel. 226-1111

- **Vu's***   *European/Fusion*
  Emirates Towers Hotel
  Sheikh Zayed Road
  12:30-3pm and 7:30-11:30pm
  Tel. 319-8088

Three of the city's best cafes include:

- **Cafe Ceramique**
  Jumeirah Town Centre
  Mall of the Emirates

- **Lime Tree Café**
  Ibn Battutu Mall
  Jumeirah Beach Road
  Tel. 349-8498

- **XVA Café**
  Bastakia
  Tel. 353-5383

Since Friday is the weekly holiday, the following restaurants offer all-you-can-eat-and-drink Friday brunches:

- **Andiamo** (Grant Hyatt)
- **Double Decker** (Al Murooj Rotana)
- **Dusit Dubai** (Dusit Dubai)
- **Focaccia** (Hyatt Regency)
- **Glasshouse** (Hilton Dubai Creek)
- **JW Marriott** (JW Marriott Hotel)
- **Marina Seafood Restaurant** (Jumeirah Beach Hotel)
- **Mediterraneo** (Shangri-La Hotel)
- **Al Qasr** (Al Qasr)
- **Thai Kitchen** (Park Hyatt Dubai)
- **Traiteur** (Park Hyatt)
- **Yalumba** (Le Meridien Dubai)

Dinner Cruises

A frequently recommended dining experience is to join an evening dinner dhow cruise along Deira Creek in Dubai. These are traditional wooden dhows converted into dinner cruise showboats. The 2-to 2 1/2-hour cruise usually involves drinks, entertainment (live music and maybe a belly dancer), shisha, and a combination Arabian/International buffet served below deck in air-conditioned comfort. The typical cost is Dhs.300-500 (US$82-136) per person. Wine and other special drinks, which are readily marketed to diners, are extra.

You may enjoy this type of "must-do-when-in-Dubai" tourist activity, especially if you are with a group or are looking for a romantic river/dining cruise. However, it's not for everyone, and once is usually enough. The evening views of the river traffic, shoreline, and skylines of both the old and new city are very interesting, but the food is often mediocre (an exception being the Al Mansour Dhow, which is noted for its excellent seafood).

The following companies offer dinner cruises along Dubai Creek:

- **Al Mansour Dhow**: Le Meridien Mina Seyahi, Tel. 205-7333

- **Bateaux Dubai**: Tel. 399-4994 (www.bateauxdubai.com)

- **Creek Cruises**: Tel. 393-9860 (www.creekcruises.com)

- **Creekside Leisure**: Tel. 336-8406 (www.tour-dubai.com)

- **Danat Dubai**: Tel. 351-1117

- **Lama Dubai**: Tel. 334-4330

Abu Dhabi Restaurants

Abu Dhabi's dining scene is not as extensive as Dubai's. Nonetheless, if you are visiting Abu Dhabi, you will find several excellent restaurants. Like Dubai, the best and most expensive restaurants in Abu Dhabi are found in hotels and clubs, places that also can serve alcohol and offer live entertainment.

Abu Dhabi's top restaurants will be found in the major hotels, especially the opulent Emirates Palace (11 food and beverage outlets at present and several more to come) and the well established Hilton Abu Dhabi, Le Royal Meridian, and Sheraton.

Three good print resources on restaurants in Abu Dhabi are:

- *Time Out Abu Dhabi* (weekly magazine with a restaurant section)

- *The Good Food Guide: The UAE's Best Restaurants and Bars* (reviews over 100 restaurants in Abu Dhabi)

- *Abu Dhabi: The Complete Residents' Guide* (includes a restaurant review section)

Also, check out the restaurant section on Time Out's website devoted to Abu Dhabi:

www.timeoutabudhabi.com

Restaurants in hotels include a 10% service and a 6% municipality tax (tourism fee) in their food prices. Other restaurants tend to add these to your bill. The same tipping rules we outlined for Dubai apply to Abu Dhabi—don't double-tip but give cash if you want to reward your server.

Some of Abu Dhabi's best restaurants and cafes include:

- **Al Fanar***   *International*
  Le Royal Meridien (Revolving restaurant)
  12:30-3pm and 7-11pm
  Tel. 695-0583

- **Al Majlis**   *Café*
  Emirates Palace
  690-9000

- **Al Mawal**   *Arabic/Lebanese*
  Hilton Abu Dhabi
  Tel. 681-2773

- **Anar**   *Persian*
  Emirates Palace Hotel
  Tel. 690-8888

- **Bam Bu!**   *Chinese*
  Abu Dhabi Marina
  Tel. 645-6373

- **Benihana**   *Japanese*
  Beach Rotana Hotel
  Tel. 644-3000

- **Bice***   *Italian*
  Hilton Abu Dhabi
  Tel. 681-1900

- **Finz***   *Seafood*
  Beach Rotana Hotel
  Tel. 644-3000

- **Hemingway's***   *Bar food*
  Hilton Abu Dhabi
  Tel. 692-4567

- **Il Paradiso***   *Seafood*
  Sheraton Abu Dhabi Resort & Towers Hotel
  Tel. 677-3333

- **Jazz Bar**   *International*
  Hilton Abu Dhabi
  Tel. 681-1900

- **Marakesh**   *Moroccan*
  www.millenniumhotels.com/ae/
  millenniumabudhabi/restaurant/marakesh.html
  Millennium Hotel
  7pm-3am
  Tel. 626-2700

- **Messaluna****   *Italian*
  Emirates Palace
  Tel. 690-9000

- **Nihal**   *Indian*
  Next to Sands Hotel
  Zayed Second Street (Electra or 7th)
  Tel. 631-8088

- **Oceans**   *Seafood*
  Le Royal Meridien
  Tel. 674-2020

- **Rodeo Grill**   *Steakhouse*
  Beach Rotana Hotel
  Tel. 644-3000

- **Sayed***   *International*
  Emirates Palace
  Tel. 690-8888

- **Soba**   *Japanese*
  Le Royal Meridien
  Tel. 674-2020

- **Talay***   *Thai*
  Le Meridien
  Tel. 644-6666

- **THE One Café**   *Café*
  Next to BMW showroom
  Tel. 681-6500

- **Vasco's***   *International*
  Hiltonia
  Tel. 681-1900

- **Zari Zardozi***   *Indian*
  Le Royal Meridien
  Tel. 695-0583

Dubai Entertainment

The UAE is full of many surprises, especially when it comes to entertainment. Indeed, most visitors are amazed to discover how much alcohol, music, and dancing are permitted in this ostensibly Muslim country. Compared to many other cities of the world, where sex and gambling are not big drawing cards, Dubai's nightlife is second to none. It has a reputation as being one of the world's most tolerant and swinging Muslim cities for non-Muslims who wish to indulge in typical Western nightlife activities. The settings are often opulent, the views spectacular and romantic, and the audiences diverse and eclectic. Admission is usually free, although at times "discriminating."

Dubai's young, single, and financially flush expatriate professionals party hard until the wee hours of the morning. Each night between 10pm and 3am the city comes alive as hundreds of bars, pubs, and nightclubs in hotels and private clubs entertain thousands of expatriates and tourists with popular DJs and live music. As might be expected, all the DJs and live entertainers are expatriates or foreigners who include Dubai on their international employment circuits.

Shopping and Dining

As we noted earlier, entertainment for many locals in the UAE is closely tied to shopping and dining. The streets and malls become very busy at night. In fact, driving through the Bastakiya area of Bur Dubai and along Sheikh Zayed Road on weekend nights (Friday and Saturday) can be extremely frustrating because of gridlock traffic.

The largest shopping malls are designed with the notion that they should be family-oriented entertainment complexes—complete with cinemas, theaters, play areas, sports activities, and day spas. They also include numerous cafes, fast food outlets, and restaurants. Best of all, they maintain shopper—and entertainment-friendly hours—open from 10am to 10pm and sometimes closing at 1am.

Hotels and Private Clubs

Visitors looking for something to do in the evening, other than shopping and dining, need to only look toward the many hotels and private clubs that offer music, drinking, and dancing. You'll find many bars, pubs, cafes, and nightclubs offering the latest music with DJs, live bands, and professional acts. If you are into jazz, pop, soul, R&B, Arabic, Latino, or fusion music, you'll have no problem finding the right entertainment venue for enjoying your favorite music.

Night Owls

Bars, pubs, and nightclubs usually get started after 10pm and close early in the morning—between 1am and 3am—even on weekdays. Many clubs don't come alive until around 1am. Friday and Saturday nights are very busy for these places. During weekdays (Sunday through Thursday) many bars, pubs, and nightclubs advertise special promotions, organize themes, and push ladies' nights.

Membership, Dress Codes, Cover Charges

Some places will have a "Members Only" sign posted. However, don't be deterred by such restrictive signage. If you look good, come with a companion of the opposite sex, arrive when the place isn't packed, and talk nicely to the gatekeepers, chances are you may get in without a membership. Such signs are notorious for allowing clubs to discriminate against anyone they don't like for any reason, be it race, ethnicity, age, dress, attitude, or accompanying guests.

Most places have relatively relaxed dress codes—casual or business casual. Avoid arriving in shorts, T-shirts, or sandals.

With a few exceptions, bars and nightclubs rarely have cover charges. The costs of food and drinks can be relatively reasonable depending on where you go and what you order in the wine and spirits department. However, many exclusive clubs, such as Trilogy and Kasbar, can be very expensive. A night on the town starting with a restaurant and then moving on to a pub, bar, and nightclub may cost you a princely sum!

Useful Resources

For the latest information on evening entertainment in the UAE, be sure to pick up copies of these weekly magazines, or visit their websites. They include updated listings on the UAE's entertainment scene:

- *Time Out Dubai* (www.timeoutdubai.com)
- *Time Out Abu Dhabi* (www.timeoutabudhabi.com)

Mumtazz (www.mumtazz.com) includes a guide to upcoming club events. The annual *The Good Food Guide: The UAE's Best Restaurants and Bars* includes a section on bar food, which covers the most popular bars in the UAE.

Popular Bars

Some of Dubai's most popular and trendy bars—offering food, drink, music, and special ladies' nights—include:

- **Boudoir**
  www.myboudoir.com
  Dubai Marine Beach
  Jumeirah
  Tel. 345-5995

- **Buddha Bar**
  www.grosvenorhouse.lemeridien.com
  Grosvenor House
  Marsa Dubai
  Tel. 399-8888

- **Ginseng**
  www.wafi.com
  Wafi City
  Umm Hurair
  Tel. 824-8200

- **Lotus One**
  www.lotus1.com
  Dubai International Convention Centre
  Trade Center 2
  Tel. 329-3200

- **Sho Cho's**
  www.dxbmarine.com
  Dubai Marine Beach Resort & Spa
  Jumeirah
  Tel. 346-1111

Bars With Great Views

Bars with great views, including some boasting wonderful sunsets and views of the illuminated Burj Al Arab Hotel at night, include:

- **360°**
  www.jumeirahbeachhotel.com/dining/360_degrees
  Jumeirah Beach Hotel
  Umm Suqeim
  Tel. 348-0000

- **Bahri Bar**
  www.madinatjumeirah.com/mina_a_salam/dining/bahri_bar
  Mina A'Salam
  Madinat Jumeirah
  Umm Suqeim
  Tel. 366-8888

- **Barasti Bar**
  www.lemeridienminaseyahi.com
  Le Meridien Mina Seyahi
  Al Sufouh
  Tel. 399-3333

- **Koubba**
  www.madinatjumeirah.com/al_qasr/koubba
  Al Qasr Hotel, Lobby
  Madinat Jumeirah
  Umm Suqeim
  Tel. 366-8888

- **Skybar**
  www.burj-al-arab.com/dining/skyview_bar
  Burj Al Arab Hotel
  Tel. 301-7600

- **Rooftop Lounge & Terrace**
  www.oneandonlyroyalmirage.com
  One&Only Royal Mirage
  Tel. 399-9999

- **Uptown**
  www.jumeirahbeachhotel.com/dining/uptown
  Jumeirah Beach Hotel
  Umm Suqeim
  Tel. 406-8181

- **Vu's Bar**
  www.jumeirahemiratestowers.com/dining/vus_bar
  Emirates Towers
  Trade Centre 2
  Tel. 319-8088

Live Music Venues

Popular bars, pubs, restaurants, and clubs with live music include:

- **Aussie Legends**
  www.rydges.com
  Rydges Plaza Hotel
  Tel. 398-2222

- **Bar Zar**
  www.jumeirah.com
  Souk Madinat Jumeirah
  Umm Suqeim
  Tel. 366-6348

- **Barasti Bar**
  www.lemeridien.com/minaceyani.com
  Le Meridien Mina Seyahi
  Al Sufouh
  Tel. 399-3333

- **Blue Bar**
  www.novotel.com
  Novotel World Trade Centre
  Trade Centre 2
  Tel. 332-0000

- **Go West**
  www.jumeirahbeachhotel.com/dining/go_west
  Jumeirah Beach Hotel
  Umm Suqeim
  Tel. 406-8999

- **Irish Village**
  www.aviationclub.ae
  Aviation Club
  Garhoud
  Tel. 282-4750

- **Jambase**
  www.jumeirah.com
  Souk Madinat Jumeirah
  Umm Suqeim
  Tel. 366-8888

- **Jimmy Dix**
  Moevenpick Hotel
  Bur Dubai
  Oud Metha
  Tel. 336-8800

- **Malecon**
  www.dxbmarine.com
  Dubai Marine Beach
  Jumeirah
  Tel. 346-1111

- **Rock Bottom Cafe**
  www.rameegroup.com
  Regent Palace Hotel
  Bur Dubai
  Tel. 396-3888

- **Trader Vic's**
  Souk Madinat Jumeirah
  Umm Suqeim
  Tel. 366-5646

Nightclubs

Dubai's popular nightclubs include:

- **Chameleon**
  www.waficity.com
  Wafi City
  Umm Hurair
  Tel. 324-8200

- **iBO**
  www.9714.com
  Millenium Airport Hotel
  Garhoud
  Tel. 282-1844

- **Kasbar***
  www.oneandonlyresorts.com
  One&Only Royal Mirage
  Al Sufouh
  Tel. 399-9999

- **MIX**
  www.dubai.grand.hyatt.com
  Grand Hyatt Dubai
  Umm Hurair
  Tel. 317-1234

- **Oxygen**
  www.rotana.com
  Al Bustan Rotana
  Garhoud
  Tel. 282-0000

- **Peppermint Lounge**
  Fairmont Hotel
  Sheikh Zayed Road
  Tel. 552-2807

- **Trilogy***
  www.madinatjumeirah.com/dining_at_souk_madinat/trilogy
  Souk Madinat Jumeirah
  Umm Suqeim
  Tel. 366-8888

- **Zinc**
  www.crowneplaza.com
  Crowne Plaza
  Trade Centre 1
  Tel. 331-1111

Concerts

Dubai also hosts many popular concerts with international artists, such as Elton John, Mariah Carey, Sting, Lionel Richie, and Robbie Williams. Most are held outdoors at the Tennis Stadium, the amphitheater at Media City, and the Dubai Autodrome. For schedules and tickets to upcoming events, visit these websites:

- www.itp.net/tickets
- www.boxofficeme.com
- www.aviationclub.ae

Theaters

Dubai's limited theater scene is centered in two shopping malls, which also have popular cinemas. For theatrical performances, most of which come from abroad, check out these places:

- **Dubai Community Theatre & Arts Center (DUCTAC)**
  www.ductac.org
  Mall of the Emirates
  Tel. 341-4777

- **Madinat Theatre**
  www.madinattheatre.com
  Souk Madinat Jumeirah
  Umm Suqeim
  Tel. 366-8888

Comedy

For comedy, visit The Laughter Factory website: www.thelaughter factory.com. Popular with expatriates, the comedy scene here is centered on comedians who come from the UK's Comedy Store. They usually do monthly performances in the region—Dubai, Abu Dhabi, Bahrain, Doha, and Muscat. The website includes information on upcoming performances in Dubai that usually take place at **Zinc** (Crowne Plaza), **Jimmy Dix** (Moevenpick), **Rainbow Room** (Aviation Club), and the **Courtyard Marriott** (Green Community).

Abu Dhabi Entertainment

Entertainment in Abu Dhabi follows the Dubai pattern—centered in hotels and private clubs and offered through restaurants, bars, pubs, and nightclubs. However, entertainment in Abu Dhabi is very tame and quiet in comparison to in-your-face Dubai. You will find a few sports bars and pubs that are popular with expatriates, but don't expect much. A lovely dinner with entertainment (try Il Paridiso at the Sheraton Abu Dhabi Resort & Towers) might be the highlight of your evening entertainment!

Abu Dhabi's most popular evening entertainment venues include the following:

- **Blitz**
  Novotel Centre Hotel
  Tel. 633-3555

- **Captain's Arms**
  Le Meridien Abu Dhabi
  Tel. 644-7800

- **Hemingways**
  Hilton Abu Dhabi
  Tel. 692-4567

- **Heroes**
  Crowne Plaza Hotel
  Hamdan Street
  Tel. 621-0000

- **Jazz Bar**
  Hilton Hotel
  Corniche Road
  Tel. 681-1900

- **LAB**
  Beach Rotana Hotel
  (next to Abu Dhabi Mall)
  Tel. 644-3000

- **Mood Indigo Piano Lounge**
  Novotel Centre Hotel
  Tel. 633-3555

- **P.J. O'Reilly's**
  Le Royal Meridian Abu Dhabi
  Tel. 674-2020

- **Rock Bottom**
  Al Diar Capitol Hotel
  Meena Street
  Tel. 678-7700

- **Sax Restaurant Club**
  Le Royal Meridien
  Khalifa Bin Zayed Street
  Tel. 674-2020

- **Tavern**
  Sheraton Abu Dhabi Resort & Towers
  Tel. 697-0260

- **Trader Vic's**
  Beach Rotana Hotel
  Next to Abu Dhabi Mall
  Tel. 644-3300

- **Zenith**
  Sheraton Abu Dhabi Resort & Towers
  Corniche Road
  Tel. 697-0358

Daytime Entertainment

Aside from shopping and dining, daytime entertainment usually involves **observing** sports events or **participating** in sports activities. Indeed, this is a very active sports-oriented country. The ruling families love sports and accordingly sponsor major international competitive events, from horse and camel racing to golf and motor sports. Such events draw thousands of visitors to the UAE each year and involve the ruling elite in attending events and giving out awards that often involve very lucrative purses (US$6 million for the Dubai World Cup in 2007, which is sponsored by the well capitalized national airline, Emirates Airline).

Despite the UAE's reputed high heat and humidity, most of these activities and events take place outdoors during the cooler parts of the year, especially October through April. February and March are usually very busy months for major international sports events:

- Dubai Tennis Open (www.dubaitennischampionships.com)
- Dubai Desert Classic (www.dubaidesertclassic.com)
- Dubai World Cup (www.dubaiworldcup.com)
- International Arabian Horse Championship (www.diahc.ae)

Sports Events/Spectator Sports

Major sports events and activities for both spectators include:

- **Camel racing:** An extremely popular sport. Camel racing season (www.zipzak.com) runs from October to April. Races usually take place twice a day (7:30am and 2:30pm) on Thursday, Friday, and Saturday. UAE has 15 racetracks and approximately 14,000 racing camels. President Zayed reputedly owns 14,000 camels and employs 9,000 workers for their upkeep!

- **Cricket:** Matches in October, November, March, and April in Sharjah.

- **Football (soccer):** Regularly played throughout the country.

- **Golf:** Dubai Desert Golf Classic (www.dubaidesertclassic.com) held at Emirates Golf Club.

- **Horse racing:** Regular races (www.emiratesracing.com) and the Dubai Racing Carnival, but highlighted with the world's richest cup in March—Dubai World Cup (www.dubaiworldcup.com)—held at Nad Al Sheba.

- **Motor sports:** Centered at the Dubai Autodrome and Business Park, which includes a 5.39-kilometer motor racing track and a grandstand that can accommodate 7,000+ spectators. Special events include Emirates Rally Championship, 1,000 Dunes Rally, Autocross Championship, Desert Challenge, FIA Marathon World Cup, Marlboro Desert Challenge, and Formula One Grand Prix (starting in 2009 in Abu Dhabi).

- **Rugby:** Competitions centered at the Dubai Exiles Rugby Club (www.dubaiexiles.com). Popular Rugby Sevens (www.dubairugby7s.com) in November.

- **Running:** Dubai Marathon (www.dubaimarathon.org) which takes place in January.

- **Sailing:** International Sailing Week Regatta in February and Offshore Powerboating in December. Contact: Dubai International Marine Club (www.minascyahidubai.com)

- **Tennis:** Dubai Tennis Championships (www.dubaitennischampionships.com) in February.

Participant Sports

We consider **mall-hopping** to be a unique indoor (shopping) and outdoor (getting there) sports activity that should be added to the UAE's

seemingly endless list of compelling sports activities. In fact, you can easily walk—even power walk—several kilometers a day as you cruise the city's many shopping malls, especially the shopping resorts, and participate in their air-conditioned sports activities.

If you are active in sports, or just want to sample Dubai's and Abu Dhabi's many unique offerings, including falconry in the desert and snow skiing in the shopping mall, check out this rather exhaustive menu of choices. Most participant sports can be arranged on your own or through hotels or tour groups:

- Archery
- Badminton
- Birdwatching
- Boating
- Bowling
- Canoeing
- Cycling
- Desert safaris
- Dune bashing
- Exercise (fitness centers)
- Falconry
- Fishing
- Flying
- Golfing
- Hiking
- Horse riding
- Hot air ballooning
- Ice skating
- Jet skiing
- Karting
- Kayaking
- Kitesurfing
- Martial arts
- Mountain biking
- Paintballing
- Parasailing
- Polo
- Rock climbing
- Rollerblading
- Rowing
- Running
- Sailing
- Sandboarding
- Scuba diving
- Shooting
- Skydiving
- Snorkeling
- Snow skiing
- Snowboarding
- Spas
- Swimming
- Tennis
- Water parks
- Water skiing
- Windsurfing

Golf

Golf is big business in the UAE. If you enjoy golfing, you'll find several world-class golf courses in Dubai, many of which were designed by Greg Norman, Robert Trent Jones II, Colin Montgomerie, and Karl Litten, and are frequently visited by Tiger Woods and other celebrity sports figures:

- Al Badia Golf Resort
- Arabian Ranches Golf Club
- Dubai Country Club
- Dubai Creek Golf and Yacht Club

- Emirate Golf Club (site for the Desert Classic)
- Jebel Ali Golf Resort and Spa
- Montgomerie Golf Club
- Nad Al Sheba Club

And more golf courses are being built to accommodate the UAE's growing local and international population of golf enthusiasts. However, this may or may not be an expensive sport, depending on what you are used to in the golfing world. For example, greens fees for visitors range from Dhs.400 (US$108) to Dhs.600 (US$164). Renting a shared cart and golf clubs will run about Dhs.150-250 (US$40-68). All totaled, you can easily spend over US$200 on 18 holes of golf.

PART II

Oman

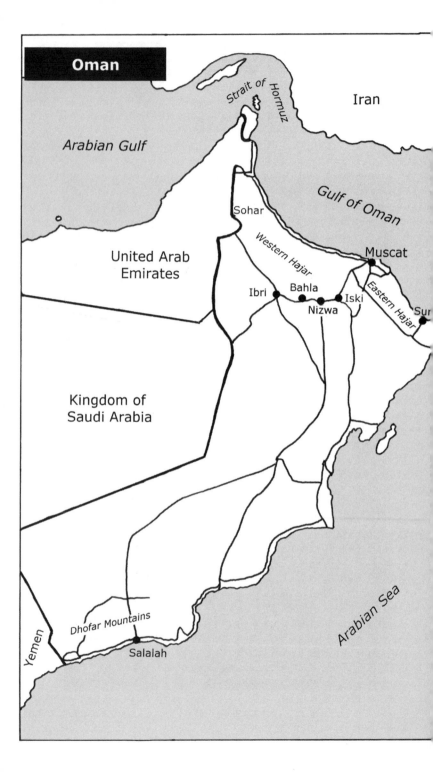

7

Welcome to the
Sultanate of Oman

WELCOME TO ONE OF the Middle East's most intriguing
destinations where culture, economics, and population go
hand in hand. It's a land made famous by the Queen of Sheba,
Alexander the Great, Vasco de Gama, Lawrence of Arabia, the
Portuguese, Ottomans, British, and nomadic Bedouins.

Known for its frankincense, metalwork, souks, forts, deserts,
beaches, sultans, warring and seafaring traditions, Zanzibar connection,
international oil companies, tourism, and new property developers, once
sleepy and backwater Oman has quickly become an important business
and tourism center on the Arabian Peninsula. It especially appeals to discerning travelers in search of a very special place not overrun by tourists
but still offering all the amenities of a five-star destination.

Welcome to undiscovered and surprising Oman. It's a friendly and
hospitable place where you will be left alone to enjoy the country's
many unique treasures and pleasures.

An Interesting History

Oman traces its history to 5,000 BC, when southern Oman, or present day Dhofar, with its idyllic monsoon season, was the center for the lucrative frankincense trade. Oman also became famous for its copper production. Exporting these key resources, the locals become noted sailors and merchant traders who regularly traded with Egypt, Greece, Rome, India, China, and Africa.

A tribal society ruled by imams and sultans, various parts of Oman have been invaded and ruled by the Portuguese, Persians, British, French, Ottomans, and Saudis. The many castles, forts, and walls that  dot the cities, towns, and countryside testify to the importance of wars and tribal conflicts in Omani history.

The Omani Empire in the first half of the 1800s played an important role in the African slave trade through its colonies in east Africa, especially Mombasa and Zanzibar. Indeed, it maintained a special relationship with the island of Zanzibar. From here Oman managed much of the east African slave trade until slavery was outlawed by the British in the mid-1800s, which led to the near collapse of the Omani economy and the flight of thousands of Omanis from Muscat to Zanzibar. In the latter half of the 1800s, one of Sultan Said's sons became the Sultan of Zanzibar. Today, Omani influences are still very apparent in Zanzibar's architecture and religion.

In 1951 the Sultanate of Muscat and Oman received independence from Great Britain. At that time Oman remained relatively poor, illiterate, backward, conflict-ridden, and inward looking. In fact, Oman was relatively closed to the outside world until tourists were first permitted to visit in the 1980s. In 1967 the country began to export oil. Today modest oil revenue is the major income source (75 percent) for the government, which manages to finance major infrastructure and development projects, especially irrigation, roads, and tourism, for diversifying the Omani economy.

Under the enlightened leadership of Sultan Qaboos, who seized power from his father in a 1970 palace coup, Oman has undergone a major transformation to modernize the country while retaining its many cultural and religious traditions. New roads, irrigation schemes, telecommunications, port facilities, airports, and educational institutions provide the necessary infrastructure for diversifying the Omani economy from dependence on oil revenue to greater reliance on trade, tourism, recreation, and property development. While the country relies a great deal on expatriate labor, its "Omanization" program is attempting to bring more and more educated and trained Omanis into the modern labor market.

The Oman you will visit today is a very new and visionary Oman. Tourism is still in its infancy, with a major emphasis on luxury accommodations and ecotourism. You'll especially see this new Oman in the impressive new expressways, streets, mosques, shopping centers, hotels, and restaurants in Muscat. If you visited Muscat 20 years ago, you'll have difficulty recognizing this place. History buffs will enjoy visiting Muscat's many museums, which showcase bygone eras of colonial powers, tribes, forts, weaponry, and seafaring trade.

For a quick overview of Omani history, visit these informative websites:

- http://en.wikipedia.org/wiki/History_of_Oman
- www.arab.net/oman
- www.omaninfo.com/oman/history.asp

The New Oman

Whatever image you have of Oman will most likely change upon arrival. If you've just come from the UAE, you're in for some surprises. Despite its oil riches, which are modest in comparison to other Gulf States, Oman has purposefully decided not to follow the frenetic high-rise development path of Dubai or Abu Dhabi, nor encourage mass tourism. Instead, it has focused on developing a few strategic low-rise business and tourism communities, mainly centered in and around Muscat, for attracting wealthy investors and upscale travelers.

Oman is much more than a challenging land of rugged mountains, sand, gravel, heat, humidity, forts, and souks. Indeed, you are about to experience a society undergoing rapid change because of the impact of oil, tourism, and expatriates on its booming economy, and especially in and around the capital city of Muscat in the north. When you visit Oman, you'll encounter a laid back and convenient country that offers some very special travel and shopping experiences. Sparsely populated with an unusually striking landscape, this is a relatively empty country with only a few significant population centers along the northern coast and interior. Indeed, you may feel you're one of only a few travelers who has the privilege of exploring this fascinating place.

Population

Boasting a population of 3.3 million, nearly 20 percent of Oman's residents are English-speaking expatriates who operate vital sectors of Oman's economy. These expatriates make up nearly two-thirds of Oman's workforce. In fact, many of the contacts you will make in Oman will most likely be with members of various expatriate communities, especially Indians, Pakistanis, Filipinos, Egyptians, Jordanians, Bangladeshis, and a few other Asians and Middle Easterners who are the real work horses of the Omani economy. These expatriates operate most hotels, restaurants, and shops as well as maintain roadways, construct buildings, and haul trash. Government officials and a few taxi drivers and shopkeepers in the souks are Omani.

Religion

Oman was one of the first Arab states to convert to Islam in the 7th century AD. Today it remains a moderately conservative Islamic state dominated by the Ibadhi sect, although some Omanis are Sunni and Shi'a Muslims.

Religion plays an important role in Oman. As such, the Omanis observe the five daily calls to prayers, fast during the month of Ramadan, give alms, and plan to make the pilgrimage (known as Hajj) to the holy city of Mecca in Saudi Arabia.

Oman is tolerant of other religions, especially Hindu and Christian expatriates and tourists, who are permitted to practice their faiths. The government actively promotes Islam through the many beautiful mosques found throughout the country, and especially in Muscat and Nizwa. If you visit only one mosque in all of Oman, make sure it's the fabulous

Sultan Qaboos Grand Mosque in the Al Khuwaye section of Muscat (open to visitors, 8am to 11am, Saturday to Wednesday). Friday is holy day in Oman, a time of abbreviated commerce.

Exotic and Modern

While Oman is both exotic and traditional, it's also a very modern and convenient country. Drive its impressive highways and navigate the frantic traffic circles of expansive Muscat and you'll think you're in another world altogether. But descend into the traditional souks of Nizwa and Muscat, climb its many over-restored forts, pass through sleepy towns and villages where you can observe the slow pace of life, watch fishermen bring in their latest netted hauls, visit a mosque, experience the near complete shut-down of communities between 1:00pm and 4:30pm each day, or try to buy a beer, and you know that many things remain the same in Oman.

This is both a traditional and modern nation that takes its religion, Islam, very seriously. The mosques in Muscat are truly impressive. Men dress in the traditional *dishdashah*, women wear *hijabs* and *abayas*, drive the latest model cars, use cell phones and computers, and frequently visit Starbucks and McDonald's. Oman also builds some of the most beautiful mosques you'll find anywhere in the Arab world.

Area and Geography

Located on the northeast corner of the Arabian Peninsula, the Sultanate of Oman boasts 2,092 kilometers (1,300 miles) of coastline, several rugged mountain ranges, and thousands of square kilometers of desert sands and scrub. This is a land of great geographic contrasts. It's the third largest country on the Arabian Peninsula. Sharing 3,466 kilometers (2,154 miles) of borders with Saudi Arabia and the United Arab Emirates in the west and Yemen in the southwest, and surrounded by the Strait of Hormuz in the north and the Arabian Sea in the east, Oman's 309,500 square kilometers are approximately the size of Italy or Poland or the U.S. states of Kansas or New Mexico.

This is a rugged, hot, and humid land of deserts, mountains, and coastal plains laced with an excellent road system. Large sections of the main paved roads are even lined with street lights, a rather unusual feature for roads seemingly in the middle of nowhere! Indeed, Oman offers some of the most spectacular scenery on the Arabian Peninsula, from the ruggedly beautiful Musandam Peninsula jutting out into the Strait of Hormuz in the far north to deserts of the central and western regions to the tropical southern area of Dhofar. Most of the country consists of valleys and deserts (82 percent) along with mountain ranges (15 percent) and narrow coastal plains (3 percent). It boasts a stunning landscape consisting of sand and gravel plains, a vast Empty Quarter

(Rub Al Khali desert) extending into Saudi Arabia and the UAE, salt flats (*sabka*), lagoons (*khwars*), oases, mountain ranges, riverbeds (*wadis*), spectacular desert dunes, a green tropical monsoon-washed area (Dhofar) in the south, and fjords at Musandam in the strategic northeast (dubbed the "Norway of Arabia"). It even boasts its own "Grand Canyon"—Wadi Ghul. Most of the population lives along the coast, especially around Muscat in the north. Nomadic Bedouin tribes live in the desert regions.

Oman's climate is varied and sometimes unpredictable. While the coastal areas are generally humid, much of the desert interior is hot and dry. This climate is moderated somewhat by mountains, with the highest mountain reaching over 3,000 meters.

While rains are usually light and unpredictable, the southern Dhofar area experiences monsoon rains from May to September. These rains turn this area into a tropical paradise, which attracts thousands of Arab tourists who come here to escape the scorching summer heat elsewhere in the Arabian Peninsula and Gulf area. They especially enjoy the arid interior and grassy hills of the beautiful Dhofar area.

In June 2007 Muscat was unexpectedly hit by a horrific cyclone (Tropical Cyclone Gonu) that flooded major sections of the city, including several hotels and shopping centers near the oceanfront as well as the nearby main mosque, the Sultan Qaboos Grand Mosque. The storm also uprooted trees, overturned vehicles, and destroyed streets. Even McDonald's in the Al Qurm shopping area went eight feet under. It took over six months for the city, including one of Muscat's top five-star properties, The Chedi, to recover from the devastation.

Getting There

The quickest way to get to Oman is to fly from Dubai directly into Seeb International Airport, which is located about 40 kilometers west of Muscat. Several airlines service Muscat from Dubai and Abu Dhabi.

Both national carriers, Oman Air (www.oman-air.com) and Gulf Air (www.gulfair.com), have daily direct flights from London to Muscat. Oman Air also flies from several destinations in the Middle East, India, and Africa.

If you visit the UAE before Oman, consider renting a car in Dubai or Abu Dhabi and driving to Oman. It's a very convenient, easy, and interesting drive along excellent highways in both the UAE and Oman. Border crossings are relatively easy—30 to 45 minutes to pass through immigration—and the drive between Dubai and Muscat takes no more than six hours. Just make sure, as we noted earlier in the driving section on the UAE, that you rent a car from a company that allows you to drive into Oman. Most companies will not permit you to take their car across the border. Check with Dollar, Avis, and Hertz, which permit you to drive back and forth across the border. Also, make sure you have an insurance policy from your car rental company valid for Oman. Once you're in Oman, the car will come in handy for exploring the country, especially for shopping in our two major destinations—Nizwa and Muscat.

You'll also find convenient tour buses that connect Dubai with Muscat. Many visitors use this service and then rent a car once they arrive in Muscat.

The UAE has six border crossings with Oman. The major ones are at Hatta and Buraimi (near Al Ain). Getting a visa and processing passports at these border crossings will take a little time since the seemingly over-staffed and under-worked bureaucracy can be a bit slow. They tend to process local passports and tour groups before passports of independent international travelers. Be patient and friendly. Expect to spend nearly an hour making this crossing, although it could be much faster depending on who is in line and staffing the counters when you arrive.

Most nationalities can get a visa upon arrival at any entry point (land, sea, or air). The cost is RO6 (US$15.60) for a single—entry visa or RO10 (US$26.00) for a multiple-entry visa which is good for 30 days. Health cards are not required for entry as a tourist.

Safety and Security

Except for traffic, Oman is a very safe and civil country, probably more so than in your home country. Omanis are famous for their hospitality, which is related to their legendary Arab and Bedouin traditions that welcome and take care of visitors. Indeed, you can walk and drive in most places without fear of encountering difficulties. While there is little theft in Oman, it's always good to take sensible precautions with your valuables.

Travelers should always remember that safety begins at home—you must take responsibility for your own personal safety. In other words, don't provide opportunities for others to take advantage of you.

Like many other countries, in Oman the biggest danger is being involved in an automobile accident. So watch where you walk, drive defensively, and be very observant of your surroundings.

While it's convenient and relatively easy to rent a car and drive in Oman, be careful when doing so. You need to drive defensively as well as avoid reckless off-road driving. In fact, Oman reports increasing rates of highway accidents and injuries. Local drivers—many of whom are expatriates from Asian countries where they acquired poor driving habits—are known for aggressive driving and speeding, including suddenly changing lanes, making unexpected stops, and overtaking vehicles on the inside lane.

Be particularly careful when navigating Muscat's many round-abouts and making turns. Drivers inside the roundabouts have the right of way Right turns on red are illegal in Oman.

Similar to the UAE, Oman uses fixed cameras and radar to catch speeding drivers. Both traffic and parking fines can be expensive.

Unexpected dangers, such as the cyclone that hit Muscat and the northern coast in June 2007 and flash floods, do occasionally occur as acts of God.

Health and Medical Care

You'll find both public and private healthcare providers in Oman where the standard of healthcare is generally high. In addition to handling routine health problems, the facilities in Muscat also specialize in a variety of areas, including cosmetic surgery. Government health facilities, which are free for local residents, are primarily reserved for Omanis. Private healthcare providers (hospitals, health centers, clinics, and doctors) offer services for expatriates and tourists and are usually preferred over public healthcare providers—shorter waiting periods, more comfortable facilities, and English-speaking staffs.

Travelers should avoid tap water and ice as well as uncooked vegetables, especially salads. Stay with bottled water and other bottled drinks, which are readily available throughout Oman.

Money Matters

The **local currency** is called the Omani Rial (RO or OR). In 2008 the exchange rate was US$1 = RO.38621. In other words, ROl = US$2.60.

The Omani rial is divided into 1,000 baisas. Bank notes are issued in denominations of rials 50, 20, 10, 5, 1, 1/2 (500 baisas), 1/4 (250 baisas), 200 baisas, and 100 baisas. Coins are available in denominations of 50, 25, 10, and 5 baisas.

ATMs are widely available at banks, shopping malls, the airport, and along various streets in Muscat.

Money exchanges are found all over Muscat and they often give a better exchange rate than banks. Exchange houses are open from 8am to 1pm and 4-7pm daily.

Most major hotels, restaurants, and shops accept **credit cards**. Small shops and merchants in souks only deal in cash.

Many hotels and restaurants include service charges, which run at least 5% of the total bill. Be sure to check your bill before leaving a tip. At the same time, mandatory service charges usually go to the house rather than the staff. Small cash tips, such as a few hundred baisas, are greatly appreciated when given directly to the person offering a service.

Do plan to bargain for most purchases made in souks and shops. However, don't be surprised if some merchants, especially in Nizwa, are unwilling to discount. In many cases the first quoted price is reasonable. In other cases, you may be able to negotiate a 20- to 50-percent discount. It depends on the merchant and your bargaining skills.

Distances

For a country the size of Italy or New Mexico, distances between major cities and sites are not very great, and the main paved highways are very good. For example, the drive from Muscat to Nizwa takes only 90 minutes, and the drive from the UAE border to Muscat takes from four to six hours. However, driving from Muscat in the north to Salalah on the far southern coast, which is the capital of Dhofar and the country's second largest city (population of 100,000), takes about 12 hours to drive the 1,030-kilometer distance. The flight (Oman Air) from Muscat to Salalah takes nearly 90 minutes.

Most major cities, towns, and villages of interest to visitors staying in Muscat can be reached by 4WD within one to two hours. Estimated distances and driving time to Oman's major cities, towns, and areas via paved roads from Muscat are as follows:

City/town/area	Area	Kilometers From Muscat	Hours driving time
Bahla	North/interior	210	2
Barka	North/coast	65	$^3/_4$
Ibra	East/interior	150	$1^1/_2$
Ibri	North/interior	300	3
Musandam Peninsula	North/coast	500	6
Nizwa	North/interior	175	$1^1/_2$
Rustaq	North/interior	145	$1^1/_4$
Salalah	South/coast	1,030	12
Sohar	North/coast	230	2
Sur	East/coast	335	4

You also can reach Sur via a spectacular 240-kilometer unpaved coastal road, which takes about 3^1/$_2$ hours to drive.

Sample Itineraries

Shoppers will want to spend most of their time in and around Muscat and Nizwa and venture into a few towns and villages in northern and eastern Oman. If you have three days in Oman and have access to a car, we suggest visiting the following places:

Day 1:	Muscat
Day 2:	Nizwa, Bakla, Barka, Rustaq, Nakhl, and Al Hazm
Day 3:	Muscat

If you have a week to 12 days in Oman, consider visiting the following places:

Days 1-2:	Muscat
Day 3:	Barka, Rustaq, Nakhl, and Al Hazm
Day 4:	Nizwa and Bakla
Day 5:	Muscat and Sur
Days 6-7:	Salalah
Days 8-9:	Muscat and Sohar
Days 10-11:	Musandam Peninsula
Day 12:	Muscat or the UAE

Some visitors may want to spend more time in Muscat from where they can go deep sea fishing, diving, dhow cruising, dune bashing, and wadi exploring. Indeed, Muscat is a convenient base from which to arrange a nearby desert or mountain safari or explore other parts of Oman.

Getting Around

Airport to City

If you arrive by airline at Seeb International Airport in Muscat, take one of the orange-and-white taxis, which are in abundance just outside the arrival hall. Since taxis do not have meters, you need to agree on the price before getting into a taxi. The standard fare from the airport to Old Muscat is about RO10. The 40-kilometer trip takes about 30 minutes. The taxi fare to The Chedi, InterContinental, or Grand Hyatt hotels will be about RO7, and the trip takes about 15-20 minutes.

Rental Cars

It's relatively easy and very convenient to rent a car and drive in Oman. Many visitors rent a car in the UAE and drive to Oman. However, only a few rental car companies, such as a Dollar, Avis, or Hertz, permit you to take their cars into Oman. You may want to wait until you arrive in Dubai before renting a car since making online reservation systems do not provide details on taking cars into Oman.

You may want to rent a car once you arrive in Muscat. You'll find several rental car agencies with desks at the Seeb International Airport as well as at major hotels. The following rental car companies, which have websites, offer competitive rates:

- Avis   www.avisoman.com
- Budget Rent-a-Car   www.budget.com
- Car With a View   www.carwithaview.com/oman-muscat.html
- CheaperThanCars.com   www.cheaperthancars.com/Country/Oman
- Europcar   http://car-rental.europcar.com/car-OMAN.html
- Hertz National Travel and Tourism   www.nttoman.com
- Mark Rent-a-Car   www.marktoursoman.com/rentacar
- Al Maskry Car Rentals   www.almaskryrentacar.com
- Nizar Rent-a-Car   www.shanfari.com/ncr/about.htm
- Oman Car Rental Guide   www.omancar.net
- Sixt   www.sixt.com/main/car-rental/Oman/Muscat/index.php
- Thrifty Car Rental   www.thriftyoman.com
- Value Plus Rent a Car   www.valueoman.com
- Zubair Automotive   www.zubairautomotive.com

You'll also find many other car rental companies, which do not have websites, operating in Oman. It's best to check upon arrival at the airport or at your hotel for information on these companies. Expect to pay from RO15 to RO30 (US$39 to US$78) per day or RO90 to RO150 (US$234 to US$390) per week for a self-drive car. Since many of these companies also operate as full-service transportation and tour companies, they can arrange for a car with driver along with several different types of customized tours.

Taxis

It's relatively easy to get around in Oman by the ubiquitous orange-and-white taxis. Just hail them along the streets or roads. Since taxis are not metered, you'll need to agree upon the fare before taking off for your destination. You can also call the following taxi companies: City Taxi (2460-2211, 2460-3363), Bid Bid Taxi (2469-3377), Comfort Line (2470-2191), Al Dar Taxi (2470-0555, 2470-077), and Hello Taxi (2460-7011, 2460-7012).

Minibuses

Minibuses are the cheapest way to navigate Oman, and especially Muscat and the suburbs. They charge by destination. You can hail them at several bus stops along streets and roads.

Getting to Know You

While there is much to see and do in Oman, especially for active travelers who wish to explore Oman's varied landscape and enjoy a variety of water sports, our primary focus is on shopping and traveling to Oman's major commercial centers in the north—Muscat and Nizwa. While all towns have souks, these two places offer the best shopping opportunities for visitors in search of unique handcrafted items. Muscat also offers the best in accommodations and restaurants. Since these are relatively small and convenient places to visit, three to four days in this area should be sufficient to cover most of the major shopping and sightseeing.

Nizwa

If you are driving from the UAE, we recommend taking the interior road from Al Ain to Muscat via Ibri, Bahla, Nizwa, and Izki. This excellent road will take you quickly through the mountains and desert and past several small towns and forts. The largest town and oasis in this area is Nizwa, which has a population of approximately 75,000 and is known as a bastion of conservatism. Once the capital of Oman (6th and 7th centuries), Nizwa has variously served as an important center for education, art, and religion. Today it's a bustling interior town primarily known for its large souk, fort, and impressive blue-domed mosque (Sultan Qaboos Mosque), all of which are conveniently located next to one another.

Nizwa is Oman's second most popular destination for tourists. For many visitors, it's their favorite town in Oman. While Nizwa has several good hotels and restaurants, it's really not necessary to stay overnight here since this is a very conservative town with not much to do other than walk the streets and visit the souk, fort, and mosque. If you are driving between the UAE and Muscat, a two-hour stop in Nizwa may be sufficient to cover the major shopping and sites. If you are staying in Muscat, you can easily reach Nizwa (175 kilometers) in less than two hours by car. However, a stop in Nizwa on the way to or from Muscat is the best use of your travel time, especially if you're also planning to stop at a few other towns and forts along the way.

You can't miss the **souk** since it lies next to both the impressive fort and mosque. You'll find plenty of parking in front of this complex. The souk consists of several sections—livestock (auctions on Thursday and Friday mornings), fruits and vegetables, dates and nuts, meat and fish, household goods, and arts and antiques. The locals tend to frequent the older food and household goods sections of the market, which becomes especially lively between 9am and 11am daily. The newer and cleaner section of the souk—the Heritage Market—which is frequented by many tourists and collectors, includes several small shops and workshops offering a limited but good selection of silver and antiques. Here you should be able to get some excellent buys on locally produced silver boxes, guns, swords, daggers (*khanjars*), shields, jewelry, copper, pottery, textiles, and leather goods. This is one of the best places to buy old copper frankincense boxes. Indeed, Nizwa is renowned for its silver craftsmen and for good buys on silver work.

While you should bargain for everything in this souk, don't expect to get much of a discount in doing so. Much of the silver is sold by weight, with the daily price of silver being the major determinant of price. Since the merchants here are not very flexible on price, you may have to pay the first quoted price, which is often good to begin with.

Muscat

Muscat is where the action is—Oman's major commercial economic, leisure, and government center where you will find the largest concentration of hotels, resorts, restaurants, shops, museums, galleries, and sightseeing attractions. A city of over 1 million people, Muscat is a sprawling metropolis with a small-town feel. From the airport at Seeb in the northwest to Al Bustan and Bandar Al Jissah in the southeast, the city stretches for nearly 50 kilometers along a narrow strip of land. Hugging a dramatic coastline wedged between rugged mountains and the Gulf of Oman, this is a sparkling white,

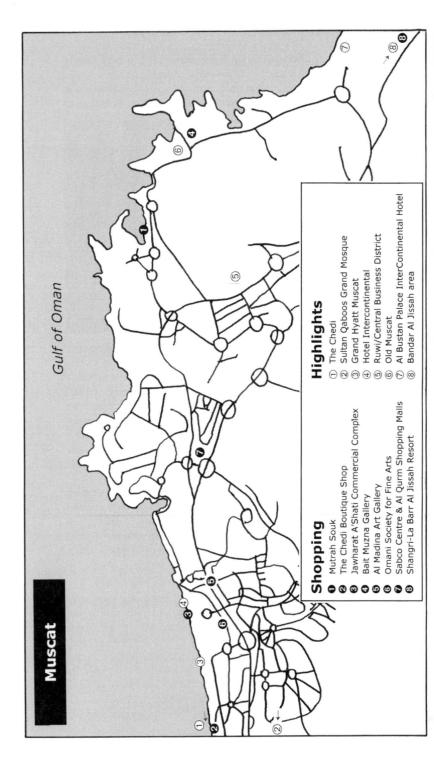

Muscat

Gulf of Oman

Highlights
1. The Chedi
2. Sultan Qaboos Grand Mosque
3. Grand Hyatt Muscat
4. Hotel Intercontinental
5. Ruwi/Central Business District
6. Old Muscat
7. Al Bustan Palace InterContinental Hotel
8. Bandar Al Jissah area

Shopping
1. Mutrah Souk
2. The Chedi Boutique Shop
3. Jawharat A'Shati Commercial Complex
4. Bait Muzna Gallery
5. Al Madina Art Gallery
6. Omani Society for Fine Arts
7. Sabco Centre & Al Qurm Shopping Malls
8. Shangri-La Barr Al Jissah Resort

modern, clean, and inviting city of suburbs and commercial centers. Its oceanfront location, dotted with palm trees, hills, roundabouts, expressways, green- and blue-domed mosques, minarets, port facilities, forts, souks, and beautiful whitewashed residential and diplomatic quarters, makes this one of the most attractive cities on the Arabian Peninsula. In fact, Muscat was designated the most beautiful city on the Arabian Peninsula by the Arab Cities Prize Organization in 1995.

While Muscat consists of several residential and commercial areas connected by expressways and roundabouts, six major areas are of most interest to visitors—Mutrah, Old Muscat, Al Qurm, Ruwi, Al Bustan, and Bandar Al Jissah. Each has its own special characteristics and attractions for visitors:

❑ **Mutrah:** Wedged between the sea, hills, and neighboring Qurm, Ruwi, and Old Muscat, the bustling Mutrah area is famous for the Mutrah Souk, Fish Souk, Mutrah Corniche, Riyam Park (can't miss its big white iconic incense burner perched on the hill), port facilities, restaurants, and budget accommodations. Running for nearly three kilometers along the oceanfront, this picturesque area is where the shopping action is for anyone interested in sleuthing through relatively sanitized traditional markets and street shops for everything from tacky souvenirs and glitzy jewelry to genuine antiques, handicrafts, spices, frankincense, and traditional clothes and fabrics. In  fact, this is Oman's major souk that overflows with both locally produced and imported goods as well as floodwaters that occasionally wash through the souk from the nearby hills that experience unexpected heavy rains. You can easily spend a day here shopping the souk, exploring nearby shops, visiting the open-air fish market (7-10am), sampling restaurants, seeing nearby sites, and enjoying a stroll along the lovely corniche and Riyam Park. Passengers from cruise ships frequently disembark here and head straight for the Mutrah Souk and nearby shops for an hour or two of retail therapy.

❑ **Old Muscat:** If you enjoy history, museums, and traditional Omani architecture, this area has much to offer for a morning or afternoon of sightseeing and shopping. It's the historical area of Muscat. Located on the eastern side of greater Muscat, between Mutrah to the west and Sidab and Al Bustan to the south, this area is home to Sultan Qaboos's waterfront gold and turquoise Alam Palace, two forts, (Jalali and Mirani), city wall, the Al Zawawi Mosque, Muscat Gate House Museum, Omani French Museum (Bait Fransa), and the Bait Al Zubair Museum. It includes a few museum shops. The major shop here is the attractive **Bait Muzna Gallery**, which showcases local artists as well as offers antiques and framing services. Much of this historical area has to be seen from a distance since the palace and adjacent forts are off limits to visitors.

❑ **Al Qurm:** Located in the center of greater Muscat, this area houses Muscat's major shopping centers. North of the Qurm Roundabout you'll find a complex of five shopping centers—Al-Araimi Complex, Sabco Centre, Capital Commercial Center (CCC), Al Harthy Complex, and Al Khamis Plaza. Four of Muscat's major hotels also are located here: Chedi, InterContinental, Grand Hyatt, and Crowne Plaza. This area also is home to many embassies and diplomats who maintain beautiful white-washed residential compounds. Just north of this area in Shatti Al Qurm, and next to the InterContinental Hotel is the small but very inviting Jawaharat A'Shati Complex for shopping and dining.

❑ **Ruwi:** This is Muscat's central commercial district. Here you'll find numerous small shops, office buildings, residential areas, business hotels, and Indian and Arabic restaurants. This area is especially popular with local residents and businessmen. A few tourists come here to visit the Sultan's Armed Forces Museum and National Museum as well as the Ruwi Souk, which is basically a collection of small street shops. If you are driving in Muscat, you can easily get lost in this congested area by making a wrong turn as you try to find your way to other areas that lie to the north and southeast of Ruwi, especially when trying to connect with the road to Bandar Al Jissah.

❑ **Al Bustan:** Located eight kilometers south of Old Muscat and 35 kilometers east of the airport, this area is home to the famous Al Bustan Palace InterContinental Hotel, one of the great hotels in the Gulf region. Nestled along the coast with spectacular views of the Gulf of Oman, the hotel sprawls over 200 acres of lush gardens and sandy beaches with a dramatic backdrop of mountains. Until the nearly Bandar Al Jissah area was opened to resort development, the Al Bustan Palace InterContinental Hotel was the number one resort in Oman. Recently undergoing a multi-million dollar renovation, the resort complex continues to offer impeccable five-star service, including its famous "high tea" in the Atrium Tea Lounge. Once re-opened, it should offer some good shopping opportunities.

❑ **Bandar Al Jissah:** Farther south of Al Bustan is the newly developed Bandar Al Jissah area, which is the center for the sprawling and relatively isolated and self-contained Shangri-La Barr Al Jissah Resort and Spa complex. Located in a rugged mountainous area dotted with a few beautiful coves and beaches (Qantab and Jassah), this is also a noted area for diving, snorkeling, and fishing. The massive Shangri-La Barr Al Jissah Resort and Spa complex consists of three hotels, each catering to different groups of travelers—Al Bandar (general), Al Waha (family), and Al Husn (luxury). It also includes numerous restaurants and shops. The Bandar Al Jissah development is the first of three major development projects that are expected to dramatically transform Muscat's tourism and leisure industries in the decade ahead.

Muscat is in the process of reinventing itself with a series of multi-million dollar property development schemes aimed at expatriates and foreign nationals in search of investment opportunities. Within the very near future, Muscat will be completing two major integrated resort and residential complexes built on reclaimed land along the coast and modeled after the ambitious and newly completed Barr Al Jissah (Shangri-La) complex: The Wave and Blue City. These developments will include luxury hotels, restaurants, shops, hospitals, golf courses, amusement parks, marinas, sports villages, and theaters.

Since Muscat is spread out over a large area, which is connected by an excellent road system, you may want to rent a car during your stay in Muscat. Indeed, having your own car will be very convenient for exploring this whole area. Once you understand how to navigate Muscat's numerous roundabouts as well as locate the various areas on a map, you should be able to drive this area with relative ease. However, it's also very easy to get lost in the jungle of roads and streets where signage will occasionally fail you. Expect to often ask directions from locals on how to get back to the main roads. Except for streets around the Mutrah Souk, most places in Muscat also have ample free parking.

Shopping Muscat

Shopping in Muscat is relatively laid back compared to other parts of the Gulf states. Indeed, you won't find shopping touts or encounter many hassles when shopping in Muscat. For the most part, you will find friendly merchants who will leave you alone so you can shop on your own. If you need help, you'll need to ask. The most aggressive merchants will be the very competitive Indians who operate shops and stalls in the Mutrah Souk and a few shopping centers.

Many of the products you find in Muscat's shops are imported from other countries, including arts and crafts that appear to be local in origin. Indeed, you'll find lots of kitsch from India that you may think comes from Oman.

Shopping is spread out in a variety of places—traditional souks, shopping malls, street shops, hotels, galleries, and supermarkets. The best quality shopping will be found in hotel shops, galleries, and a few shopping malls. But the real fun shopping is found in the popular Mutrah Souk.

Since shopping is so spread out in Muscat, you'll need local transportation to take you to the various shopping areas and neighborhood galleries.

While prices are generally fixed in shopping malls and hotel shops, you can bargain in the souks and street shops. However, don't expect to receive very large discounts through your bargaining efforts. Bargaining is not as widespread as often reported. Many prices are relatively fixed, with little room to negotiate. If you manage a 10—to 30-percent discount, consider yourself fortunate! At the same time, a few Indian handicraft shops that primarily cater to tourists, especially cruise ship passengers, may have widely fluctuating prices that could result in 50- to 70-percent discounts. Be sure to do comparative shopping for such items since prices can vary greatly from one shop to another. Keep in mind that both locals and tourists shop in the souk, and prices can fluctuate greatly for the tourist audience.

In Muscat you'll encounter a very diverse mix of expatriate merchants with different degrees of aggressiveness—Indians, Kashmiris, Pakistanis, Iranians, Lebanese, and British. Since many speak English, you should have little difficulty communicating when shopping. The most aggressive merchants will be found in the souks where tourists tend to congregate and where prices are subject to negotiation. But even there the merchants are relatively friendly, relaxed, and accommodating.

The quality of shopping in Muscat is generally very good. You can usually trust what you are buying is genuine. Expect to encounter good quality gold and silver jewelry as well as some of the world's best quality frankincense and myrrh.

Most shopping centers are open daily 8:30am to 12noon and 4:30-

9:30 or 10pm. Many shops close in the afternoon between 1pm and 4:30pm, which makes shopping somewhat inconvenient for those who enjoy spending their afternoons shopping!

What to Buy

You'll find a large selection of attractive products in Muscat's many shops. Look for the following:

❏ **Antiques:** While some antiques come from Oman and neighboring Yemen, don't expect to find many quality antiques in Muscat. Very few antiques remain in the marketplace. Look for the traditional *khanjar* (decorative curved dagger/knife worn by men in their waistband), swords, guns, bullets, incense burners, copper pots, boxes, chests, doors, silver jewelry, pottery, and oil lamps.

❏ **Art:** A few art galleries offer paintings and drawings by expatriates. Most of these galleries also offer a few antiques, handicrafts, and framing services. The Omani Fine Arts Society also promotes local painters and sculptors.

❏ **Handicrafts:** Look for Omani *khanjars*, coffee pots, incense burners, bags, leather goods, and lots of brass and bronze items from India.

❏ **Pottery:** Oman is famous for its pottery, which is produced in several regions throughout the country—Dhofar, Musandam, Bahla, Manah, Nakhl, Wadi Al Ma'awil, Fanja, Bilad bani bu Hassa, and Saham. The town of Bahla, which is located just west of Nizwa, is Oman's largest and most popular center for pottery production.

❑ **Clothes and accessories:** You'll find lots of clothes for locals and South Asian expatriates. Look for *dishdashah* or *thawb* (men's traditional outerwear—an ankle-length shirt), *kummas* (caps), *massar* (turban), *surwal* (trousers for women), *lihaff* (shawl for women), and Indian saris and pashimas, along with handbags. This is not a fashion center for tourists—few men and women wear Western trousers, dresses, or T-shirts.

❑ **Foods and spices:** Souks and supermarkets offer a good variety of Dhofar mountain honey, dates, nuts, and spices.

❑ **Jewelry:** Look for traditional 22-karat gold jewelry along with Bedouin silver jewelry (necklaces, bracelets, anklets, rings) in the souks. Much of the silver comes from silversmiths in the towns of Nizwa and Rustaq as well as from neighboring Yemen. A great deal of the gold jewelry is imported from the UAE and India. Shopping centers include several fine jewelry stores offering everything from exquisite diamond jewelry to Chopard and Rolex watches imported from Europe and Asia.

❑ **Furniture:** Shopping centers, galleries, and markets include everything from traditional antique Omani chests (hard to find good quality ones these days) to reproduction furniture imported from India.

❑ **Basketry:** Look for woven baskets and mats produced in various villages throughout Oman.

❑ **Textiles:** You'll find lots of textiles imported from India, especially saris, pashminas, and fabrics sold by the meter. You also can find some Omani tribal woven goods as well as rugs and carpets from Iran and India.

❑ **Frankincense and myrrh:** Several merchants in the Mutrah Souk offer raw frankincense and myrrh in small bags as well as frankincense candles. This is some of the best quality frankincense and myrrh you will find anywhere in the Middle East. If you purchase frankincense, you'll want to make sure you have a frankincense burner. The best ones (copper or silver boxes) are found in the market in Nizwa.

❑ **Perfumes, natural oils, and sandalwood:** You can't miss the smells when you enter the Mutrah Souk. You'll find several small shops offering a good selection of perfumes, natural oils, and sandalwood.

❑ **Imported items:** It's often difficult to sort out what is locally produced from what is imported from India. Indeed, the souks, shopping malls, and hotel shops are jam-packed with products from India, especially handicrafts, textiles, carpets, and furniture. If you're looking for something uniquely Omani, you'll need to ask about the country of origin before making purchases. Better still, educate yourself by picking up the two-volume set of Omani craft books—*The Craft Heritage of Oman* (Neil Richardson and Marcia Door), which is readily available in many hotel and resort bookstores, especially Turtles.

Where to Shop

Shopping in Muscat is centered in several places. The best quality shopping will be found in a few hotel shops, shopping centers, and galleries. The most interesting shopping for many visitors is found in the famous Mutrah Souk. If you have limited shopping time, focus your attention on these places:

❑ **Mutrah Souk:** This is Oman's single most popular shopping complex and one of the few remaining traditional souks on the Arabian Peninsula. It's open Saturday through Thursday, 8am to 1pm and 4pm to 10pm, and Friday, 4pm to 10pm. Located near the port, just off the corniche at the clock tower in Mutrah, this one-stop covered market includes hundreds of small shops offering a wide range of arts, crafts, clothing, jewelry, antiques, spices, and household goods. It's popular with both locals and tourists. You can easily spend a couple of hours wandering through the major thoroughfare and narrow winding maze of lanes sleuthing for local treasures as well as taking in the whole market  atmosphere. Many visitors are especially interested in the gold market, which is located on the right side of the souk, near the antique shops. It includes several jewelry shops offering a large variety of traditional gold jewelry (bangles, bracelets, rings, necklaces). You'll also find a few arts and crafts emporiums selling a wide variety of inexpensive jewelry as well as brass and bronze items from India. Much of this stuff is tourist kitsch. Also look for raw frankincense, which is sold in clear plastic bags. Some of the best antiques in Oman can be found in a few shops but they may be difficult to find. Most are concentrated on the outer lane on the right side of the souk—you can enter this area from the street (100 meters to the right of the main entrance) rather than from the front entrance to the souk. If you have difficulty finding this section, keep to your right and ask where the antique and gold shops are located or ask for the Al Turath Centre, which is one of the best antique shops in the souk.

❑ **Hotel shops:** The best quality hotel shops are found at the Chedi, InterContinental, Al Bustan, and Grand Hyatt hotels and at the Shangri-La Barr Al Jissah Resort complex. The **Chedi** has the best hotel gift shop, which is stocked with top quality products (jewelry,

 textiles, clothing, ceramics, tableware, books) from Asia. The **Grand Hyatt** includes Al-Raid for watches, gifts, and carpets. The **InterContinental** has a few carpet and handicraft shops, but the best shopping here is found at the small shopping center at the bottom of the circular drive near the entrance to the hotel—Jawharat A'Shati Commercial Complex. Here you'll find the Tahani Antique Gallery and Omani Heritage Gallery. The **Shangri-La Barr Al Jissah Resort and Spa** complex includes several shops offering jewelry, carpets, art (Art Gallery), resortwear, and books (Turtles) as well as a traditional arts and crafts center (Omani Heritage Village) with several small demonstration shops showcasing frankincense, woven baskets and mats, daggers, chests, caps, books, clothes, bags, and pottery.

❑ **Art galleries:** Muscat has a few art galleries, which include a mixture of paintings, drawings, crafts, furniture, and antiques. Most of these places are especially known for their bread-and-butter business—framing services. Look for the Bait Al Munza Gallery, Al Madina Art Gallery, and the Omani Society for Fine Arts. The various hotels within the Shangri-La Barr Al Jissah Resort and Spa showcase some of the best quality art in all of Oman.

❑ **Shopping malls:** Air-conditioned shopping malls are extremely popular with locals in Muscat. The largest concentration of these centers is found in the Qurm area. Here you'll find the Al Araimi Complex, Al Harthy Complex, Capital Commercial Centre, Al Khamis Plaza, City Plaza, and Sabco Commercial Centre. Most of these places cater to the shopping needs of local residents. Few shops appeal to visitors. If you shop at any of these places, we recommend focusing on the two-level **Sabco Commercial Centre**, which is Muscat's oldest shopping mall and includes several upscale jewelry and clothing stores as well as a mini-souk (jewelry, arts, crafts, textiles, frankincense) on the ground floor. One of our favorite small shopping centers is the **Jawharat A'Shati Commercial Complex** (www.jascomplex.com), which is located next to the InterContinental Hotel in the Shatti Al Qurm area. The **Markaz Al Bahja**, which is located near the airport (Al Mawaleh roundabout in the Seeb area), includes several upscale shops and a food court. Nearby is the **Muscat City Centre**, which is anchored by the huge Carrefour supermarket and noted for shops that are popular with locals.

Best Shops

While you will find many places to shop in Muscat, we found the following shops to offer some of the best quality products for visitors in search of unique quality items:

Antiques

❑ **Tahani Antique Gallery:** *Ground Floor, Jawharat A'Shati Commercial Complex (next to the InterContinental Muscat Hotel), Shatti Al Qurum, Tel. 2456-2589. E-mail: tahani@omantel.net.om. Website: www.tahanioman.com.* This is one of our favorite shops on the Arabian Peninsula. Owned by the Tahani Company, a Lebanese company that primarily specializes in upscale clothes and accessories, this exclusive antique shop nicely displays in two large rooms one of the best collections of copper incense burners,  boxes, pots, Omani chests, *khanjars*, silver jewelry, rugs, guns, camel baskets, and old cameras, radios, and wall clocks you will find anywhere in Oman. The quality here is first rate and prices (fixed) are reasonable. If you are looking for something very special, be sure to visit this shop.

❑ **Al Turath Centre:** *Shop 1775/1771, Lane No. 1431, Mutrah Gold Market, Mutrah Souk, Tel./Fax 2471-1565.* Somewhat difficult to find, this small but well established traditional antique, jewelry, and handicraft shop is tucked along the right side of the Mutrah Souk. Its owner, Tariq, offers a good selection of antique Omani silver jewelry, *khanjars*, boxes, Rhino shields, swords, chests, old lamps,

and coffee pots. You may see village women dressed in black visiting this shop with their families to sell their old silver jewelry by gram weight. Be sure to check out the small room in the back of the shop as well as ask to see the owner's three mini-warehouses nearby, which are jam-packed with un-reconditioned old Omani wedding chests. Also, be sure to visit Tariq's father's shop, which is located three doors from this shop and includes similar items in a less crowded space.

Handicrafts

❑ **Omani Heritage Gallery**: *Ground Floor, Jawharat A'Shati Commercial Complex, Shatti Al Qurum, Tel. 2469-6974, Fax, 2469-6568. E-mail: lhgmg@omantel.co.om. Website: www.omaniheritage. com.* This small shop offers a good selection of good quality locally produced arts and crafts. Look for copper and ceramic pots, woven baskets, camel blankets, clothing, jewelry, *khanjars*, leather goods, incense burners, scented oils, frankincense, and fabrics. For an overview of their products, be sure to visit their website.

❑ **Omani Craftsman's House:** *Sarouj, Qurum (located across the street from the Sabco Commercial Centre), Tel./Fax 2456-8553 or 2456-8553.* This is the first shop sponsored by the government's Public Authority for Crafts Industries to showcase the Omani crafts industry. The emphasis here is on quality products drawn from villages throughout the country. Look for ceramics, woven baskets, copper trays, frankincense bowls, textiles, silver jewelry. A very nice showroom with attractive displays. Additional shops should open at the airports, borders, and ports in the future.

❑ **Omani Heritage Village:** *Located on the grounds of the Shangri-La*

Barr Al Jissah Resort complex. This crafts center, developed by the former Minister of Culture, includes several small demonstration shops showcasing frankincense, woven baskets and mats, *khanjars*, chests, caps, books, clothes, bags, and pottery. One central shop offers a wide variety of traditional arts and crafts for sale. While this center is an interesting attempt to showcase Oman's major arts and crafts in a village setting, we don't recommend making a special trip here just to see this place. Come here only if you are staying at the resort or visiting the restaurants and shops elsewhere in the resort complex.

❑ **Souks:** In **Muscat**, visit the many small shops that occupy the Mutrah Souk and the mini-souk in the Sabco Commercial Centre. In **Nizwa**, be sure to visit the silver and handicraft souk for some of the best buys on Omani silver. If visiting the town of **Rustaq**, check out both the old and new souk for handcrafted items.

Books

❑ **Turtles:** *Al Bandar Hotel at the Shangri-La's Barr Al Jissah Resort (Tel. 2477-6682), InterContinental (2468-0000, ext. 8379), and Seeb Airport.* Offers a good selection of English language books on Oman as well as many bestselling paperbacks, children's books, travel guides, self-help books, and newspapers and magazines.

Art

❑ **Bait Muzna Gallery:** *Old Muscat, next to Bait Al Zubair, Tel. 2473-9204, Fax 2473-9204, or e-mail: baitmgal@omantel.net.om. Website: www.omanart.com. Open Saturday through Thursday, 9:30am to 1:30pm and 4:30pm to 8pm.* This charming art space—housed in the former home and villa of Her Highness Sayyida Muzna bint Nadir of the Omani royal family with a courtyard and fountain—includes a good selection of paintings, prints, old maps, jewelry, ceramics, books, cards, furniture, antiques, gifts, souvenirs, and crafts displayed in several rooms. Be sure to check out the art gallery upstairs which showcases both local and international painters, sculptors, and photographers. Like many other art galleries, this

one offers framing services as well as professional art sourcing services, advice, and consultancy.

❑ **Al Madina Art Gallery:** *145/6 Al Inshirah Street (aka Ther Service Road), Tel. 2469-1380, Fax 2469-1370, or e-mail: almedgai@ omantel.net.om.* This two-story residential art gallery is affiliated with the Creative Arts Centre gallery in Dubai. It includes a nice collection of paintings, old map prints, cards, small chests, ceramics (from South Africa), books, candles, soaps, and jewelry. One of its specialties is making tables from old Omani doors. Two expatriate artists, David Webber and L. Shephard, are featured in this gallery.

❑ **Omani Society for Fine Arts:** *Located next to the Ramada Hotel near the Al Sarooj roundabout. Tel. 2469-4969 or e-mail: omanarts @omantel.net.om. Website: www.omanartsociety.org.* Located on the second floor, this organization helps promote the development of artists and photographers—amateurs, professionals, and even hobbyists—by providing them with a place where they can work as well as exhibit their paintings and photography. Two rooms on the second floor are devoted for painters and sculptors, many just getting started, who work on projects. The Society regularly hosts exhibitions and meetings. It's a good idea to check the website (www.omanartsociety.org) before visiting this place since the website showcases the artworks of its many members. It also includes links to several Arab artists and galleries within the region. If you just walk into this building, you may find it somewhat disorienting since no one seems to be in charge and they may be between exhibitions. You may meet a few amateur painters at work here. This is a good place to make contact with and buy directly from the more than 100 artists affiliated with the Society.

❑ **The Art Gallery:** *Shangri-La Barr Al Jissah Resort complex.* This is a relatively new art gallery, which showcases paintings of both local and international artists. However, the best quality art is literally found throughout the resort property. Indeed, the owners of this property have emphasized the importance of art and display it accordingly—in the lobby areas, hallways, and meeting rooms. If you find something that catches your interest, ask about it at the front desk. The resort may put you in contact with the artist.

Gifts

❑ **Chedi Boutique Shop:** *The Chedi Muscat: 133 Al Khuwair, Tel. 2452-4400, Fax 2449-3485. E-mail: thechedi@omantel.net.om. Website: www.chedimuscat.com.* Offers a fine collection of gift items, many of which come from the Chedi properties in Southeast Asia. Look for jewelry, clothing, textiles, tableware, and books. The Chedi also includes a fine arts gallery.

Furniture

❑ **Village Arts and Crafts:** *Majid Trading Enterprises, Sohar House (next to Sabco Commercial Centre), Tel. 2456-2370. Also includes shops at the Al Araimi Complex, Al Harthy Complex, and the Grand Hyatt Hotel.* Popular with expatriates, this huge three-story emporium includes a wide range of furniture (tables, chairs, chests, cabinets), accessories, and handicrafts from India, Kashmir, Pakistan, Indonesia, Oman, and Yemen. Look for both old and new carved furniture, including many Indian doors and panels, brassware, papier-mache pieces, walnut furniture (primarily from Kashmir), gift items, handmade carpets, handwoven silks, pashminas, marble tables, jewelry, and objects d'art. Includes a small workshop and packing area for preparing shipments to be sent abroad. Since the quality and product mix here varies, you'll need to spend some time finding the really good stuff. But it's all here.

Accommodations

Five-Star Properties

Muscat boasts several five-star properties that cater to both business and leisure travelers. The top properties include:

❑ **The Chedi Muscat**: *133 Al Khuwair (P.O. Box 964), Muscat, Sultanate of Oman, Tel. 968-2452-4400, Fax 968-2449-3485, E-mail: thechedi@omantel.net.om. Website: www.chedimuscat.com.* Set along 370 meters of private beach with palm gardens and water gardens, The Chedi is 15 minutes from the airport and 20 minutes from the Muscat city center. Designed in the style of traditional Omani architecture, the resort's sleek and minimalist lobby, hallways, and manicured gardens feature Omani artwork and photography. The 151 guestrooms and suites, which reflect modern minimalist Arabian design, are comprised primarily of terrazzo floors stylishly combined with marble and dark woods. Everything about the hotel, within the guestrooms, the public

areas and the grounds, is designed, with great success, for its aesthetic appeal. Convenience and function are lost on occasion, however. For example, there is no bathtub and the rainforest-type showerhead centered in the shower area makes bathing without getting one's hair wet extremely difficult. There is no physical separation between the bath/dressing area and the bedroom/sitting area, so if guests come over for a before-dinner drink you had better be ready before their arrival!

The flavors of the world are brought to The Chedi at *The Restaurant* where an a la carte menu offers selections from Asian to Arabic, and Indian to Mediterranean. Guests can enjoy the spectacle of dinner being prepared in any of the four open-display kitchens. The breakfast buffet is one of the best—anywhere! More choices than you can imagine and excellent quality and service. The *Restaurant Bar* houses an extensive wine collection. The art gallery/boutique, located off the main reception area, offers one of the largest selections of quality items available in Muscat. These items are drawn from several regions, especially Southeast Asia, rather than primarily from Oman.

Offers fully equipped gym; flood-lit tennis courts; two swimming pools and Spa.

❑ **Shangri-La's Barr Al Jissah Resort & Spa**: *P.O. Box 644, Postcode 113, Muscat, Sultanate of Oman, Tel. 968-2477-6666, Fax 968-2477-6677, E-mail: simu@shangri-la.com. Website: www.shangri-la.com.* Located 20 minutes from downtown and 45 minutes from the airport, Shangri-La's Muscat resort nestles against the backdrop of rugged mountains and faces out to the waters of the Gulf of Oman. The 124-acre property actually consists of three resort hotels. The five-star **Al Waha** (means "the oasis"), with 262 rooms, is focused for leisure stays and offers family-oriented activities. The resort's children's club, "Little Turtles," is based here offering a wide range of supervised activities. Babysitting facilities are available. **Al Bandar** ("the town"), a five-star deluxe property with 198 sea-facing guestrooms, is oriented towards the conference and incentive market as well as leisure guests. The exclusive **Al Husn** (the castle), with 180 guestrooms, is branded as a "six-star" hotel and focuses on both leisure and business

guests. Guests at Al Husn are welcome to enjoy facilities of the entire three-hotel resort, while the services and facilities of Al Husn are for the exclusive use of guests staying in the hotel. Guestrooms feature balconies, terraces, or patios, and have separate bathtub and shower, coffee and tea making facilities, computer data port with broadband Internet access and other amenities expected at a five-star hotel.

Recreation facilities include a 600-meter private beach, 500-meter "lazy river," 6,000-square-meter total area of swimming pools, four tennis courts, health club, Chi Spa, sauna, steam room, and Jacuzzi. Boat excursions are offered and a dive center offering PADI dive instruction and certification, scuba diving, snorkeling, sailboats, and wind surfing.

The Omani Heritage Village offers an opportunity for guests to watch typical crafts being produced, and many are offered for sale in the adjoining retail shop. A hotel gift shop and 11 retail outlets are on the premises. A shuttle is available to take guests to the Old Mutrah Souk.

With 24 food and beverage outlets, guests have plenty of choices, from *Samba*, a South American/Argentinean restaurant, *Al Tanoor* for Middle Eastern selections, or *Capri Court* for Italian cuisine.

Offers Business Center; Fitness Facilities; Conference/Banquet Facilities.

❑ **InterContinental Muscat:** *P.O. Box 398, P.C. 114, Muscat, Sultanate of Oman, Tel. 968-2468-0000, Fax 968—2460-0012, or e-mail: muscat@interconti.com. Website: www.intercontinental.com.* Located between the pale sand of the Gulf coast and an upscale residential section which is home to many of Oman's embassies and with the Hajjar mountains in the distance, the InterContinental is conveniently located (by car) to Muscat's main business centers. We especially liked the small shopping center (Jawharat A'Shati) located at the foot of the car ramp that circles in front of the hotel. The shopping center had a wonderful antique shop, a handicrafts shop, Starbucks, and an Italian restaurant. With 258 guestrooms and 11 suites, the Intercontinental offers executive suites and executive floors. The only negative was that, being an older hotel, the standard guestroom bathrooms have only one sink and a shower/tub combination. But that was quickly offset by the warmth of the efficient staff and the location.

Several restaurants provide choices for many ranges of palates. *Musandam Café & Terrace Restaurant*, open daily for breakfast, lunch, and dinner, is an informal venue featuring international and Mediterranean cuisine and offers a buffet or a la carte selections. *Trader Vic's*, located adjacent to the hotel, features award-winning Polynesian cuisine for lunch or dinner. *Senor Pico's*, open for lunch and dinner, presents authentic Mexican selections. *Al Ghazal Pub*, serving lunch and dinner, presents award-winning food, live sports and live bands on selected days. *Majlis El Shams*, located in the main lobby, serves French pastries, coffees, and teas. *Tomato* is located poolside and serves lunch and dinner in an open-air setting overlooking the pool and gardens.

Offers a Business Center; Health and Fitness Center features two swimming pools, Jacuzzi, steam room, sauna, plunge pool, gym and an aerobics studio as well as six outdoor floodlit tennis courts and two squash courts. Conference/Banquet Facilities.

❑ **Al Bustan Palace InterContinental:** *Mutrah, Tel. 968-2479-9666. Website:* http://al-bustan.intercontinental.com. One of the finest hotels on the Arabian Peninsula. Currently undergoing a multi-million dollar renovation. A spectacular property which boasts a five-star+ reputation. Famous for its beautiful grounds, gorgeous setting and views, fine French restaurant, popular high tea, and water sports activities.

❑ **Grand Hyatt Muscat:** *Shatti Al Qurum, Tel. 968-2464-1234. Website:* www.muscat.grand.hyatt.com. This large and rather ornate and ostentatious property—Arabic rococo—is known for its excellent service, beachfront location, restaurants, and entertainment venues. It includes one of the best Italian restaurants in Muscat—*Tuscany*—and three popular entertainment venues—the Copacabana Nightclub, Club Safari, and a piano bar (John Barry Bar) offering soft jazz and R&B.

Other properties worth considering include the following, which primarily cater to business people:

- **Crowne Plaza Muscat:** *Ruwi, Tel. 968-2466-0660. Website: www.crowneplaza.com.* Located in the central business district and popular with the business crowd.

- **Radisson SAS:** *Al Khuwair, Tel. 968-2448-7777.*

- **Sheraton Qurum Resort:** *Qurm. Tel. 968-2460-5945.* A relatively small beachfront property.

- **Sheraton Oman:** *Ruwi, Tel. 968-2477-2772.* Located in the central business district and popular with the business crowd.

While most of Muscat's major properties are relatively expensive (US$200-$600 a night), you will find some mid-range and budget accommodations. Many of the budget accommodations are nicely located along or near the corniche in Mutrah:

Mid-Range Properties

- **Coral Hotel Muscat:** *Ruwi, Tel. 968-2469-2121, Fax 968-2469-4404, or e-mail: bwmuscat@omantel.net.om. Website: www.coral-international.com/muscat/index.aspx.*

- **Holiday Inn Muscat:** *Seeb, Tel. 968-2448-7123, fax 968-2448-0986, or e-mail: mcthinn@omantel.net.om.*

- **Oman Beach Hotel:** *Mina al Fahal, Tel. 968-2469-6601, Fax 968-2469-7686, or e-mail: info@omaninfobeachhotel.com. Website: www.omanbeachhotel.com.*

- **Ramada Muscat:** *Qurm Beach and embassy row area (near InterContinental), Tel. 968-2460-3555, Fax 968-2469-4500, or e-mail: ramadaom@omantel.net.om.* Website: *www.ramadamuscat.com.* Located in the Qurum Beach area, near the InterContinental hotel and the embassy row, and a few doors down from the Omani Society of Fine Arts.

Over the next few years, look for several new luxury hotels and resorts tied into the three large resort and residential complexes being built along Muscat's expansive coastline: Barr Al Jissah, The Wave, and Blue City. The Fairmont Hotel, for example, plans to build a luxury property at The Wave. Other major international luxury hotels and resorts will soon follow as the whole accommodations, restaurant, and leisure scene changes dramatically during the next decade.

Restaurants

Muscat's expatriate community is responsible for a large variety of excellent restaurants. From hotels to shopping centers and neighborhoods, you'll find a wide range of international cuisines. Not surprisingly, the best and most expensive restaurants, which attract international chefs, are found in the major hotels, such as The Chedi Muscat and the Shangri-La Barr Al Jissah Resort and Spa complex. In fact, the Shangri-La has the largest number of quality international restaurants in Muscat among its 24 food and beverage outlets. If you're not sure where to dine in Muscat, just head for the Shangri-La where you will have lots of interesting international choices, from casual to fine dining.

As more and more luxury hotels open here, expect to see an even more robust fine dining scene catering to discerning travelers. At the same time, you'll also find a few excellent restaurants outside the hotels.

Most hotel restaurants and some independent restaurants are permitted to serve alcohol to visitors during the hours of 12noon to 3pm and 6pm to closing. Shopping centers include many restaurants and food courts. You'll also find several international fast-food restaurants and coffee houses, such as McDonald's, Burger King, KFC, Pizza Hut, Papa John's Pizza, Starbucks, and Costa Coffee.

For the latest information on the best restaurants in Muscat, be sure to check with your hotel or pick up a copy of the latest edition of TimeOut's *Muscat for Visitors* and *Oman Explorer: The Complete Residents' Guide*. As we go to press, some of the best restaurants in Muscat include the following:

International

❏ **The Restaurant:** *The Chedi, 133 Al Khuwair, Tel. 2452-4343. Website: www.chedimuscat.com. Open 7am to 10pm.* Simply outstanding! A very exceptional and chic open restaurant (includes four display kitchens) offering both indoor and outdoor dining. The breakfast buffet is sumptuous and best enjoyed outdoors with a lovely garden and oceanfront view. The dinner menu includes excellent choices of Asian, Arabic, Indian, and Mediterranean dishes. A very popular restaurant operated by one of Oman's top international chefs. If you dine at only one fine restaurant in Oman, make sure it's this one!

❑ **Trader Vic's:** *InterContinental Muscat, Shatti Al Qurum, Tel. 2460-0500. Website: www.muscat.oman.intercontinental.com. Open Saturday through Thursday, 12noon to 2:45pm and 7pm to 11:15pm.* Includes an extensive menu of favorites (steaks, grilled seafood, curries) along with signature drinks that have made this international chain of Polynesian restaurant/bars famous. In a romantic setting with an excellent view of the sea.

Arabic and Middle Eastern

❑ **Kargeen Café:** *MQ Complex, Tel. 2469-2269. Open Sunday through Wednesday, 9am to 12 midnight. Also has two other less atmospheric locations—City Plaza and Al Harthy Complex.* This quirky Lebanese-owned canopied restaurant is a favorite with many locals and visitors who enjoy the outdoor setting complete with shisha served at the relaxing tables with pillowed benches. Its garden setting with lanterns hanging from trees and wood tables with jewelry and artifacts encased in glass make this one of Muscat's most unique atmospheric restaurants. The menu is a mixture of Arabic foods, soups, pastas, pizza, burgers, and hot dogs. Includes an extensive list of nonalcoholic drinks. Be sure to try the hot Arabic bread.

❑ **Al Tanoor:** *Al Bandar Hotel, Ground Level, Shangri-La Barr Al Jissah Resort and Spa, Tel. 2466-6565. Open 6am to 10am, 12noon to 3pm, and 6:30pm to 11pm.* Used for breakfast in the morning, this intimate restaurant comes to life in the evening with its excellent sampling of cuisines from around the Arabian Gulf region. It's laid out with Arabian tents and pottery. Dishes are prepared at several open food stations. In addition to Arabian cuisine, the restaurant offers Iranian, Turkish, Indian, and Mediterranean dishes along with such tempting dessert favorites as baklava, creme brulee, and ice cream. It also includes an a la carte menu.

Turkish

❑ **Turkish House:** *Al Khuwair, Tel. 2448-8071. Open 12noon to 1am.* Especially popular with locals, this restaurant serves excellent breads, salads, fresh fish, and mezzes.

Italian

❑ **Tuscany:** *Grand Hyatt Muscat Tel. 2464-1234. Open 12noon to 3:30pm and 7pm to 11pm. Closed for lunch on Friday.* This authentic Italian restaurant offers both indoor and outdoor dining. Includes an extensive menu of classic Italian dishes. An award-winning restaurant with excellent service and a charming atmosphere.

❑ **Capri Court:** *Al Bandar Resort, Shangri-La's Barr Al Jissah Resort and Spa, Tel. 2477-6666. Open 7pm to 11pm.* This small, brightly lit, and cheery restaurant offers an extensive menu and wine list along with excellent breads. Includes both indoor and outdoor dining (the latter is preferred for watching the sunset over the ocean).

❑ **O Solé Mio:** *Jawharat A'Shati Shopping Complex, Shatti Al Qurum, Tel. 2460-1343.* Popular with expatriates, this restaurant offers an extensive menu of fine Italian dishes. The pastas, lobster dishes, and desserts are especially good. Somewhat dark and kitschy setting. Excellent service and good value.

Indian

❑ **Mumtaz Mahal:** *Near Qurum National Park, Tel. 2460-5907. Open Saturday to Thursday, 12noon-3pm and 7:30—11:45pm, and Friday, 1-3pm and 7:30-11:45pm.* This popular restaurant is known for its spectacular hilltop view along with excellent dishes and service. Serves great soups and curries.

Chinese and Thai

❑ **Golden Oryx:** *Opposite the Bank of Muscat in Ruwi, Tel. 2470-2266. Open Saturday through Thursday, 12noon-2:45pm and 7-11:45pm, and Friday, 1-2:45pm and 7-11:45pm.* This long-established and very popular restaurant includes an extensive Chinese and Thai menu. It's especially known for its fish and seafood dishes. Try the Mongolian Barbecue, which is a house specialty. Reasonably priced.

Tex-Mex

❑ **Pavo Real:** *Madinat Sultan Qaboos, near Pizza Hut and Kargeen Café, Tel. 2460-2603. Open Saturday through Thursday, 12noon to 3pm and 6pm to 11:30pm.* This quirky Tex-Mex restaurant serves lots of typical Tex-Mex fare in a party atmosphere of cowboys (Indian waiters), karaoke, dancing, and kids. Reasonably priced.

Café

❑ **D'Arcy's Kitchen:** *Jawaharat A'Shati Complex, Tel. 2431-7143. Open 8am to 10pm.* Famous for their all-day breakfast and pineapple pancakes. Good for burgers, steaks, and fish and chips. Offers both indoor and outdoor seating.

Enjoying Your Stay

There's much to see and do in Oman, from sightseeing and recreation to entertainment, in addition to shopping in Muscat and Nizwa,

Sightseeing

Within Muscat, plan to visit the following places:

Ruwi

❏ **National Museum:** *Way 3123, Near Al Falaj Mercure Hotel and beside Adb Reza Mosque, Tel. 2470-1289. Open Saturday to Wednesday, 8am to 1:30pm, and Thursday, 9am to 1pm.* Features highlights of Omani history. Many displays of items from the old Muscat palace, jewelry, clothes, pottery, boats, guns, and more.

❏ **Sultan's Armed Forces Museum:** *Bait Al Falaj Fort, Mujamma Street, Tel. 2431-2654. Open Saturday to Wednesday, 8am to 1:30pm, and Thursday and Friday, 8-11am and 3-6pm.* Showcases Oman's military history, including tribal disputes, foreign forces, cannons, swords, and guns.

Old Muscat

❏ **Bait Al Zubair Museum:** *Al Saidiyah Street, Tel. 2473-6688. Open Saturday to Thursday, 9:30am to 1pm and 4 to 7pm.* Heritage displays of Omani lifestyle and traditions, including clothes, jewelry, weapons, and household items along with photos.

❏ **Omani French Museum:** *Near Police Station, Al Saidiyah Street, Tel. 2473-6613. Open Saturday through Thursday, 9am to 1pm. Extended hours (4 to 7pm) from October to March.* Focus is on 19th century colonial period in Muscat.

❏ **Muscat Gate Museum:** *Al Bahri Road, inside city gates, Tel. 9932-8754. Open Saturday through Thursday, 9:30am to 12:30pm and 4:30 to 7:30pm.* Summarizes the history of Oman and Muscat.

Madinat As Sultan Qaboos (MSQ)

❏ **Omani Museum:** *Al Alam Street, Way 1566, near Ministry of Information, Tel. 2460-0946. Open Saturday to Wednesday, 8:30am to 1:30pm, and Thursday, 9:30am to 12:30pm. Extended hours (4pm to 6pm) from October to March.* Showcases Omani artifacts, agriculture, architecture, weaponry, jewelry, minerals, trade routes, dhows, and arts and crafts.

❑ **Sultan Qaboos Grand Mosque:** Open to visitors from Saturday to Wednesday, 8am to 11am. One of the largest and most beautiful mosques in the Arab world. Has the capacity to accommodate 20,000 worshipers.

The following sites can be seen from a distance, but they are not open to visitors unless you are a dignitary with a special invitation:

Old Muscat

❑ Sultan's (Alam) Palace

❑ Al-Jalali Fort

❑ Al-Mirani Fort

Mutrah

❑ Mutrah Fort

Recreation

If you love water sports, the outdoors, and an active lifestyle, you will find lots of appealing recreational activities in Oman:

- Archery
- Bird watching
- Bull fighting
- Camel riding and racing
- Camping
- Canoeing
- Canyoning
- Caving
- Climbing
- Cricket
- Cycling
- Desert safari
- Dhow cruise
- Diving
- Dolphin and whale watching
- Fishing

- Golf
- Hiking
- Horseback riding
- Ice skating
- Jetskiing
- Kayaking
- Kitesurfing
- Motorcycling
- Mountain biking
- Rugby
- Running
- Sailing
- Sandboarding/skiing
- Snorkeling
- Squash
- Surfing
- Swimming
- Tennis
- Turtle watching
- Visiting nature reserves and parks
- Wadi and dune bashing (4WD into remote areas)

Most hotels and tour operators can arrange these activities. If you pick up a copy of ***Oman Explorer: The Complete Residents' Guide***, you will find listings of organizations and tour operators that specialize in various recreational and sporting activities.

Some of the most well established and reliable tour operators in Oman include:

Arabian Sea Safaris	www.arabianseasafaris.com
Desert Discovery Tours	www.desert-discovery.com
Eihab Travels LLC	www.omanvalueholidays.com
Empty Quarter Tours	www.emptyquartertours.com
Golden Oryx Tours LLC	www.goldenoryx.com
Gulf Leisure	www.gulfleisure.com

- Gulf Ventures Oman   www.gulfventures.ae
- Hormuzline Tours
  & Cruises   www.hormuzlinetours.com
- Khasab Travel & Tours   www.khasabtours.com
- Mark Tours   www.marktoursoman.com
- Muscat Diving &
  Adventure Center   www.omandiving.com
- National Travel
  & Tourism   www.nttoman.com
- United Tours   www.unitedoman.com

If you're interested in exploring Oman by 4WD, including the popular and fun sports of wadi and dune bashing, be sure to pick up a copy of Explorer's **Oman Off-Road**.

Entertainment

When it comes to entertainment and alcohol, Muscat is not Dubai, at least not yet. Oman remains a moderately conservative society. Indeed, there's not a lot to do in Muscat in the evening other than spend a few hours dining out at a restaurant with live entertainment, shisha, karaoke, and/or a lovely view of the city or oceanfront at sunset, or booking a dinner cruise. Oman is relatively liberal in permitting alcohol to be served to non-Muslims at hotels and resorts and a few licensed restaurants. Most Western entertainment venues are found in hotels and resorts, especially the Grand Hyatt.

Remember, this is conservative Oman—not a popular center for international musicians, entertainers, and hookers. If you're looking for evening entertainment centered around expensive alcohol, music, and dancing, try the following hotels, pubs, and restaurants:

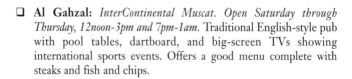

❑ **Copacabana Nightclub:** *Grand Hyatt Muscat, Tel. 2464-1234. Open Monday to Thursday, 10am to 3pm.* Best nightclub in the city, although very retro and expensive.

❑ **Club Safari:** *Grand Hyatt Muscat, Tel. 2464-1234. Open 6pm to 2am.* Popular for drinking and dancing and watching sports shows on TV screens.

❑ **Al Gahzal:** *InterContinental Muscat. Open Saturday through Thursday, 12noon-3pm and 7pm-1am.* Traditional English-style pub with pool tables, dartboard, and big-screen TVs showing international sports events. Offers a good menu complete with steaks and fish and chips.

❏ **John Barry Bar:** *Grand Hyatt Muscat, Tel. 2464-1234.* A relatively sophisticated piano bar offering live entertainment (soft jazz and R&B).

❏ **Duke's Bar:** *Crowne Plaza, Al Qurum, Tel. 2466-0660.* Offers excellent bar food and service along with live entertainment.

❏ **The Piano Lounge:** *Al Bandar Hotel, Shangri-La Barr Al Jissah Resort & Spa, Tel. 2477-6666. Open 6pm-2am.* Relaxing bar with a good cocktail menu, including regular promotions.

❏ **Uptown:** *Ruwi, opposite Golden Oryx, Tel. 2470-6020.* Along with the usual large-screen TV featuring international sports events, this popular bar offers a daily happy hour and live entertainment.

❏ **Sarai Pool Bar:** *The Chedi, Tel. 2452-4343. Open 12noon-10:30pm.*

❏ **Kargeen Café:** shisha and people watching

❏ **Pavo Real:** cowboys and karaoke

❏ **Dinner cruises:** Most leave from the Marina Bandar Al Rosdha. It's easiest to book through Arabian Sea Safaris (www.arabiansea safaris.com, Tel. 2469-3223) or through a tour operator.

Day Trips Outside Muscat

There are several interesting towns and villages near Muscat which you can easily reach within a couple of hours. Be sure to visit the souks at **Nizwa**, which is located 175 kilometers southwest of Muscat. Nizwa is renowned for its fine silverwork and in-triguing souks. The

town of **Bahla**, which is located 30 kilometers west of Nizwa, is noted for its pottery production. Far-ther west is the town of **Ibri**, which is famous for its fort and lively souk, including a morning auc-tion for dates, honey, fruits, livestock, and cam-els. The town of **Ibra**, which is located 100 kilo-meters south of Muscat, is especially noted for its women's only souk (big on toiletries, cosmetics, and perfumes) on Wednesdays (7:30am to 11am)—the only such souk in Oman. The pleasant trading town of **Rustaq**, which is about 160 kilometers west of Muscat and is known for its fine silver work, includes both an old and new souk as well as one of the oldest forts in Oman (great views of the town from the top of the fort). The town of **Barka**, 75 kilometers west of Muscat, is famous for its bullfights, textiles, fort, and fish souk along the oceanfront.

Recommended Resources

The following books and websites are well worth reviewing as you plan your trip to Oman. While some are available outside Oman (visit www.impactpublications.com), many of them can be found in bookstores and hotel shops in Muscat, especially Turtles at the Shangri-La. The website www.soukofoman.com includes an extensive section on hard-to-find books on Oman:

Travel Guides/Companions

- *Oman: The Bradt Travel Guide*, Diana Darke and Sandra Shields, 2006.
- *Oman Off-Road*, Explorer Group (www.Explorer-Publishing.com).
- *Oman, UAE, and the Arabian Peninsula*, Lonely Planet, 2007.
- *Traveler's Survival Kit Oman and the Gulf*, Dan Boothby, Vacation-Work
- *Travellers Oman*, Thomas Cook Publishing.

Muscat City Guides

- *Muscat for Visitors*, TimeOut, Biannual magazine guide.
- *Oman Explorer: The Complete Residents' Guide*, Explorer Group, annual (www.Explorer-Publishing.com).

History of Oman

- *Beyond the Veil in Arabia: Women in Oman*, Unni Wikan, University of Chicago Press
- *A Modern History of Oman*, Francis Owtram, I.B. Tauris. *Oman Under Qaboos: From Coup to Constitution, 1970-1996*, C.H. Allen and W.L. Rigsbee, Frank Cass Publishers.

Travelogues on Oman

- *Sultan in Oman*, Jan Morris, Sickle Moon Books

Pictorial Books on Oman

- *Architecture of Oman*, Salma Samar Damluji
- *The Craft Heritage of Oman*, Neil Richardson and Marcia Door, Motivate Publishing (www.craftheritageofoman.com)
- *Heritage of Oman*, Ozzie Newcompe

Magazines

Business Today	www.apexstuff.com/bt/200803/index.asp
Review	www.oeronline.com
Oman Today	www.apexstuff.com/ot/200803/index.asp

Newspapers

Oman Daily Observer	www.omanobserver.com
Oman Star	www.omanstar.com
Oman Tribune	www.omantribune.com
The Week	www.theweek.co.om/home.aspx
Times of Oman	www.timesofoman.com

Websites

- http://wikitravel.org/en/oman
- http://en.wikipedia.org/wiki/Muscat,_Oman
- http://en.wikipedia.org/wiki/Nizwa
- http://en.wikipedia.org/wiki/Oman
- www.arab.net/oman
- www.destinationoman.com
- www.nizwa.net
- www.omanaccess.com
- www.omanet.om
- www.omaninfo.com
- www.oman.org/tourism.htm
- www.omantourism.gov.om

PART III

Yemen

8

Welcome to Stunning and Seductive Yemen

WELCOME to beautiful, compelling, magical, and seductive Yemen, one of the world's best kept travel and shopping secrets. Only recently opened to the outside world, this is one of the most friendly, adventuresome, romantic, and unspoiled countries you will ever encounter. Little known to most travelers, this ancient land is a travel-shopper's paradise for handcrafted products reflecting the country's rich ethnic, tribal, and religious traditions. As you will quickly discover, this is a very special place for anyone sleuthing for unique treasures and pleasures.

Yemen also is one of the poorest Arab countries in the world with a per capita income of US$2,400 per year. Contrast this to relatively wealthy Qatar, which is located on the northern shores of the Arabian Peninsula and boasts a per capita income of US$75,000 per year as well as the UAE (US$55,000) and Oman (US$19,000).

Given Yemen's less than stellar economic performance, don't expect to find a well developed tourist infrastructure, such as five-star hotels, fine restaurants, and paved roads. Yemen still has a long ways to go to compete with the UAE, Oman, and other Arab countries for tourists.

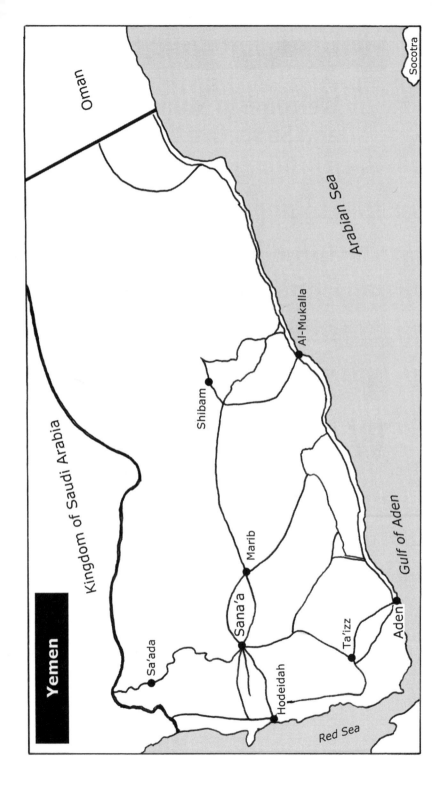

Seductive Arabia Felix

Visit Yemen and you'll be enthralled by this rugged country of biblical proportions where time often seems to stand still. You'll especially be impressed with its stunning landscapes, ancient architecture, vibrant culture, unique history, and extremely friendly and hospitable people who make this such a special place to visit. If you only allow a few days in Yemen, chances are you'll want to come back to explore it further. After all, this is one of the world's few remaining authentic destinations, a place relatively untouched by mass tourism and exuding a great deal of charming chaos. For independent travelers, Yemen is a dream come true!

Dubbed Arabia Felix—Happy Arabia, Arabia the Blessed, or Fortunate Arabia—by the ancient Romans, who encountered a very prosperous and relatively green civilization on the Arabian Peninsula, Yemen indeed remains a very special place today. For photographers and first-time visitors unprepared for Yemen's uniqueness, this is a visually stunning place for its natural beauty and striking people. In fact, you'll wonder why so few people have discovered this land of spectacular baked gingerbread and tower architecture (in Sana'a, seemingly laced with icing and topped with satellite dishes), breathtaking landscapes, World Heritage sites, fertile valleys, and unspoilt beaches punctuated with aging towns,  colorful markets, noisy and chaotic streets, and delightful people (especially playful children) who enjoy welcoming foreigners, posing for photos, and generally having lots of fun in what is ostensibly a barren and forbidding country known to outsiders for its poverty, kidnappings, and terrorist activities.

Encounter the Real Thing

If you've traveled to other parts of the Arab world, you'll quickly discover that Yemen is "the real thing." Everything about this place shouts "unique," "authentic," and "exotic"—from buildings and markets to music, food, and people. Exhibiting strong tribal traditions, with over 1,300 distinct tribes, this is the real Arab world before all the plastic, asphalt, steel, department stores, shopping malls, and expatriate labor transformed many other parts of the oil-rich Arab world, especially on the northern shores (the Gulf States) of the Arabian Peninsula.

If you've visited the UAE and Oman before coming here, you may experience some culture shock when you first arrive in Yemen. It looks and feels unfamiliar. The small and worn airports, aging and  battered vehicles, rough and dusty roads, crumbling buildings, and rugged-looking yet friendly men chewing *qat* leaves, dressing in traditional attire (head turban, sport coat, and full-bodied white shirt/skirt), and displaying the trademark curved Yemeni dagger (*jambiya*) tucked in their waistband may give you reasons to initially pause and take in the local character of this interesting place. These people look simultaneously exotic, fierce, and mysterious, and more so once they are around their fully veiled women who are covered from head to toe in public with the black abaya. After a few hours it will all come into focus and start making eminent sense. This is a friendly and humorous place where everyone seems to be having a good time with the basics of living. Indeed, Yemen will quickly embrace you as Arabia Felix!

This is a very poor country rich in history, culture, and ancient legends for Christians and Muslims alike. It exhibits all the chaos normally associated with such places, and much more. From the moment you step off the plane, pass through immigration, and find transportation to your hotel, to when you encounter charming and picturesque cities, towns, and villages, explore traditional bustling markets, and marvel at the unique architecture and landscapes, you know you're in a very special place that beckons you to explore its many hidden treasures and pleasures.

Location and Images

Situated on the southeastern part of the Arabian Peninsula—south of Saudi Arabia, west of Oman, and surrounded in the south and east by the Arabian Sea and Red Sea—legendary Yemen is the land of ancient kingdoms, Cain and Abel, Noah's Ark, the Queen of Sheba, coffee, spices, frankincense, and myrrh. Most recently it has developed a reputation as an international danger zone, because of its fierce tribalism, kidnappings, terrorist activities, draconic socialism, civil war, and a heavily armed population (the world's third largest per capita gun ownership after the U.S. and Finland). Somewhere between these two images lies one of the world's most fascinating and undiscovered places—a paradise for architecture and nature lovers, hikers, campers, divers, and shoppers.

Size, Population, and Religion

Yemen occupies an area of 555,000 square kilometers (214,287 square miles). As such, it's approximately the size of France, Thailand, or the U.S. states of Nevada and Colorado combined.

Yemen's population of over 22 million in 2008 ranks it as the 51st most populous country in the world, just behind Romania, Ghana, and Taiwan. It has a relatively young population with 48 percent of the population being under the age of 15. It also has a relatively high birth rate (43.07 births/1,000 population), which translates into an annual population growth rate of 3.5 percent.

Population estimates for Yemen's various cities are notoriously inaccurate and confused with larger administrative statistics that encompass both urban and rural areas. They are at best guesstimates since figures tend to be drawn from different decades and most are based on questionable ground counts. In addition, population figures for the larger administrative units called "governerates" are often confused with actual city boundaries. For example, you'll find Sana'a's population variously reported at 1 million, 1.5 million, 1.8 million, and 2.1 million. The city of Ta'izz's population is sometimes reported at 2.2 million when in fact this is the population for the whole governerate. Some visitors are told the population for the famous mud tower-house city of Shibam is 1.1 million. Once they get there they encounter a relatively quiet and deserted town of only 7,000! Here are our best guesstimates for 2008:

Sana'a	1,200,000
Aden	700,000
Hodeidah (Al-Hudaydah)	350,000
Ta'izz	320,000
Al-Mukalla	220,000
Sa'ada	35,000
Shibam	7,000
Marib	6,000

The first five cities are Yemen's major economic centers whereas the last three are small but popular tourist towns for exploring some of Yemen's most interesting archeological and architectural sites.

Yemen is one of the poorest Arab countries (45 percent earn less than US$2 a day) with 73 percent of the population residing in rural areas.

This is a very tribal country where loyalty to one's clan and family takes precedence over loyalty to a nation. Yemen's recent history (since World War II) has witnessed major divisions and conflicts between the north and south, including separate governments, which were finally reunified into the Republic of Yemen on May 22, 1990.

While 98 percent of the country is Muslim, Yemen is also divided along two major religious lines—the Shi'a (Zaidi sect) Muslims in the north and northwest (45 percent of population) and the Sunni (Shafa'i sect) Muslims in the south and southeast (53 percent of the population).

Borders and Neighbors

Yemen shares a sometimes contentious 288-kilometer border in the northeast with Oman and a 1,800-kilometer border in the north with Saudi Arabia. Its 3,165 kilometers of coastline face both the Arabian Sea and the Red Sea as well as the African nations of Eritrea, Djibouti, and Somalia. Yemen is currently dealing with a large influx of refugees from war-torn Somalia who cross the Gulf of Aden in overcrowded boats to the southern shores of Yemen. Aden in the south, with a population, of nearly 700,000, is Yemen's major port and faces the Gulf of Aden, which connects the Red Sea to the Arabian Sea. Yemen also has over 200 islands, most of which are located in the Red Sea. Yemen's largest island, the extremely intriguing Socotra, is located nearly 400 kilometers off the southeastern coast. There is some talk about building one of the world's largest bridges to connect the southwest tip of Yemen with the African nation of Djibouti.

Images of Yemen

For visual images of Yemen, visit the following websites:

Photo Galleries

- www.pbase.com/bmcmorrow/yemen
- www.yemenweb.com/gallery
- www.hansrossel.com/fotos/fotografie/yemen/index.htm
- www.infohub.com/pictures/images_yemen_248.html
- www.world66.com/asia/middleeast/yemen/lib/gallery
- www.ishoparoundtheworld.com/yemen/yemen_photoalbums.html

Videos

- http://youtube.com/watch?v=7tuQagz4C68 (Sana'a)
- http://youtube.com/watch?v=Dp1x79pWmq8
- http://youtube.com/watch?v=fU9Rl63_DAA (Socotra Island)
- http://youtube.com/watch?v=7LmNba66lFA (Socotra Island)
- www.youtube.com/watch?v=9iaR2XkeD_c
- www.youtube.com/watch?v=ndWqz2pDtec (Aden)
- http://youtube.com/watch?v=Ehn1ob4nelU (Sana'a—Jambiya)
- www.youtube.com/watch?v=Vtt2emodFvw
- www.youtube.com/watch?v=bdySdolF6JA

Getting There

Yemen is most conveniently reached by air, with the capital city of Sana'a being the major gateway entry point. While various international airlines fly into Sana'a International Airport (Royal Jordanian, Emirates, Gulf Air, Qatar Air, Lufthansa, Ethiopia Airlines, Syrian Air, Turkish Airlines, Egypt Air), the national carrier, **Yemenia Airways** (www.yemenia.com), offers the most extensive connections to major cities in Europe, the Middle East, Africa, and Asia. The flight from Dubai to Sana'a, for example, takes approximately two hours. Flights from London, Paris, and Frankfurt take from seven to nine hours. A few airlines also service Yemen's four other international airports, which are located in Aden, Ta'izz (Al-Janad), Seiyun (Sayan), and Riyan Mukalla.

You also can enter Yemen at six seaports along the Arabian Sea and Red Sea (Aden, Hudaydah, al-Khawkha, al-Mokha, Nashtoon, and al-Mukalla), four land crossings with Saudi Arabia (from east to west—Haradh, Alab, al-Buqa', and al-Wadee'ah), and two land crossings with Oman (Serfayt in the south and Shahan in the north). However, your easiest entry points will be via air through the international airports in Sana'a, Aden, Ta'izz, Seiyun, and Riyan Mukalla.

Visas and Entry Requirements

With the exception of citizens from Jordan, Syria and Egypt and nationals of the GCC (Gulf Cooperation Council)—Bahrain, Kuwait, Qatar, Oman, Saudi Arabia, and the United Arab Emirates—all visitors to Yemen are required to enter the country with a valid passport (good for at least six months before expiration) and visa.

While many nationalities, including most Europeans, Americans, and Australians, can now acquire a visa upon arrival at border crossings and airports, be sure to check with a Yemeni embassy on the latest rules before you finalize your travel plans. You may want to play it safe and arrange your visa prior to departing from your home country. For information on visa requirements for U.S. citizens, visit the Yemeni Embassy home page: www.yemenembassy.org. This site also includes a downloadable visa application form. The basic requirements are two passport-size photos, a completed application, a valid passport, a self-addressed prepaid express mail envelope (no special delivery services), and a money order made payable to The Embassy of Yemen for the amount of either $27 (3-month tourist visa) or $62 (6-month tourist visa). It usually takes a week to 10 days to process a visa application. Nationals of other countries should visit their country-relevant Yemeni Embassy website for similar instructions and downloadable forms.

If you wish to apply for a visa in person at the Yemen Embassy in Washington, DC, be sure to check the embassy's website for application hours (currently 10am to 1pm, Monday through Thursday). The embassy does observe both U.S. and Yemeni holidays, which may conflict with your planned visitation time.

Yemen follows an anti-Israeli position in solidarity with other Arab and Gulf States. If you carry an Israeli passport or have an Israeli stamp in your passport, you will not be allowed entry into Yemen. However, if it is obvious the traveler must have been in Israel because of an exit stamp from another country that would have necessitated entry to Israel, the visitor could be denied entry. Some travelers with an Israel stamp in their passport, get a new passport before applying for a visa. Others planning to travel to Israel prior to arrival in Yemen ask Israeli immigration officials to not stamp their passport—only stamp a separate piece of official paper. This may satisfy their government regulations and allow them to enter Arab countries with a "clean" passport.

Photography Do's and Don'ts

Yemen is a photographer's paradise for stunning landscapes, beautiful sunsets, unique architecture, and portraits of its fascinating people. Whatever you do, be sure to stock up on lots of film, flash cards, and batteries to record the many memorable people and places you will encounter throughout Yemen.

Taking photographs of people can be a bit tricky in Yemen. While most people, especially children, are very easy to photograph—indeed many eagerly pose for photographers and some even demand to be photographed!—do not photograph the mysteriously veiled women, who are usually all females over the age of 14. Indeed, you can quickly earn the wrath of such women and their families if you photograph them without their permission. And few will give you such permission. Consequently, you may need to be very discreet in planning your shots by literally shooting from the hip not knowing exactly the quality of your shots!

Some older people don't like to have their photographs taken without their permission, but many others don't care. Many welcome such attention and are delighted to see themselves in digital format.

While a few people, usually a tourist-savvy young girl, may ask for money when photographed, most do not. Your camera may become an excellent icebreaker for meeting the locals. You'll become very popular with your subjects if you use a digital camera or camcorder and share your shots with them. In fact, children love to see themselves in digital or video format and will give you a thumbs up if they like the result!

Safety and Security

You should be aware of a few safety and security issues when planning your trip to this country. Indeed, Yemen has received some bad press in North America and Europe for being a hotbed for terrorists, for occasional terrorist activities and kidnappings, for violent tribal clashes, and for its politically incorrect leanings—widespread sympathy for Saddam Hussein, Hezbollah, and al-Qaeda. These are legitimate concerns supported by some scary facts on the ground. Much of this image stems from the October 2000 bombing of the USS Cole in Aden that killed 17 U.S. sailors; the presence of Yemeni nationals in al-Qaeda cells in many parts of the Middle East, Africa, Asia, and Europe; the July 2007 suspected al-Qaeda suicide car bombing that killed seven Spanish tourists and two Yemenis at the Queen of Sheba Temple in Marib; and three exploding mortars possibly aimed at the U.S. Embassy (but hit a neighboring girls' school instead, killing one guard and one student) in Sana'a (March 18, 2008). More such problems are expected in this turbulent region.

Yemen also has a long history of banditry, warfare, and kidnappings—a certain degree of lawlessness associated with a tribal society with grievances against the central government, which has yet to effectively govern from Sana'a. In many respects, this is a poor and wild frontier country of heavily armed semi-autonomous tribes—all 1,300+! Yemen's gun culture includes 60 million guns in circulation among a population of only 22 million. While the government has banned carrying guns in public and has begun confiscating weapons, nonetheless, this remains the world's third most heavily armed population.

The irony is that many visitors fear coming to Yemen but once there they usually feel very safe—no thievery, muggings, rapes, or other crimes normally associated with tourism. Indeed, a comparison of crime statistics between Kansas City, Missouri and Sana'a in 1999 found that the crime rate in Kansas City was 97 times higher than in Sana'a. And Kansas City is considered to be relatively safe by American standards! Yemen's main safety issue tends to relate to political violence associated with al-Qaeda activities and kidnappings because of tribal issues with the government. In fact, Yemen's jails and prisons include some very scary people associated with al-Qaeda who have some deadly political and religious agendas aimed at governments and foreigners.

Despite media reports and U.S. Department of State warnings to the contrary, Yemen is a relatively safe place to travel to as long as you

take sensible precautions and plan your stay accordingly. Wherever you visit in Yemen, and especially if you are an adventure traveler heading into the more remote and unstable regions of Yemen, particularly the north, you are well advised to travel with an experienced local guide who is familiar with the current security situation. The city of Sana'a, for example, is a very safe place to visit—you need not worry about your personal safety here other than watch out (look both left and right) for the speeding traffic when crossing busy intersections and stay away from the American Embassy. Your chances of becoming a target of a pickpocket, mugging, kidnapping, or al-Qaeda terrorist activities are about the same as being struck by lightning.

Do put such travel reports in perspective. However fearful visitors might be, with the exceptions of **Sa'ada**, which is located 240 kilometers north of Sana'a, and **Marib**, which is located about 150 kilometers east of Sana'a, and require police escorts, most reports are irrelevant to tourists. Indeed, after visiting Yemen, you may wonder what this security fuss is all about. And keep Kansas City in mind—they have some serious safety issues compared to Sana'a. No one can guarantee your safety—anywhere in the world at home or abroad.

If you travel outside the major cities, be sure to check on the current security situation. A few parts of the country, which are noted for tribal tensions, should be approached with caution because of reported kidnappings and violence that could affect tourists. Unfortunately, some foreign tourists have been killed when they ventured unescorted into areas designated as dangerous by the government. Local travel warnings should be taken seriously and you should not tempt fate by wandering off on your own.

Soft kidnappings do occur, but they are usually quickly resolved through government intervention. Most such kidnappings relate to tribal grievances against the government—issues about infrastructure and incarcerated tribal members. Kidnapped individuals often report being inconvenienced but treated well. Indeed, a few visitors have been known to actually look forward to being kidnapped in order to get some good photos of the experience! A few years ago our own tour guide was kidnapped by some enterprising individuals who actually asked him to hold their AK47s while they enjoyed being treated to ice cream, which was offered by our guide. Unharmed and treated to traditional Yemeni hospitality, he was released within hours after arranging for a nominal exchange of money. This was the third time he had been kidnapped in 10 years!

Check out the latest travel advisories before planning any adventures outside the major cities, especially in northern Yemen (Sa'ada) which has experienced a great deal of turbulence during the past three decades. U.S. Department of State travel advisories tend to be preoccupied with al-Qaeda terrorist activities and thus their advisors often lump traditional tribal warfare into their terrorist warnings. For example, in July 2007, suspected al-Qaeda operatives attacked a tour group at the Belquis Temple in Marib, killing eight Spanish tourists and two Yemenis. On January 2008, two Belgian tourists and two Yemini nationals were murdered in Hadramant. In February 2006, 23 convicts, including known affiliates of al-Qaeda, escaped from a high-security prison in Sana'a. To the great displeasure of the United States and the United Kingdom, some of these individuals were involved in the 2000 bombing of the USS Cole and the 2002 attack on the French oil tanker Limburg.

But again, such security warnings are largely irrelevant to most tourists who spend the majority of their time in and around Sana'a. Nonetheless, you should be aware of your surroundings and work with an experienced tour company that is well aware of the current security situation and does not take unnecessary risks that could endanger you. Also, check out recent security warnings available on these official U.S. and U.K. websites: http://travel.state.gov and www.fco.gov.uk).

Money Matters

The local currency is called the Yemeni rial or riyal (YR). Notes are printed in the following denominations: YR1,000, 500, 200, 100, 50, and 20. Coins are available in three denominations: YR10, 5, and 1.

In 2008 the exchange rate between the U.S. dollar and the Yemeni rial was nearly 200 rial per U.S. dollar.

Dollars can be easily exchanged at banks, hotels, and exchange bureaus (*bureaux de change*). Some shops also will accept U.S. dollars. However, you are well advised to travel primarily with new (issued

after 2005) US$100 bills. Older bills are often rejected as possibly counterfeit. Since you don't want all your cash to be in $100 bills, make sure your smaller denomination bills are the most recent year issued. The year varies by denomination. The new multi-colored bills, which are harder to counterfeit, are most likely to be accepted. Here's a useful **money tip** that will help you avoid potential exchange problems: Ask your local bank to stock up on new $100 bills at least six weeks before you travel to Yemen. Many banks are short on such notes and thus have difficulty coming up with such bills a couple of days before your departure.

It's best to carry cash in U.S. dollars since few places outside hotels accept credit cards, ATMs are limited (primarily found at the airport and banks and may or may not work for you), and traveler's checks are not accepted in most places. Carrying lots of cash should be safe since robbery and thievery are relatively unheard of in Yemen. Indeed, you will see many locals carrying large wads of cash. However, be very discreet where you carry cash and how much you show at a time.

Tipping

Tips are not expected in local restaurants, but a 10-15 percent service charge is often added by restaurants catering to tourists. Major hotels add a 22-percent service charge and government tax to your bill. Porters, waiters, tour guides, and drivers expect tips. Porters expect a US$.50-$1 (YR100-200) tip for their services.

Sample Itineraries

Shoppers will want to spend most of their time in and around Sana'a and venture into a few towns in villages in central and western Yemen. If you have three days in Sana'a and arrange a car, driver, and guide, we suggest visiting the following places:

Day 1:	Thula, Wadi Dhahr, Shibam, Kawkaban
Day 2:	Old Sana'a
Day 3:	Greater Sana'a and Old Sana'a

If you have a week to 12 days in Yemen, consider doing the following by region:

Days 1-3:	**Sana'a and Environs:** Sana'a, Thula, Wadi Dhahr, Shibam, Kawkaban
Days 4-6:	**West and Southwest Yemen:** Shahara, Al Hajjarh, Manakha, Hodeidah, Bayt Al-Faqih, and Zabid
Days 7-8:	**Southern Yemen:** Yarim, Jiblah, Ibb, Ta'izz, Al Mokka, and Aden
Days 9-10:	**East and Southeastern Yemen:** Shibam, Seiyun, Tarim, and Al-Mukalla
Days 11-12:	**Island in Yemen:** Socotra

Some visitors may also want to visit the historic towns of Marib and Sa'ada. However, these two places remain on security lists due to killings of tourists in these areas. Approach them with extreme caution and with a very knowledgeable and armed tour/ escort group.

Local Transportation

Despite the often crowded traffic conditions in Sana'a, it's relatively easy to get around by car, taxi, or minibus. Since taxis do not have meters, you'll need to negotiate each fare. A taxi from the airport to most destinations in Sana'a, for example, should cost about US$10 (YR2,000). Within the city, most rides cost about US$1 (YR200), although taxi drivers may try to double or triple the prices for tourists. While taxis and minibuses are very inexpensive, you may have difficulty communicating with taxi and bus drivers and finding places with ease. Since good maps are difficult to find, you may often feel lost trying to navigate the streets and lanes of Old Sana'a. But you'll soon find your way around, especially if you carry a compass for reorienting yourself.

Unless you are on a shoestring budget, have lots of time to kill exploring an unfamiliar place, and seek numerous street-level cultural experiences, it's most convenient to hire your own car, driver, and guide. Whatever you do, don't be penny-wise but pound foolish in navigating Sana'a. A travel service, such as the ones mentioned below, will quickly take you to and from various places, wait for you while you explore sites, carry your shopping treasures, field any security issues, and share with you inside information on the who, what, where, and why of Sana'a. If you want a car and driver for part of a day, check with your hotel. Most can make such arrangements for you.

Tours and Tour Operators

Several tours groups in Yemen can assist you with local transportation and sightseeing arrangements. Our personal preference is:

- **Abu Taleb Group**
  P.O. Box 25321
  Sana'a, Yemen
  Tel. 967-1-441-260
  Fax 967-1-441-259
  E-mail: info@atg-yemen.com
  Website: www.atg-yemen.com

Operating since 1972, this very experienced full-service tour operator offers customized group and individual tours throughout Yemen, including sightseeing, trekking, hiking, and diving trips via four-wheel drive Toyota Land Cruisers, camels, donkeys, and foot. Our experience with this company was exceptional—very experienced and informative local guide who spoke impeccable English and went out of his way to ensure that we experienced the very best of Yemen, including its many colorful shops and markets. Try to contact them several weeks before you arrive to ensure a well organized trip. They will initially meet you at the airport, where they also have an office, and make all local arrangements for a safe and comfortable trip.

Several other tour operators offer a variety of local travel services, from rental cars to fully organized 21-day tours:

- Universal Touring Company   www.utcyemen.com
- Future Tours Industries   www.ftiyemen.com
- Yemen Old Splendor Tours   www.yostours.com.ye
- Cameleers Tours   www.cameleerstours.com
- Gold Moore Tours   www.g-m-tours.net
- Yamanat Tours   www.yamanat.com
- Yemen Explorer Tours   www.al-bab.com/yet

- Acacia Tours   www.acaciatours.com
- Yemen Explorers   www.yemen-explorers.com
- Shibam Tour Operator   www.y.net.ye/shibam-tours
- Arabian Horizons   www.arabian-horizon.com
- Universal —Yemen   www.universalyemen.com
- Ashtal Travel and Tourism   www.ashtal.com
- Al-Nasim Travel & Tourism   www.alnasim.com.ye
- Summer Tours & Travel   www.summer-yemen.com
- Al-Mamoon Group   www.al-mamoon-group.com
- Yemen Tourism Company   www.y.net.ye/ytc
- Yeman Tours   www.al-bab.com/yemantours
- Sinbad Tours   www.al-bab.com/sinbad
- Dubai Tours   www.al-bab.com/dubaitours
- Yemeni Dreams   www.yemeni-dreams.com
- Alzahra Tourism Agency   www.al-bab.com/alzahra
- GuideMe   www.gmyemen.com

All of these companies offer some variation of sightseeing, trekking, hiking, sailing, fishing, birding, snorkeling, and related trips for individual and group travelers that involve a combination of hotel and camping accommodations. If you review several of their websites, some of which are very basic and filled with spelling and grammatical errors, you'll get a good feel for the different types of tours and trips you can join or organize in Yemen. Since we've not worked with any of these other groups, we are unable to make personal recommendations. As you will soon discover, all are not equal. You need to do your homework before selecting a company that will be responsible for your personal safety and well being. You might also want to check out the Tourism Promotion Board's list of licensed tour operators which can be found here:

www.yementourism.com/services/travelagency/index.php

If you arrange a car and driver through any of these local tour companies, expect to pay from US$80 to $150 per day. Accommodations, of course will be extra, running anywhere from US$30 to US$200 a day, depending on the quality of accommodations.

Only a few international tour operators include Yemen in their itineraries. You may want to check out the offerings of these specialty travel groups that sometime cover Yemen:

- Bestway Tours and Safaris   www.bestway.com
- Spiekermann Travel Service   www.mideasttrvl.com
- Adventure Center   www.adventurecenter.com
- Geographic Expeditions   www.geoex.com
- Caravan-Serai Tours   www.caravan-serai.com
- Adventures Abroad   www.adventures-abroad.com
- Worldwide Travel Ltd.
- Explore Worldwide Ltd.   www.explore.co.uk
- Responsible Travel   www.responsibletravel.com

Most of these companies charge from US$3,000 to US$6,000 per person, including airfare, for a two- to three-week tour package.

Primary Focus on Sana'a

While there is much to see and do throughout Yemen, our major focus is on the capital city of Sana'a and a few surrounding towns and villages, especially Al Rawdah, Thula (Thilla), Wadi Dhahr, Shibam, and Kawkaban, which are within an hour's drive from Sana'a. These places offer the best shopping opportunities in Yemen, and they are safe destinations to visit. Our recommendation: Plan a minimum of three days in Sana'a in order to see the many sites and shop the various markets and intriguing street shops that define Yemen's fascinating shopping culture.

If you have a week to 12 days, you may want to extend your stay to visiting the interesting World Heritage city of Shibam (located 800 kilometers east of Sana'a)—dubbed "the Manhattan of the desert" for its unique tower architecture—and the once booming port city of Aden in the south as well as explore the special island of Socotra, which is located nearly 400 kilometers off the southeastern coast of Yemen. All of these places can be conveniently and safely reached by air from Sana'a.

Getting to Know Sana'a

From the moment you arrive at the small worn Sana'a International Airport to when you depart for other parts of the world, you're in for a real treat. Located at an elevation of 7,200 feet and boasting a population of 1.2 million (some say 2 million+), this place quickly grows on you after initial exposure to excessive pollution, noise, congestion, and visual chaos—especially after you discover the many

treasures and pleasures found in the city within the city, **Old Sana'a** (Old City).

While Dubai may be a Wow! destination, because of its concentration of modern high-rise commercial buildings, luxury hotels and resorts, massive shopping malls, and expansive expressways, Sana'a is a Wow! destination of a different kind—a completely coherent ancient and exotic city with sights and sounds unlike any you may have encountered elsewhere in the world. It includes historical biblical and Koranic bragging rights such as being founded by Noah's son Shem (Aden boasts being established by Cain and Abel and the launch point for Noah's Ark) and being the world's oldest continuously inhabited city (a claim also made for Damascus and Aleppo in Syria and a few other cities around the world). No question about it—Sana'a is an old city, with all the signs of an ancient past only recently preserved from over-population, pollution, and crumbling neglect.

Indeed, compelling Sana'a may well become one of your favorite destinations. Colorful and full of character, this city and its surrounding area beg to be explored for several days. In fact, you may think you've discovered a Shangri-La that has not been overrun by the excesses of unplanned modernity and chaotic development found in many cities throughout the world. Except for stringy electrical wires, exposed pipes, rooftop satellite dishes, and the constant ringing of cell phones, Sana'a truly maintains and preserves its ancient and exotic character, which is terrific news for visitors in search of authentic Yemen not yet overrun by tourism, or even 20th-century development!

Located nearly 2,200 meters (7,200 feet) above sea level along a plateau in the central highlands and surrounded by imposing mountains (Jebal Nuqum and Aiban), the sprawling capital of Sana'a is the country's gateway city. While the port city of Aden, which is located 370 kilometers (230 miles) south of Sana'a, is the economic capital, Sana'a is Yemen's political and communication capital.

Sana'a also is a working urban tribal museum well worth sleuthing for unique treasures and pleasures. The noisy and bustling Old City section of Sana'a, which is located in the center of the city along a dry north-south riverbed called The Sailah, includes a striking collection of over 6,500 (some say 14,000) well-preserved mud brick multi-storied tower buildings, 103 mosques, 14 *hammans* (baths), and numerous green patches of tidy gardens. A self-sustained residential and commercial city within a city, Old Sana'a is home to nearly 250,000 local residents. A UNESCO World Heritage site since 1988,

this is the major destination for most visitors who fall in love with the city because of its ancient core. In fact, until the early 1960s, most of Sana'a was synonymous with the Old City. Today Sana'a continues to expand rapidly beyond the Old City walls and gates.

The Heritage area begs to be explored on foot and with a camera and shopping bag. This is a great place to easily get lost and found while marveling at the ginger-bread architecture and stained-glass windows, listening to the exotic sounds, taking photos, meeting interesting locals, playing with the uninhibited children, having a few laughs, and shopping the main streets and narrow lanes that are filled with local treasures and people going about their daily shopping and religious routines. Spend a full day exploring this area and you will quickly come in touch with the many exotic peoples, products, sights, and sounds of this delightful city.

Sana'a is one of the world's oldest and most fascinating cities noted for its old walls and unique stone, brick, and mud buildings designed as four- and five-story tower-houses accented with elaborate friezes and plastered with white gypsum. The best views of this city are from the roofs of a few choice hotels (we vote for the rooftop of the classy Burj Al Salam Hotel) that are found in the heart of the Old City as well as the walk-

way along the top of the main gate or *bab*, Bab al-Yemen (access via the Bab Al-Yemen Gallery—www.nizar-art.com).

While you can easily explore the Old City on your own with the help of a basic, but not particularly informative, hotel map available to guests, the best way to approach the Old City is with a guide who can take you through the maze of streets and lanes to highlight the various sites and shop the intriguing Souk al-Milh. While this is a much more open and festive area than the narrow and enclosed souks of Morocco (Fez and Marrakesh) and Syria (Damascus and Aleppo), a guide is still useful for navigating the Old City.

This partially walled city includes several gates that define the main entrances to the city. The main entry point is the 700-year old gate called **Bab al-Yemen**, which is located in the middle of the imposing and well maintained southern wall of the Old City. A busy and noisy area, here you'll see and hear all kinds of street activities on both sides of the wall, from shouting street vendors selling men's clothing, candies, and spices to honking buses, minivans, and taxis dropping off or waiting to pick up passengers leaving the Old City. From this gate you also can quickly enter the central souk, **Souk al-Milh** (Salt Market), which is located just a few minutes directly north of this entrance. This ancient market,  with its combination of clothes, accessories, household goods, souvenirs, and foodstuffs, is the main attraction and shopping experience for most visitors to Sana'a.

Alternatively, you may want to enter the Old City via the western gate called **Bab Al-Sabah** (look for the popular gold souk here) and then meander east toward the Burj Al Salam Hotel and then southeast into Souk al-Milh. While you will pass a few mosques along the way, these religious compounds are off limits to nonbelievers. Take your time just enjoying the many sights and sounds, getting a sense of the Old City, observing the daily activities of many colorful and expressive people. As you move closer to the central souk, you'll encounter a bee-hive of activity. You'll see men buying and chewing the ubiquitous *qat*, black-clothed and completely veiled women buying gold jewelry and colorful garments for home use only, vendors pushing wheelbarrows filled with goods and others displaying their goods on the ground, open-air restaurants and juice bars, and children playing in the streets and lanes.

Outside the Old City, there's not much of interest to see and do beyond a few museums, hotels, restaurants, universities, supermarkets, and embassies that service the local and international population. Best covered by car, this part of the city is relatively worn and chaotic, suffering from an excess of unimaginative construction, little urban zoning and planning, and heavy and polluting traffic. In many respects, the charming Old City is an ancient oasis and fortress facing the negatives of urbanization in Yemen.

Shopping Treasures

For us, Sana'a is a great place to shop for all kinds of interesting local products that reflect the history, art, culture, and skills of the Yemenis. If you want to meet the locals and learn about Yemen, be sure to spend several hours shopping in Sana'a. Indeed, shopping in Yemen is an interesting economic, social, and cultural experience. Your main destination will be the shops and stalls lining several streets and lanes that define Souk al-Milh in the heart of the Old City.

What to Buy

The shops and markets of Sana'a are filled with a wide range of locally produced and imported items. Look for the following:

- **Weapons:**
    - daggers (*jambiyas*)
    - swords
    - guns

- **Handicrafts**
    - model tower-houses
    - waterpipes (*mada'a*)
    - baskets
    - brass, copper, and ceramic pots
    - incense burners
    - lanterns (folding and collapsible)
    - musical instruments
    - Hadhrami hats

- **Jewelry:**
    - traditional silver
    - gold

- **Antiques**
  - silver
  - daggers
  - boxes

- **Foodstuffs**
  - raisins
  - honey
  - tea
  - coffee

- **Paintings and prints**
- **Clothes**
- **Fabrics**
- **Shawls**
- **Spices**
- **Frankincense and myrrh**
- **Henna and traditional makeup**
- **Music (tapes and CDs)**

Some of the favorite treasures appealing to visitors include:

❑ **Jambiyas:** These are traditional ceremonial curved daggers tucked in a wide belt and worn by men around their waists. For a man to be completely dressed in traditional attire, he needs to wear his jambiya in the center of his waistband. These daggers come in many different qualities and designs—from inexpensive souvenir daggers to antique collector's daggers. Prices range from US$10 to over $50,000. In fact, one famous Yemeni politician is the proud owner of a US$1 million+ jambiya. When shopping for a jambiya, pay particular attention to the quality of the handle and case. The most expensive jambiyas are made with rhino horn (most now are made of buffalo horn from India) and cases include intricately designed Jewish silver work and sometimes also gold and jewels. The dagger blade itself is usually disappointing. If you want a souvenir or antique that is truly representative of Yemen, check out the jambiya selections that are found in Sana'a's many antique, jewelry, and handicraft shops.

❑ **Jewelry:** Yemeni jewelry primarily comes in two major forms—traditional silver tribal jewelry and gold jewelry. You'll find lots of intricately designed old tribal ornamental jewelry in the form of necklaces, pendants, and bracelets. Indeed, many shops that offer jambiyas also have a large collection of traditional silver jewelry. Much of this jewelry includes semiprecious stones. Be aware that most of the new jewelry is imported from India. Yemeni jewelry tends to be heavier and bulkier than the Indian imports. Other silver jewelry is hammered into nicely designed bracelets and sold by weight. Many gold shops offer a good range of locally designed rings, bracelets, and necklaces in 18 and 22 karat gold. Most of this jewelry also is sold by weight. Be sure to check out the gold souk near Bab Al-Sabah, the western gate, which is a worthy competitor to the gold souk in Souk al-Milh near Bab Al-Yemen, the southern gate.

❑ **Antiques:** Being an ancient land with many tribes and old villages and towns means having lots of heirlooms available for trade and sales. Many of these items end up in art, souvenir, and jewelry shops. You'll encounter lots of antique jewelry, silver boxes, jambiyas, swords, oil lamps, lanterns, candle stands, guns, shields, chests, pots, and household items that were once family heirlooms but sold off to shops. Be ware that there are legal restrictions on exporting antiques, although enforcement is very spotty. Most shopkeepers will tell you there's "no problem" taking their particular antiques out of the country. Also, be aware that not all purported to be old is actually old, and some things may come from Morocco, Oman, and India rather than from local artisans. Some of the best collections of antiques can be found at the two World Friend shops in Sana'a.

❑ **Art:** Sana'a has a few art galleries that display the works of local and expatriate artists. Keep in mind that this is a Muslim country where religious doctrines normally prohibit the portrayal of images, people, and scenery. As a result, local art tends to be produced by non-Muslims, geared toward the tourist market, and very limited and often uninspired. Nonetheless, you may be able to find some interesting paintings and drawings that depict the scenes and

peoples of Yemen, especially those produced by local artists Fuad Al Futaih and Mazher Nizar who both have art galleries in the Old City (National Art Center and Bab Al-Yemen Gallery respectively). Mazher Nizar, who works with many local artists through the Graphic Art Society whose members meet at the Bab Al-Yemen Gallery every Thursday, claims there are more than 250 creative artists in Yemen. None are able to support themselves through their art work alone.

❑ **Handicrafts:** Yemeni artisans produce a wide range of handicrafts that appeal to visitors in search of souvenirs and gift items. Many are produced in the Old City of Sana'a whereas others come from villages all over Yemen. Many also are imported from Morocco, Syria, Oman, and India. Look for woven baskets and boxes, pots, waterpipes (*mada'a*), Hadhrami hats, lanterns (collapsible and folding), incense burners, coffee pots, textile bags and costumes, natural cosmetics, recycled crafts, fiber goods, wall hangings, model tower-houses, toys, henna, and stained glass window decorations made of gypsum. For a good overview of Yemeni handicrafts sponsored by the Social Fund for Development, including photos of individual items, be sure to visit www.yemen-handicraft.com.

❑ **Music:** You'll find several stores offering a combination of audio tapes and CDs of Yemeni and other Arab music. Most audiotapes sell for around US$.75. CDs go for US$1.00. If you enjoy collecting local music when traveling, this is one of the best buys you can find anywhere!

❑ **Food and incense products:** Sana'a's markets and shops are filled with many tempting foodstuffs, especially raisins, dates, honey, dried fruits, tea, coffee, and spices. Yemen is especially noted for its fine honey. You'll find Yemen's famous frankincense and myrrh available in markets next to incense and spices.

How to Shop and Bargain

Contrary to what some observers may tell you, in Yemen you **are** expected to bargain. If you don't, you'll be paying anywhere from 10 to 60 percent above retail.

Few prices are fixed in Yemen, including the cost of taxi rides. The general shopping rule is to nicely bargain for everything. Discounts will

vary depending on the items, merchant, your ability to bargain, and your nationality. For example, don't expect to get much of a discount on a kilo of raisins or bag full of *qat*—quoted prices on such items are close to the day's street price.

Quoted prices will vary depending on where you come from. In fact, a merchant may first ask your nationality before giving you a price—an important piece of information for setting their initial price. Americans, for example, are often quoted lower prices than Italians

because Americans have a reputation for not bargaining much—they often turn around and walk away after given a price they think is too high. Italians, on the other hand, seem to enjoy the art of bargaining and thus are often given an initial high price to allow them to engage their bargaining skills. Consequently, an American may be quoted a price 10 percent above the final price whereas the Italian might be quoted a price 50 percent above the same final price. The final agreed price will be about the same for both nationalities.

Don't be disappointed if a merchant only gives you a 10-percent discount after an attempt to bargain for a 50-percent discount. Some simply don't bargain much. Others, especially those who frequently sell to tourists, may approximate the 50-percent discount model. In either case, offer anywhere from 40 to 50 percent of the initial quoted price and work your way to a final price with a series of offers and counter offers. Few merchants are aggressive bargainers (except in the town of Thula!) and some may take offense if you are extremely aggressive. Always keep the process light-hearted and humorous if possible. Aggressive and clever bargainers may be told *"You bargain like a Bedouin!,"* which is both a compliment and an observation that you're a tough buyer.

Don't be surprised if you are given an **extra gift** after settling on a final price—a T-shirt, piece of inexpensive jewelry, a handicraft, or postcard. This may or may not indicate you paid too much for the item you purchased. Accept it even though you may neither need it or want it. You can always re-gift it further down the road if you don't want to carry it home.

Be sure to do comparison shopping before making any purchases. Since many shops carry similar items, and they are located near each other, it's relatively easy to compare prices for similar items. For example, we found an attractive antique bird teapot in one shop with an initial asking price of US$2,000.

We found the identical pot in another shop for US$950. The first shop was unwilling to bargain much (claimed the item was on consignment and the owner difficult to reach) whereas the second shop would have discounted the pot by 30 percent. In addition, the pot was not as old as the first shop claimed (in the end, they

really didn't know much about it). The lesson learned here was clear: don't take the first explanation and quoted price as indications of the true value of an item; shop around to get a sense of "the going rate" before bargaining for a final price.

The exception to this rational "shop around for comparative prices" rule is when you find an item you absolutely love but decide to look elsewhere for the same item at a cheaper price. You would be distressed if, after having no luck in "looking around," you came back to the first shop and found the item had been sold. In this situation, shopping around to gain a price advantage becomes a form of buyer's remorse when it results in missing out on acquiring something you really love. This has happened to us on more than one occasion and we've regretted it ever since. Hindsight told us we should have quickly tested our bargaining skills (tried to get the best deal we could) and then bought the item before leaving the shop. Such shopping experiences also warn us not to fall in love when shopping—such material love can be costly!

While shopkeepers tend to be relatively honest, always be skeptical of claims of authenticity. Many shopkeepers may not be as knowledgeable about their products as they claim. The top shops, many of which we feature below, tend to be the most knowledgeable since many of them also are operated by their owners.

One final buying tip for visitors interested in buying the best quality items available in the shops of Yemen. Sometimes the really good quality arts, crafts, antiques, and jewelry may be kept in a separate room and drawer or encased behind the counter. If you indicate that you are interested in the best-quality items, the merchant may direct you to a back or side room, pull out a special drawer, or present you with a box or bag of the "really good stuff." For example, if you are interested in buying a jambiya, the merchant will initially show you all the similar US$50 to US$300 ones hanging on the walls or displayed behind glass counters, which are appropriate for most tourists. However, if you indicate you're interested in something very special, the merchant may go into a back room and open a special drawer where he keeps his antique US$1,500, $5,000, and $20,000+ daggers, which appeal to serious collectors. In other words, assume that many shops have another level of products that will not become apparent unless you indicate an interest in seeing the best quality items.

Where to Shop

Within Sana'a, the best places to shop are the shops and stalls in and around **Souk al-Milh** and the shopping arcade in the **Moevenpick Hotel**. The city also has a few shopping malls (Sana'a Mall on Ring Road and Libyan Centre on al-Jazaar Street), but these are of most interest to local residents in search of relatively uninspired clothes and household goods. The really good stuff for visitors is found in Souk al-Milh and the Moevenpick Hotel.

Souk al-Milh

As noted earlier, **Souk al-Milh** (Salt Market) is the highlight of any visit to the Old City. Despite its name, there's very little salt to be

found in this comprehensive consumer and handicraft market. An ancient market that has nicely evolved into the 21st century for both local residents and tourists, this is first and foremost a local consumer market and only secondarily one that caters to tourists. Both buying groups coexist nicely in what is basically an authentic Yemeni market. Indeed, you can spend several hours exploring the many stalls and shops along the crowded maze of streets and lanes that define this fascinating market. It's both a buyer's and photographer's paradise.

You may want to explore this area with the assistance of a guide. Since Yemeni guides are not known for taking commissions from shops (most claim it's against their Islamic values to take advantage of others), they will generally try to take you to the best places.

The fastest way to get to this market is via Bab Al-Yemen on the southern section of the Old City walls. From here walk directly north for about five minutes and you'll be in the heart of the market.

The first thing you need to know about this market is that it is still organized by specialty products and **submarkets**—firewood market, blacksmith market, silver and gold market, brassware market, spice market, raisin market, carpet market, salt market, caps market, grain market, coffee husk market, jambiya market, handicraft market, cloth and silk market, and *qat* market. If you're interested in jewelry, head for all the shops that congregate in the gold and silver (jewelry) submarkets. Nearby you'll also find hundreds of small shops and stalls offering a wide selection of handicrafts, including many antiques. The jambiya market (Souk al-Janabi) is jam-packed with shops and stalls offering a wide range of locally crafted jambiyas, al-though collectors should head to the handicraft and jewelry sections to look for antique jambiyas. However, at times the specialty sections may merge into more general consumer goods. The raisin market (Souk al-Zabeeb) is a fascinating place to sample 15 varieties of raisins stacked high in storage bags.

The best way to explore this market is to simply wander around by foot for a few hours. In so doing, you'll have many serendipitous experiences along the way that make this market such a rewarding visual, cultural, and buying experience. While this market operates all day, it begins transforming itself by mid-afternoon with the arrival of the daily male *qat* chewing ritual. Early in afternoon, for example, you'll most likely encounter the crowded lanes of the noisy *qat* market where men with puffed cheeks busily examine and purchase bags full of fresh *qat* to satisfy their daily chewing addiction, which usually ends their already limited productivity by mid-afternoon. Indeed, by 4pm many of these men have chewed themselves into a low-level narcotic buzz and are happily socializing with other men over food and drink.

The sights and sounds of this place are unforgettable as you observe the locals going about their daily shopping. You'll occasionally see a few tourists, but for the most part you will be alone among the very friendly and expressive locals. At the same time, you'll want to stop and visit several of our recommended shops, such as Ali Ba Ba's Jewellery, Al-Kelabi, World Friend, Al-Ra'ae Jewelrils, Konouz Chamdan, Bab Al-Yemen Gallery, National Art Center, and Abu Imad Storets, which are profiled below.

Moevenpick Hotel

You also should visit the shopping arcade at the **Moevenpick Hotel**, which is the city's most luxurious hotel. There's one shop here that offers a fine collection of arts and antiques—World Friend. This is actually a branch of the main shop, which is located in the heart of the Old City. Somewhat pricey, nonetheless, serious collectors will want to visit both shops to see a real difference between handicrafts and antiques, which is not always apparent in the many market shops.

Nearby Towns and Villages

Outside Sana'a you'll find a few towns and villages offering some interesting shopping experiences. In fact, you should spend at least one day exploring a few towns and villages nearby Sana'a for sightseeing and shopping. Since all are conveniently reached within one hour by 4WD (usually an air-conditioned Toyota Land Cruiser) from Sana'a, it's not necessary to stay overnight in these places unless you seek a cultural experience, which might be more rewarding in by staying in a *funduq* in Old Sana'a (see the Accommodations section below). Hope for good weather since all of these towns and villages are connected via narrow dirt roads that are either muddy or dusty, depending on the weather conditions.

Al Rawdah Market

Just eight kilometers north of the city center is the town of Al Rawdah. If you're in Sana'a on a Sunday, be sure to visit the **Al Rawdah Market**, which is open from 7am to 12noon. The best time to visit is between 9am and 11am. Primarily operated by women, this bustling open-air market, jam-packed with pickup trucks filled with animals and produce, offers everything from household goods and fresh tomatoes

 and potatoes to spices, henna, and live chickens and goats. While you may not find much to buy here, the market experience itself is well worth the visit. It's a great opportunity to interact with the locals as well as take many wonderful photos of very accommodating people. Indeed, everyone seems to want to have their photo taken, including some veiled women who normally protest attempts to take their photos! While in this town, try to get a glimpse of the famous old mosque.

Thula

One of the best places for shopping is the aging fortress town of **Thula** (also spelled "Thilla"). Dating from the 11th century AD, this town of approximately 9,000 people welcomes visitors to spend some money in its many shops, which are organized for the tourist trade. Popular with visitors, Thula is noted for its well-preserved walls, aqueducts, narrow streets, imposing tower-houses, Jewish history, beggars, enterprising children, and numerous small handicraft and antique shops.

Indeed, Thula is known as the "shopping village" because of its nearly 25 small shops operated by friendly yet aggressive merchants who try to persuade visitors to "just come in and look" at their wares. Since most of the shops offer the same product mix (shawls, boxes, guns, pots, jewelry, daggers, alabaster lamps, Jewish crafted items, hanging lanterns, carpets), you can easily do comparative shopping to make sure you're not paying inflated tourist prices, which you surely will if you don't bargain. In fact, many shops will give you a 50-percent discount (*"What price you give me?"*) if you bargain aggressively (*"You bargain like a Bedouin!"*). Just don't buy at the first place you visit nor accept the first asking price until you've had a chance to look around and bargain for the true value of items. Remember, there are at least two dozen shops in this small town, all found along one circular route as you walk through the town, and these are very street-savvy merchants who are used to handling wealthy tourists. Prices seem to get better the farther you walk along the narrow cobblestone pathways and peek inside the tiny shops without buying.

Don't be surprised if some enterprising young man attaches himself to you and constantly pesters you to visit his shop. You'll have difficulty shaking him, unless you buy from him. Just ignore him and move on to other shops.

By no means should you assume this is a town of tourist kitsch shops. Among all the shops, you may find a few treasures worth acquiring. Indeed, some good antiques can be found here if you spend the time digging through the tiny shops. All totaled, you should be able to shop this town within 60 to 90 minutes.

Wadi Dhahr

Located 14 kilometers (9 miles) northwest of central Sana'a, **Wadi Dhahr** is one of the most popular tourist destinations for both locals and international visitors—a leisurely 30-minute drive from the city. This place is known for its iconic five-story tower-house, Dar al-Hajar or "Palace of the Rock," built on top of an imposing boulder. Most visitors come here to tour the multi-story building and view the surrounding mountains and valley. If you visit Friday morning (9am to 12noon) you'll be able to watch the ceremonial music and dance performance for Yemeni weddings.

One arts and crafts shop adjacent to the parking area monopolizes the Wadi Dhahr's shopping scene—**Daral Hagar Antique Shop**, which also functions as the Al-Dar Travel and Tourism (Tel. 382113 or 711617913). A one-stop tourist shop, it includes two rooms filled with silver boxes, jewelry, daggers, pots, belts, postcards, and T-shirts—everything tourists seem to need and want. While you may be able to negotiate a small discount, prices are not particularly flexible. The shop does include some good quality antique silver boxes and related items.

Shibam

Shibam, which is located 35 kilometers (22 miles) northwest of Sana'a, should not be confused with the famous "Manhattan of the desert" Shibam, a UNESCO World Heritage site and architectural masterpiece located nearly 500 kilometers (310 miles) east of Sana'a. The Shibam near Sana'a is located at the base of a rugged mountain filled with caves and laced with a trail that takes ambitious trekkers to the top where they enter the intriguing town of Kawkaban. A somewhat charming but embarrassingly trashy town in need of a good community clean up and some civic pride, Shibam is especially noted for its lively **Friday market** that draws villagers from all over the region. While you may not purchase anything here, since much of is local produce and animals and unappetizing looking foodstuffs, the market experience is interesting and offers some great photo opportunities.

Many visitors also stop in Shibam for a traditional and inexpensive (YR1,000) Yemeni lunch at the **Hamida Restaurant**, which is operated by the hard-working Madame Hamida and her daughters who manage to put on a big buffet spread for the many guests that make this an obligatory stop during their visit to Shibam.

Kawkaban

Kawkaban is a striking village perched on top of a butte overlooking Shibam. More noted for its location than its shopping or sights, Kawkaban is well worth visiting just for the panoramic views. As you approach this crumbling 700-year old village, you'll probably be met by excited boys and girls quickly pushing wheelbarrows full of handicrafts in your direction—truly mobile businesses! Not surprisingly, you represent potential new economic activity for this poor village. Shopping here is an interesting activity centered on whatever appears in the roving wheelbarrows. Look for lots of Bedouin jewelry and other handcrafted items that you may neither need nor want! This is the only place in Yemen where you can shop from a wheelbarrow while overlooking an awesome valley spotted with towns and villages—a truly breathtaking shopping experience!

Best Shops in Sana'a

While you will find many excellent shops by just wandering on your own along the streets and lanes of Souk al-Milh in the Old City, you may want to the visit the following shops which we found to be especially worthwhile. In many cases, someone in the shop spoke English. Since many of these shops do not have street addresses, you may need a guide to locate them for you:

❑ **World Friend:** *Old Silver Market of Old Sana'a (Tel. 291483, sadiqalalam@y.net.ye) and the shopping arcade of the Moevenpick Hotel (Tel. 545930, Rubaih@yemen.net.ye).* If you visit only one antique and handicraft shop in Yemen, make sure it's this one. This shop includes two very different locations and shopping experiences. The main shop is located in the heart of the silver market and next door to Al-Kelabi, another excellent jewelry and antique shop. This well established and reputable shop offers one of the best collections of quality arts, crafts, and antiques. Many locals come here to sell their heir-

looms and the owners travel to the countryside to source for quality pieces. The shop also designs jewelry and will custom-make pieces upon request. The market shop in the Old City includes a small back room on the right with some of the best quality items. Look for old chests, shields, silver jewelry, candle holders, and oil lamps. The shop also offers one of the best collections of collectible jambiya, including one that sells for US $50,000. Be sure to check out the drawers filled with jewelry, especially pearls and coral. The Moevenpick

Hotel shop showcases some of World Friend's best quality pieces. Unlike the rather crowded and cluttered market shop, the hotel shop includes more space and attractive displays. If you're looking for something very special, make sure you visit World Friend's two shops. Prices are somewhat high (we paid, for example, US$600 for an antique shield in Muscat, Oman, which for a similar quality piece had an initial asking price of US$2,200 in this shop; we also bought a copper candle holder in the market for US$40 and an apparently similar one here had an initial asking price of US$230). Bargaining is in order for both shops.

❑ **Al-Kelabi:** *Al-Mekhlas Market, Old Sana'a, Tel. 281805 or 777799196, alkelabiantiques@hotmail.com.* Located next to World Friend in the silver market of the Old City, this small shop includes a good collection of antique jewelry, and jambiyas, as well as handicrafts, including boxes from both Yemen and Morocco.

❑ **Ali Ba Ba's Jewellery:** *Al Malh Market, Tel. 711685677.* This large corner shop offers a good selection of old and new silver jewelry, especially hammered bracelets using local designs. Also look for pearls, coral, stones, daggers, boxes, lamps, and pots. Very friendly and knowledgeable service. Accepts credit cards.

❑ **Bab Al-Yemen Gallery:** *Bab Al-Yemen, Old Sana'a, Tel. 481948 or 733262972, www.nizar-art.com.* Ideally located at the Old City's major gate, Bab Al-Yemen, this two-level gallery is operated by local contemporary artist Mazher Nizar (mazher.nizar@y.net.ye) whose artistic style has been greatly influenced through his studies and work with the "Kolkutta Modern Art Group" in Calcutta, India. The gallery includes several small rooms filled with framed oils/acrylics and watercolors, prints, books, and postcards. Many of the paintings depict major city sights and veiled women along with several abstract paintings. Most unframed prints cost around US$20. One of the added advantages of visiting this shop is to gain access to the top of the wall and gate through the second floor. From here you get one of the best views of both the Old and New City, especially the pedestrian and vehicular traffic on both sides of the wall. You can easily spend a half hour here taking photos and observing the fascinating activities below. Be sure to visit the gallery's website, which includes photos of the gallery, examples of the art works, and information on purchasing the art.

❑ **Al-Ra'ae Jewelrils:** *Al-Mahl Market, Tel. 286433 or 77906328.* This popular gold shop, located near both World Friend and Al-Kelabi antique shops, includes two adjacent jewelry shops. Offers some nicely crafted pendants and broaches crafted in the form of jambiyas. If you're looking for a unique piece of gold jewelry representing Yemen, check out this shop.

❑ **Konouz Chamdan:** *Allgeia Square Zabarah Street, Tel. 286344 or 733007770.* This rather large shop offers a good selection of antique silver, jambiyas, jewelry, collapsible lamps, silver boxes, swords, chests, and candle stands. Includes a large section of jambiyas framed for hanging on the wall.

❑ **National Art Center:** *Samsarat Al-Mansurah, Tel. 296246 or 734137949, Al-Futaih@y.net.ye*. This private gallery, which showcases the works of local artist Fuad al-Futaih and a few other artists, includes two floors of paintings, prints, books, and postcards. The second floor includes temporary exhibitions.

❑ **Abu Imad Storets:** *Tel. 485495, Kelgaramani@yahoo.ec.uk*. Located in the fourth block to the left from Bab Al-Yemen, this relatively new (here since 2006) but large shop includes a nice collection of antiques and handicrafts. Look for jambiya, jewelry, silver chests, lanterns, furniture, boxes, and oil lamps.

❑ **Sheba Art Gallery:** Located on the second floor of a very large and old three-story handicraft emporium— the National Handicrafts Training Center—this sleepy gallery includes two rooms of drawings and watercolors. Most originals in the first room sell for around US$80; copies cost US$5-15. The paintings of city and people scenes in the second room go for between US$10 and US$40. Includes prints, post- cards, and velvet paintings.

❑ **Hamza Exhibition for Olsted:** This small shop includes a good collection of reasonably priced silver boxes, bowls, and candle holders.

❑ **National Women's Center for Development** *(Tel. 482-454)* and **Hope in Their Hands** *(Tel. 482455)*. *Samsarat al-Hallaqah*. Located in the same building, both of these handicraft shops operate as nonprofit organizations supporting the work of Yemeni women who are widowed or divorced.

Accommodations

The best accommodations in Sana'a are found at the relatively new five-star Moevenpick Hotel. After this opulent Saudi property, the two other so-called five-star hotels—Sheraton and Sheba—are in a different class of their own. Nonetheless, all of these properties offer adequate accommodations and excellent service. Most of the hotels in the Old City are old houses or mansions that have been converted into hotels. Rooms may be small and the climb to the top floor arduous.

New Sana'a

Five-Star Hotels

❑ **Moevenpick Hotel Sana'a:** *Berlin Street, Dhahr Hemyer, Sana'a, Yemen (P.O. Box 5111), Tel: 967-1-546666, Fax 967-1-546000. E-mail:* hotel.sanaa@moevenpick.com. *Website:* www.moevenpick-hotels. com. Since the opening of the Moevenpick, this Saudi-owned property has received rave reviews. Even the embassy staff in Washington were talking about it when we went to apply for our visa. The newest luxury hotel (and the largest) in the city boasts 338 guestrooms, including 39 suites, all elegantly decorated in contemporary style. The deluxe and executive guestrooms offer a choice of twin beds or a king-sized bed; suites are furnished with a king bed. Guestrooms include up-to-date offerings for the business traveler from modem data ports to a special safe for your laptop. Bathrooms are spacious and offer the expected amenities from hair dryer to bathrobes. With the hotel situated on a hill (about seven minutes from the city center) overlooking the town, guestrooms offer panoramic views of the city or the surrounding mountains. Guestrooms on the executive floor come with complimentary buffet breakfast, snacks, and beverages as well as a business corner.

Seven food and beverage outlets provide plenty of choices for hotel guests and city residents alike. The *Moevenpick All Day Restaurant* is recognized for the best breakfast buffet in Sana'a. Lunch and dinner utilize multiple open-buffet counters and one can select from a la carte menu or the buffet. A Friday brunch is also offered. *Dar Fez*, considered by many to be the best modern Moroccan restaurant in Yemen, serves traditional Moroccan cuisine. The *Panorama Lobby Bar*, serving pastries, coffee, tea, and light snacks, is a favorite meeting place for hotel guests and locals alike. *Horse Shoe Night Club* is open until 3:00am with nightly entertainment, and *Al Fresco* at the pool and garden is a favorite place for the shisha—also known as a hookah or hubbly bubbly— a waterpipe used for smoking flavored tobacco. The *Gourmet Shop* serves cakes, pastries, and regional specialties.

A spa, hairdresser, and gymnasium featuring cardiovascular and weight training equipment, sauna and steam rooms, Jacuzzi, squash court, and indoor and outdoor swimming pools are available on the premises. A nice antique shop (World Friend) in the arcade on the lower level offers quality and pricey pieces. Business Center. Conference/Banquet facilities are the largest in Sana'a.

❑ **Sheraton Sana'a Hotel**: *Berlin Street, Sana'a, Yemen (P.O. Box 2467), Tel. 967-1-237500, Fax 967-1-237405. E-mail:* reservations. sanaa.yemen@sheraton.com. *Website:* www.sheraton.com/sanaa. The Sheraton Sana'a is located just down the street from the Moevenpick and, until the Moevenpick's opening, was considered the best hotel in town. The Sheraton still offers luxury to its guests with its 255 guestrooms and 18 suites. New rooms on the executive floors offer additional privileges including private check-in/out in the executive lounge, upgraded amenities in guestrooms and bath, complimentary breakfast in the executive lounge, use of private meeting room facilities, and high-speed and wireless Internet connection. Several dining and entertainment venues include the *Tandoor Restaurant* serving Indian cuisine, *Chinese Palace Restaurant* offering traditional Chinese fare, and *Waves Pool Bar & Restaurant* providing a variety of snacks and beverages. *Broadway at Sheraton Bar* overlooking the city skyline and *The Tent/ Night Club* round out the choices. Fitness Center; Business Center: Conference/ Banquet Facilities.

❏ **Sheba Hotel:** *Ali Abdul Moghni Street, Tel. 967-1-272372, Fax 967-1-274129. E-mail: info@ShebaHotel.com. Website: www.shebahotel.com.* Until December 31, 2007, this hotel was known as the Taj Sheba Hotel, which was part of the Taj Resorts and Palaces chain based in India. Now locally owned and operated, this hotel has in the past received mixed reviews—not quite five-star quality compared to the Moevenpick and Sheraton properties. It includes 186 rooms along with all the amenities expected of five-star properties. Located near Tahreer Square on the western edge of the city, it's nicely situated next to the Old City (.5 kilometers from Bab Al-Yemen).

Three—and Four-Star Hotels

❏ **Sana'a International Hotel:** *Western 60's Street, P.O. Box 5501, Tel. 967-1-400666, Fax 967-1-400675. E-mail: info@sanaainterhotel.com. Website: www.sanaainterhotel.com.* A relatively nice hotel that offers 80 rooms on the two floors of the Azal Hospital.

❏ **Mercure San'a Al Saeed:** *Al-Zubairi Street, P.O. Box 5270, Tel. 967-1-212544, Fax 967-1-212487. E-mail: mercure_sanaa@y.net.ye. Website: www.yemenbusiness.net/Mercure-Sanaa.* Includes 70 rooms and a few restaurants.

❏ **Al Yamama Palace Suites:** *Tunis Street, Tel. 967-1-236230. E-mail: alyamama.com@y.net.ye. Website: www.yamama-palace.com.* Offers 30 rooms, including several two-bedroom suites, some with kitchens. Located near the airport.

❏ **Hilltown Hotel:** *Tahreer Square. Tel. 967-1-278426, Fax 967-1-278427.* Offer 65 spacious rooms just off Tahreer Square. A bit worn but good location.

Old Sana'a and the Funduq Experience

Old Sana'a is a great place to stay if you want to get a real sense of the Old City both day and night. However, don't expect normal hotel accommodations here. No drive-up entrance, swimming pool, exercise facilities, or major restaurants. These are basically bed and breakfast accommodations with lots of Old World "charm." They are especially popular with budget travelers in search of cheap sleeps and eats.

Most places designated as hotels in the Old City are known as *funduq*—traditional tower-houses or mansions converted into hotels with a lobby on the first level, rooms on the second to sixth floors, and a sitting or meeting room (*mafraj*) and restaurant at the top. Plan to climb all five to six floors to the top for breakfast. These are good places to get a nice overview of the city from the top floor. But you may find the accommodations limiting—small rooms, few furnishings (some with mattress on the floor), shared baths, and no air-conditioning. These places are at best clean, spartan, friendly, charming, and inexpensive. The closest to luxurious accommodations in this form is the Italian-run Burj Al Salam Hotel, which also includes an elevator and a separate restaurant popular with outsiders!

❑ **Burj Al Salam Hotel:** *Harat Al Fulayhi Street, P.O. Box 2898, Sana'a, Tel. 967-1-483333, Fax 967-1-483330, Mobile 7122943888. Website: www.burjalsalam.com. E-mail: manager@burjalsalam.com.* Unquestionably the city's best funduq. Great location in the heart of Old Sana'a and a quality operation. Italian designed and operated. Includes nine floors with 45 rooms and an elevator. Includes a restaurant on the top floor with one of the best views of Sana'a as well as one of the city's best restaurants, *Walema Restaurant* (open for breakfast, lunch, and dinner). Prices range from US$50 (single) to US$200 (suite).

❑ **Arabia Felix:** *Avenue Saila Al-Jeila, Tel. 967-1-287-330, Fax 967-1-287426.* E-mail: *arabiafelix@y.net.ye*. Website: *http://arabiafelix .free.fr*. Offers 44 rooms ranging in price from US$22 (single) to US$80 (suite) plus 10-percent service charge. Includes a popular garden restaurant that primarily caters to tourists.

❑ **Sultan Palace Hotel**: *Golden Street, Tel. 967-1-273766, Fax 967-1-276175.* E-mail: *sultanpalacehotel@yahoo.com*. Website: *www.al-bab.com/sultanpalace*. Popular with backpackers—rough and cheap.

❑ **Golden Daar Tourist Hotel and Restaurant:** *P.O. Box 4269, Sana'a.* E-mail: *goldendar@y.net.ye*. Basically a backpacker's hotel with an excellent location and view. Includes very basic small rooms, with some shared baths.

Food and Restaurants

Yemeni food may or may not appeal to your culinary senses. However, many visitors are pleasantly surprised and enjoy the local cuisine. Typical meats are lamb, fish, and chicken, which are usually grilled or barbecued. *Saltah* is a Yemeni staple—a stew mixture of meat broth and vegetables topped off with a froth of fenugreek and served in a heated stone bowl and eaten with flatbread. Other dishes include *fuul* (fava beans with onions, tomatoes, and spices), grilled fish and chicken, fried eggplant, and hummus served with traditional freshly baked Arabic bread (*khaboos*). Deserts may include sweet pastries drizzled with Yemeni honey.

The main meal of the day is usually lunch, which takes place from 11:30am to 1:30pm.

Many of the city's best restaurants are located in the top hotels as well as along Hadda Street. The following restaurants, which cater to Westerners, are recommended for travelers:

❑ **Dar Fez:** *Hotel Sana'a, Berlin Street, Dahr Hemyer district. Tel. 546666. Website: www.moevenpick-hotels.com.* Considered by many to be the best modern Moroccan restaurant in Yemen, this fine restaurant serves traditional Moroccan cuisine.

❑ **Al Fakher:** *Hadda Street, 11:30am to 3:30pm and 7-10:30pm.* One of the most popular Yemeni restaurants for a good selection of Yemeni specialties.

❑ **Al-Shaibani Modern Restaurant:** *Hadda Street, Tel. 440920. 6-10:30am, 11:30am-3:30pm, and 7-10:30pm.* This famous restaurant is known for its excellent Yemeni dishes.

❑ **Arabia Felix Hotel Restaurant:** *Al-Sailah Street, Tel. 287330.* A popular courtyard restaurant frequented by tour groups.

❑ **Al-Fanoos:** *Located off Hadda Street, Tel. 441042. Hours vary but usually 11:30am to 3:30pm and 7-11:30pm.* A popular Lebanese restaurant with both indoor and outdoor seating.

❑ **Walema Restaurant:** *Burj Al Salam Hotel, Old City, Sana'a, Tel. 483333 or 7122943888. Website: www.burjalsalam.com.* This Italian-inspired restaurant is open for breakfast, lunch, and dinner.

Both the Moevenpick and Sheraton hotels have restaurants serving European food.

Entertainment

Alcohol, music, and dancing—three great decadent activities associated with non-Muslims—are hard to find in Yemen. Nonetheless, Yemen offers something, including female entertainers, for everyone. Even some Muslim men from Saudi Arabia and other Gulf States lose their inhibitions in Sana'a's and Aden's seedy night spots. But you'll have to work at finding such places, which tend to keep a low profile.

Once the sun sets over Sana'a, there's not much to do beyond some relatively sedate entertainment establishments centered in the bars and restaurants of the three major hotels—Moevenpick, Sheraton, and Sheba—and a few restaurants and coffee shops serving tea and shisha (waterpipe).

Sana'a has two private membership-only recreational clubs, which you may be able to visit with a friend—**The British Club** (Hadda Street) and **The Officers Club** (Zubayri Street).

Sana'a also boasts two bars and nightclubs—the relatively classy **Horseshoe Nightclub and Bar** (Moevenpick Hotel), which primarily serves drinks, and the somewhat seedy **Russia Club** (located within the Tourist City compound across from the U.S. Embassy) that includes drinks, music, and dancing.

The southern port city of Aden has more entertainment (The Sailor's Club) and seedy nightlife, but in both places the nightlife is largely forgettable. You may find your evening routines in Sana'a center around dinner and watching CNN or BBC in your hotel room. This is always a good excuse to start early the next morning in exploring areas outside Sana'a.

Enjoying Your Stay

A recently commissioned tourist guide by the Yemen Tourist Promotion Board identifies 101 things visitors can do during their stay in Yemen. We've distilled many of these "to do" items along with our own recommendations as well as organized them by various regions into 67 things to see and do in Yemen. As such, this checklist should give you a quick overview of the many places to visit and things to do in Yemen. Some we've already covered for Sana'a and nearby towns and villages, but they are worth repeating in this checklist format.

We've put red flags on two popular destinations—Marib in the east (150 kilometers from Sana'a) and Sa'ada in the north (240 kilometers from Sana'a)—which have experienced turbulence in recent years, including the deaths of several tourists. However tempting to visit, these places should be approached with caution by smart travelers.

Within Sana'a

Sana'a's many highlights include the following:

❑ Make a grand entrance through the gates of Old Sana'a, especially **Bab Al-Yemen**. Stop to take photos and absorb all the local commercial activity.

❑ Visit the cavernous **art gallery and studio of Mazher Nizer** (www.nizar-art.com) to appreciate the watercolors of this artist's nearby hometown, Al Hajjarah.

❑ Sample the **raisin juice** served near Bab Al-Yemen.

❑ Stop at a fresh juice stall to sample the lime or lemon juice. But be sure to request that your drink be made with bottled water. These juice stalls also are found in many places outside Sana'a.

❑ Stroll through the less congested western gate, **Bab Al-Sabah**, and enjoy a leisurely walk through the residential and commercial sections of the Old City.

❑ Visit the recently restored **National Museum** (Tel. 271696, Ali Abdul Mogni Street, 9am-12:30pm, Saturday through Thursday, admission of YR500), which is reputed to be the largest such museum on the Arabian Peninsula.

❑ Observe the **blindfolded camel** walking in circles as it turns the sesame mill in the Old City.

❑ Watch the *qat* chewers go through their daily ritual of buying fresh *qat* (best crop comes from Wadi Dhahr) and consuming it in great abandonment during the afternoon, from noon to sunset. A male drug tradition, this ritual occurs all over Yemen. Some male visitors decide to go native and try chewing the *qat*. Try it once and it may be enough. Just don't swallow the stuff!

❑ Sample the ***mada'a***—the Yemeni waterpipe which is known as hubbly-bubbly or shisha elsewhere in the Middle East and Europe. Try the apricot, apple, peppermint, strawberry, or honey tobacco. The *mada'a* is found in many places throughout Yemen.

❑ Look for the tie-dyed *muckmug*, the colorful **veils** worn by Sana'ani women, in the Souq Al-Milh. Some visitors use them as tablecloths back home.

❑ Women may want to have their hands and feet decorated in the traditional **henna** designs (*naqsh*), which are used at weddings to decorate the bride. Your hotel may be able to arrange for you to see a henna artist.

❑ Pick up some **frankincense** as souvenir of Yemen. But consider also buying the frankincense burner (*mabkhara*), which is available in wood, copper, and silver.

❑ Check out Yemeni **musical instruments** (*oud, lute, mismar,* and drums) as well as acquire some tapes or CDs of Yemeni music, which include many Arabic love ballads.

❑ Look for the intricately woven and colorful round **baskets** produced by Jewish women in Sa'ada.

❑ Have a cup of **Yemeni-style coffee**, known as *qishr*. It's an infusion of coffee husks flavored with cinnamon, cardamon, and ginger.

The **Arabic coffee** called *gahwa*, a lighter mix of roasted coffee beans with cardamon, saffron, and/or a pinch of rosewater, is also worth trying.

❑ Learn about Yemen's gun culture and turbulent military history by visiting the **Military Museum** (Tel. 276635, Gamal Abdul Hasser Street, 9am-1:30pm, 3-8pm, Saturday through Wednesday, and 3-7pm, Thursday and Friday, YR200 admission fee).

❑ Walk around the great **walls** of Sana'a, which are under restoration, as well as visit the lively **markets** near the two remaining gates—Bab Al-Yemen and Bab Al-Sabah.

❑ Marvel at the grand exterior of the ancient **Great Mosque** (Al Jami' Al Kabir) in the Old City. Non-Muslims might try to sneak a peek of the interior. Try to find a few of the additional 100+ mosques in the city.

❑ Visit the **Museum of Arts and Crafts** in Dar Al Shuke (House of Gratitude), just off Tahrir Square in Sana'a (Tel. 271648, Midan at-Tahrir, 8am-12noon and 3-5:30pm, Saturday through Wednesday, YR500 admission fee).

❑ Be one of the few people to **visit the mummies** at the small museum at the Old University (open 9am-1pm every day except Friday—you may need to ask for the key!).

❑ Try the **grilled stuffed fish** with spices on bread and the traditional dessert of bananas dripped in Yemeni honey at **Al-Shaibani Modern Restaurant** (Hadda Street in front of Al Komain center, Tel. 440920).

❑ Enjoy lunch in a traditional courtyard at the **Arabia Felix Hotel** (Tel. 287330).

❑ Relax in the **heated swimming pool** at the Sheba Hotel—it charges a small fee for outside guests.

❑ Enjoy a picture-perfect **view of the city** from a hotel roof or *'mafraj'* (upstairs sitting room), from where you can see more than 100 mosques and their minarets against the background of ancient tower-houses and mountains.

❑ Feast on *saltah* before trying the *qat*.

❑ Make a guest appearance at a **Yemeni wedding**, which usually takes place on Thursday and Sunday nights in the Old City.

❑ Visit the **gardens** (Dar Al Hamad) at Bir Al Azab near Tahrir Square.

Nearby Sana'a

We also recommend seeing and doing the following things near Sana'a, which should involve no more than a one-hour drive:

❑ Enter the gates of the deserted village of **Bayt Baws**, a former Jewish settlement located south of Sana'a.

❑ **Visit Wadi Dhahr** on a Friday morning (10am-12noon) to see the bridegrooms congregate on a plateau overlooking the valley to celebrate their marriages by performing dagger dances.

❑ Tour the iconic **Rock Palace** (Dar Al Hajar) at Wadi Dhahr, which was built by Iman Yayha as a summer resident in the 1930s and is now a museum.

❑ Tour the fortified shopping village of **Thula** with the assistance of enterprising children who will take you shopping.

❑ Sample the local cuisine while dining on the floor of the *mafraj* at the popular **Hameda Hotel and Restaurant** in Shibam.

❑ From the base town of **Shibam**, make the steep one-hour walk (350 meters) up the mountain to **Kawkabam**, a village perched at the top of a plateau.

❑ View the valley from the butte-top village of **Kawkabam**, which can be reached by car.

North of Sana'a

This is one of Yemen's most troubled areas bordering on Saudi Arabia—a serious security problem which you need to approach with extreme caution if at all lest you get caught up in some real nasty local rebel activities (these are Hezbollah-type rebels, not your everyday variety kidnappers with local tribal grievances and who share Yemeni hospitality with their captives; these characters will kill you without a second thought!).

❑ Visit the ancient walled city of **Sa'ada**, the capital of the Za'idi state and perhaps the most conservative city (women beware of your attire) in Yemen. Located about 240 kilometers north of Sana'a, it's one of the few places where you will still find a community of Jewish silversmiths, which is currently under pressure by rebels to flee the area. It's also famous for its adobe architecture, completely enclosed wall (3.5 kilometers in length) with 52 defense towers and four gates, old mosque, the zaydism spiritual school of Yemeni Islamic philosophy, and lively arms market (Suq al-Talh). Be sure to check out the local security situation before visiting this sometimes troubled area. In fact, serious clashes between government and rebel forces within recent years have left several hundred dead and thousands of displaced local residents. Sa'ada is not ready for prime time tourism!

West and Southwest of Sana'a

If you head west and southwest of Sana'a, you'll soon reach the beaches along the Red Sea as well as one of Yemen's major port cities for fishing and commerce, Hodeidah (also spelled Al-Hudaydah). You'll also encounter some spectacular scenery and several fascinating fortified towns and villages.

❑ Visit the iconic 400-year-old **stone bridge** near the mountain village of Shihara, which spans a 300-meter gorge. One of the best photo opportunities in Yemen.

❑ Explore the mountaintop fortified village of **Al Hajjarh** near Manakha.

❑ View the **spectacular mountains and terraced fields** when traveling through the high (3,500 meters) Haraz mountains west of Sana'a on the way to Hodeidah, which overlooks the Red Sea.

❑ Visit the **fish market** at Hodeidah by 5:30am and watch the fresh catches come into this fishing port along the corniche.

❑ Visit the fabulous **Friday market at Bayt Al Faqih** (60 kilometers south of Hodeidah and 40 kilometers north of Zabid), which includes over 1,000 traders offering everything from food, animals, coffee, and locally produced Tihami handicrafts, textiles, and pottery—one of the largest such markets in Yemen.

❑ Explore the famous walled town of Zabid, a UNESCO World Heritage site, overlooking the Red Sea.

❑ Go beach hopping and swimming in the Red Sea along the many beaches (Al Faza, Al Jah, Al Khawkhah) south of Hodeidah.

South of Sana'a

Here lie the famous old cities and towns of Ta'izz, Al Mokha, Ibb, and Jiblah as well as Yemen's major port and economic center, Aden, which once (1950s) was the world's second largest port (thanks to British colonialism) after New York City.

❑ Drive to the top of Jebel Sabir for a panoramic view of the city of **Ta'izz** and stop for coffee in the village of Al Arus near the summit of this hill.

❑ Visit the famous **silver souq in Ta'izz** where you can pick up some of the best buys on silver in Yemen.

❑ Tour the **National Museum in Ta'izz**, once the luxurious residence of controversial Iman Ahmed who ruled parts of Yemen until his death in 1962, which resulted in a succession crisis for nearly eight years.

❑ For a specular view of Ta'izz in a luxurious setting, stay at the five-star **Sofitel** on a hill overlooking the city.

❑ Get a glimpse of the unveiled and colorfully dressed **Sabir women** working the *qat* fields and trading in the souqs of Ta'izz.

❑ Explore the famous coffee town of **Al Mokha**, once (18th century) the world's leading center for coffee production.

❑ Visit one of the most beautiful mosques in Yemen, the **Arwa mosque** in the small town of **Jiblah** (8 kilometers from Ibb, which is 50 kilometers north of Ta'izz), where non-Muslims are sometimes allowed to enter. The town was once the seat of power for one of Yemen's most admired rulers, Queen Sayyida Arwa.

❑ View the **lush green terraces** in Ibb district as well as the old fortified stone **town of Ibb**.

❑ Visit the historical port of **Aden** where you should tour the old Crater district with its 18 ancient cisterns (Aden Water Tanks or Cisterns of Taweela), souk, and Towers of Silence (funeral site of former Parsee community); Steamer Point; museums (National Museum of Antiquities, Ethnographic Museum, Military Museum); mosques; beaches; and sinful nightclubs/bars (try the popular yet seedy beachfront Sailor's Club, complete with music, dancing, liquor, and prostitutes).

❑ Enjoy the beautiful, unspoilt **Kanafa Beach**, which is only accessible by the sea from a motor launch in Aden.

East and Southeast of Sana'a

This area takes you to the important historical city of Marib, the port city of Al-Mukalla, and the desert towns of Shibam, Seiyun, and Tarim. There's lots of sand in this part of Yemen, which also encompasses the central desert region.

❑ Explore the ruins at the ancient city of **Marib**, one of the world's oldest towns and which is located only 150 kilometers (95 miles) east of Sana'a. However, be very cautious in planning a trip to this red flag area since it is the site (Queen of Sheba Temple) of the murders of seven Spanish tourists and two Yeminis in July 2007—all attributed to al-Qaeda suicide bombers. You may need an armed escort to visit here, which may be enough trouble to deter you from making the trip to this crumbling town of ill repute. You may want to make this a day trip since staying in Marib means being confined to your hotel because of security issues.

❑ Visit the flourishing port city of **Al-Mukalla** (800 kilometers or 500 miles southeast of Sana'a) on the Indian Ocean, which is famous for its fishing, mosques, and museums.

❑ Go **fishing for tuna** by hiring a motor launch from the Hadramawrt Hotel in the seaside town of **Al-Mukalla** and then proceed on to Al Burum, a one-hour journey.

❑ Visit the famous UNESCO World Heritage site of **Shibam**, located 800 kilometers (500 miles) east of Sana'a or 300 kilometers north of Al-Mukalla. This is a sleepy 2,000-year-old town (population 8,000) known as "the Manhattan of the desert" because of its famous architecture—imposing six- to eight-story tower-houses.

❑ Visit **Qasr Kaff**, the magnificent palace of the Kathiri Sultan, which is a museum in Seiyun. It's filled with displays on customs, agriculture, and cooking as well as showcases weapons, jewelry, and old photographs.

❑ Climb the **hills overlooking Shibam** to get a good view of this town's ancient skyscrapers. Just after 4pm is a great time to take **photos** from this vantage point.

❑ Tour the **tower-houses** in Shibam, which can go a high as 40 meters or eight floors. Ask some children to take you to their house—their mothers will be delighted to escort female visitors to the top and show them how they live.

❑ Drive to **Seiyun** (also spelled Sayun), which is located 25 kilometers east of Shibam, by way of the desert where you'll encounter beautiful sand dunes and perhaps have tea with the "bedu" (Bedouin) from whom you can buy their handmade jewelry.

❑ Stay at the beautiful mud brick **Al Hawta Palace Hotel** in Seiyun (Tel. 425013), which was designed and built by heritage conservation expert Marco Livadiotti.

❑ Visit the pilgrimage site (pre-Islamic tomb) of **Qubr Nabi Hud** (great grandson of Noah), which is located 85 kilometers east of Tarim (near Seiyun).

❑ Visit the pilgrimage site (tomb) of Ahmed Bin Isa Al Muhajir on the road between Seiyun and Tarim. Revered by both Shi'a and Sunni Muslims, he was a direct descendant of Ali (Prophet Mohammed's son-in law).

❑ Marvel at the 365 mosques—one for each day of the year—in the former religious teaching center of **Tarim**, which also boasts the tallest minaret in the Hadhramawt at Al Muhdhar mosque.

❑ View the many **mud brick palaces** that dot Tarim, including their fusion of Hadhrami, Southeast Asian, and colonial influences. This city once was a major trading center with India, Malaysia, and Indonesia.

❑ Visit **Wadi Do'an** (Hadhramawt) to acquire some of the world's best honey.

Island of Socotra

❑ Visit the fascinating island of **Socotra** (www.socotraisland.org), located nearly 400 kilometers off the southeast coast of Yemen. The unique flora (dragon's blood trees) and fauna of this island have earned it the reputation of being the Galapagos of the Arabian Peninsula. Since infrastructure is very basic for visitors, plan to do some camping and lots of hiking on this beautiful island that has yet to be discovered by many tourists.

Recommended Resources

The following books and websites are well worth reviewing as you plan your trip to Yemen:

Travel Guides/Companions

- *Oman, UAE, and Arabian Peninsula*, Lonely Planet, 2007
- *Yemen: The Bradt Travel Guide*, Daniel McLaughlin, 2007

History of Yemen

- *Arabia Felix: An Exploration of the Archaeological History of Yemen*, Alessandro de Maigret, 2002
- *A History of Modern Yemen*, Paul Dresch, 2000
- *A Tribal Order: Politics and Law in the Mountains of Yemen*, 2007

Travelogues on Yemen

- *Motoring With Mohammed*, Eric Hansen, 1991
- *The Southern Gates of Arabia: The Journey in the Hadhramaut*, Freya Stark and Jane Geniesse, 2002
- *Yemen: The Unknown Arabia*, Tim Mackintosh-Smith, 2000
- *Yemen: Travels in Dictionary Land*, Tim Mackintosh-Smith, 1997

Pictorial Books on Yemen

- *Queen of Sheba: Treasures From Ancient Yemen*, St. John Simpson (ed.), 2002
- *Yemen: Jewel of Arabia*, Charles and Patricia Aithie, 2007

Magazines
(primarily available in Yemen)

- *Arabia Felix*
- *Yemen Today*

Newspapers

- Yemen Daily   www.yemendaily.com
- Yemen Observer   www.yobserver.com
- Yemen Times   http://yementimes.com

Websites

In addition to the many websites identified earlier for tour companies in Yemen, visit these useful sites:

- www.al-bab.com/bys
- www.al-bab.com/yemen
- www.aiys.org
- www.lonelyplanet.com/worldguide/yemen
- www.socotraisland.org
- http://wikitravel.org/en/Yemen
- www.yemen-handicraft.com
- www.yementourism.com

Index

The Authors

WINSTON CHURCHILL put it best—*"My needs are very simple—I simply want the best of everything."* Indeed, his attitude on life is well and alive among many of today's travelers. With limited time, careful budgeting, and a sense of adventure, many people seek both quality and value as they search for the best of the best.

Ron and Caryl Krannich, Ph.D.s, discovered this fact of travel life 25 years ago when they were living and working in Thailand as consultants with the Office of the Prime Minister. Former university professors and specialists on Southeast Asia, they discovered what they really loved to do—shop for quality arts, antiques, and home decorative items—was not well represented in most travel guides, which primarily focused on sightseeing, hotels, and restaurants. While some guidebooks included a small section on shopping, they only listed types of products and names and addresses of a few shops, many of questionable quality. And budget guides simply avoided quality shopping altogether, as if shopping was a travel sin!

The Krannichs knew there was much more to travel than what was represented in travel guides. Avid collectors of Asian, South Pacific,

Middle Eastern, African, and Latin American arts, antiques, and home decorative items, they learned long ago that one of the best ways to learn about another culture and meet its talented artists and craftspeople was by shopping for local products. In so doing, they also acquired many wonderful products, met many interesting and talented individuals, and helped support the development of local arts and crafts.

But they quickly learned shopping in many countries was very different from shopping in North America and Europe. In the West, merchants nicely display items, identify prices, and periodically run sales. At the same time, shoppers in the West can easily do comparative shopping, watch for sales, and trust quality and delivery; they even have consumer protection! Americans and Europeans in other parts of the world face shopping cultures based on different principles. Like a fish out of water, they make many mistakes: don't know how to bargain, avoid purchasing large items because they don't understand shipping, and are frequent victims of scams and rip-offs, especially in the case of gems and jewelry. To shop a country right, travelers need to know how to find quality products, bargain for the best prices, avoid scams, and ship their purchases with ease. What they most need is a combination travel and how-to book that focuses on the best of the best.

In 1987 the Krannichs inaugurated their first shopping guide to Asia—*Shopping in Exotic Places*—a guide to quality shopping in Hong Kong, South Korea, Thailand, Indonesia, and Singapore. Receiving rave reviews from leading travel publications and professionals, the book quickly found an enthusiastic audience amongst other avid travel-shoppers. It broke new ground as a combination travel and how-to book. No longer would shopping be confined to just naming products and identifying names and addresses of shops. It also included advice on how to pack for a shopping trip (take two suitcases, one filled with bubble-wrap), comparative shopping, bargaining skills, and shopping rules. Shopping was serious stuff requiring serious treatment of the subject by individuals who understood what they were doing. The Krannichs subsequently expanded their work into a series of travel-shopping guides on Hong Kong, Thailand, Indonesia, Singapore and Malaysia, Australia and Papua New Guinea, the South Pacific, and the Caribbean.

Beginning in 1996, the series took on a new look as well as an expanded focus. Known as the *Impact Guides* and appropriately titled *The Treasures and Pleasures of . . . Best of the Best*, new editions covered Hong Kong, Thailand, Indonesia, Singapore, Malaysia, Paris and the French Riviera, and the Caribbean. In 1997 and 1999 new volumes appeared on Italy, Hong Kong, and China. New volumes since 2000 focus on India, Australia, Thailand, Myanmar, Hong Kong, Singapore, Bali, Egypt, Brazil (Rio and São Paulo), Vietnam, Cambodia, Turkey, Mexico, Syria, Jordan, Ethiopia, Mali, Kenya, Tanzania, South America, and Southern Africa.

The *Impact Guides* now serve as the major content for a travel-shopping website called www.iShopAroundTheWorld.com and seven regional travel websites, such as www.middleeasttravellover.com and www.africatravellover.com.

While the primary focus remains on shopping for quality products, the books and websites also include useful information on the best hotels, restaurants, and sightseeing. As the authors note, *"Our users are discerning travelers who seek the best of the best. They are looking for a very special travel experience which is not well represented in other travel guides."*

The Krannichs' passion for traveling and shopping is reflected in their home, which is uniquely designed around their Asian, South Pacific, Middle East, African, and Latin American art collections and which has been featured on CNN and in the *New York Times*. *"We're fortunate in being able to create a living environment which pulls together so many wonderful travel memories and quality products,"* say the Krannichs. *"We learned long ago to seek out quality products and buy the best we could afford at the time. Quality lasts and is appreciated for years to come. Many of our readers share our passion for quality shopping abroad."* Their books also are popular with designers, antique dealers, and importers who use them to source products and suppliers.

While the *Impact Guides* keep the Krannichs busy traveling to exotic places, their travel series is an avocation rather than a vocation. The Krannichs also are noted authors of more than 40 career books, some of which deal with how to find international and travel jobs. The Krannichs also operate one of the world's largest career resource centers. Their works are available in most bookstores or through the publisher's online bookstore: www.impactpublications.com.

If you have any questions or comments for the authors, please direct them to:

Ron and Caryl Krannich
IMPACT PUBLICATIONS
9104 Manassas Drive, Suite N
Manassas Park, VA 20111-5211 USA
Fax 703-335-9486
E-mail: krannich@impactpublications.com

Feedback and Recommendations

WE WELCOME FEEDBACK and recommendations from our readers and users. If you have encountered a particular shop or travel experience, either good or bad, that you feel should be included in future editions of this book or on www.ishop aroundtheworld.com and www.middleeasttravellover.com, please send your comments by e-mail, fax, or mail to:

Ron and Caryl Krannich
IMPACT PUBLICATIONS
9104 Manassas Drive, Suite N
Manassas Park, VA 20111-5211 USA
Fax 703-335-9486
E-mail: krannich@impactpublications.com

_____

_____

_____

_____

_____

_____

_____

_____

_____

_____

_____

_____

_____

_____

_____

_____

More Treasures and Pleasures

THE FOLLOWING TRAVEL guides can be ordered directly from the publisher. Complete this form (or list the titles), enclose payment, and send your order to:

IMPACT PUBLICATIONS
9104 Manassas Drive, Suite N
Manassas Park, VA 20111-5211 (USA)
Tel. 1-800-361-1055 (orders only)
703-361-7300 (information) Fax 703-335-9486
E-mail: query@impactpublications.com
Online bookstore: www.impactpublications.com

All prices are in U.S. dollars. Orders from individuals should be pre-paid by check, money order, or credit card (Visa, MasterCard, American Express, and Discover). We accept credit card orders by telephone, fax, e-mail, and online. If your order must be shipped outside the United States, please include an additional US$7.00 per title for air mail shipping. Orders usually ship within 48 hours. For more information on the authors, travel resources, and international shopping, visit www.impactpublications.com and www.ishoparoundtheworld.com.

Qty.	TITLES	Price	TOTAL
Travel in the Arabian Peninsula			
___	Lonely Planet Dubai	$18.99	_____
___	Lonely Planet: Oman, UAE, and Arabian Peninsula	$29.99	_____
___	Oman: The Bradt Travel Guide	$23.95	_____
___	Yemen: The Bradt Travel Guide	$25.99	_____
The Impact Guides			
___	Treasures and Pleasures of Bermuda	$16.95	_____
___	Treasures and Pleasures of Dubai, Abu Dhabi, Oman, and Yemen	$19.95	_____
___	Treasures and Pleasures of Ethiopia (2009)	$19.95	_____

___	Treasures and Pleasures of Istanbul	$19.95	_____
___	Treasures and Pleasures of Jordan (2009)	$19.95	_____
___	Treasures and Pleasures of Kenya and Tanzania (2009)	$19.95	_____
___	Treasures and Pleasures of Mali (2009)	$19.95	_____
___	Treasures and Pleasures of Mexico	$19.95	_____
___	Treasures and Pleasures of Syria	$19.95	_____
___	Treasures and Pleasures of Thailand and Myanmar	$21.95	_____

SUBTOTAL $ _____

❑ **Virginia residents** (add 5% sales tax) $ _____

❑ **Shipping/handling** ($5.00 for the first title and $2.00 for each additional book) $ _____

❑ **Shipping outside U.S.** (Ad $7.00 per title) $ _____

TOTAL ENCLOSED $ _____

SHIP TO:

Name _____

Address _____

Phone Number: _____

PAYMENT METHOD:

❑ I enclose check/money order for $ _____
   (made payable to IMPACT PUBLICATIONS.)

❑ Please charge $ _____ to my credit card:
   ❑ Visa ❑ MasterCard ❑ American Express ❑ Discover

Card # _____

Expiration date: _____/_____

Signature _____

Keep in Touch . . .
On the Web!

www.impactpublications.com

www.ishoparoundtheworld.com

www.middleeasttravellover.com

www.veteransworld.com

www.exoffenderreentry.com